HEAVY LIFTING:
THE JOB OF THE
AMERICAN LEGISLATURE

ALAN ROSENTHAL
Rutgers University

CQ PRESS

A DIVISION OF CONGRESSIONAL QUARTERLY INC.
WASHINGTON, D.C.

CQ Press
1255 22nd Street, N.W., Suite 400
Washington, D.C. 20037

202-729-1900; toll free, 1-866-4CQ-PRESS (1-866-427-7737)

www.cqpress.com

Cover design: TGD Communications, Alexandria, Va.

Printed and bound in the United States of America

08 07 06 05 04   5 4 3 2 1

⊗ The paper used in this publication exceeds the requirements
of the American National Standard for Information
Sciences—Permanence of Paper for Printed Library Materials, ANSI
Z39.48-1992.

LIBRARY OF CONGRESS CATALOGING-IN-PUBLICATION DATA

Rosenthal, Alan
      Heavy lifting : the job of the American legislature / Alan Rosenthal.
        p. cm.
      Includes bibliographical references and index.
      ISBN 1-56802-734-6 (pbk. : alk. paper)
        1. Legislative bodies—United States—States. 2. Legislation—United States—States.
I. Title.
    JK2495.R66 2004
    328.73—dc22

                                                              2004010182

To Lynda

CONTENTS

TABLES AND FIGURE

PREFACE

This book is the third I have written that covers state legislatures in broad terms. The first, *Legislative Life* (1981), attempts to describe the most significant features of the legislative institution and process. The second, *The Decline of Representative Democracy* (1998), goes further, not only exploring legislative terrain but also articulating a significant, if disturbing, trend. Now, I am taking a different perspective in my ongoing efforts to understand legislatures; the present focus is on the job of American legislatures and how they manage to do it.

My perspective here began to take shape six years ago, when I wrote an essay in which I challenged legislative scholars to take on a question that the profession had largely ignored: What is a "good" legislature?

I admit, however, that I had little standing to issue such a challenge. Until then I had pretty much ignored the question myself, although I had spent more than a decade supervising studies commissioned by state legislatures for the purpose of improving legislative organization, procedure, and performance. Just about my first encounter with state legislatures was a study I had conducted of the Maryland General Assembly, which concluded with ninety-two recommendations for improvement. It is embarrassing to acknowledge that despite my involvement in Maryland, and later in Arkansas, Connecticut, Mississippi, and Wisconsin, I had never thought seriously about what a legislature ought to be or, indeed, what a good legislature is. I simply slid around the issue. On more occasions than I care to remember I had been asked to name the best and the worst among the nation's fifty legislatures. My response to such requests was to hem and haw and then finally to come up with the top-ranking few. Yet I had not been able to offer solid justification for my evaluations. As far as "good" legislatures were concerned, like art, I was able to tell people what I liked but not exactly why.

In my 1998 essay "The Good Legislature: Getting Beyond 'I Know It When I See It,' " I took a first step in trying to figure out a way to assess legislatures by developing some standards by which to make judgments. The model of the good legislature, I suggested, is based on the performance of three principal legislative functions: representing constituents and constituencies, lawmaking, and balancing the power of the executive. *Heavy Lifting: The Job of the American Legislature* represents an effort to explore just how legislatures perform these critical functions. What legislatures do is by no means easy work; indeed, few of us appreciate how difficult it actually is. While most of the book examines legislative performance, the concluding chapters return to the question I posed some years ago and offer answers that are far from being obvious and even farther from being mechanistic.

I could not have gotten anywhere in addressing that question without the help of many people. First, I want to acknowledge the members and staffs of the legislatures in Maryland, Minnesota, Ohio, Vermont, and Washington whom I observed, interviewed, and surveyed. I owe a special debt to the following people: Warren Deschenaux, Joyce Fowler, Mike Miller, and Cas Taylor in Maryland; Pat Flahaven, Roger Moe, and Steven Sviggum in Minnesota; Rachel Faherty, Richard Finan, and Tom Manuel in Ohio; and Walter Freed, Richard Marron, William Russell, and Peter Shumlin in Vermont. I am also grateful to three legislators whose accounts of their experiences have been especially useful in my writing here. Ember Reichgott Junge, a former member of the Minnesota senate; Sandy Rosenberg, a current member of the Maryland house; and Ralph Wright, a former speaker of the Vermont house, through their penetrating observations have indirectly contributed to this book.

At the Eagleton Institute of Politics, in this particular enterprise as in many others, I have benefited from the most generous support. Specifically, I appreciate the work of Patrick Murray, who administered the survey of legislators in five states that provides much of the data that appear in chapters 2 and 3. Critical to the production of the manuscript was Joanne Pfeiffer, who may be the only person around able to decipher the handwritten pages that I continue to churn out long after the invention of word processing. I also extend thanks to Lucy Baruch, Chris Lenart, and Sandy Wetzel, each of whom makes life—which is not difficult to begin with—a whole lot easier for faculty such as myself.

I want to acknowledge the efforts of CQ Press, even though authors are not supposed to be grateful to their publishers. We authors—and this is my fifth book with CQ—all believe that if the publisher had only done a better job of marketing our book, it would have sold thousands and thousands of additional copies. I am under no such illusion. Therefore, I am grateful for what Brenda Carter, Charisse Kiino, Talia Greenberg, Gwenda Larsen, Bonnie Erickson, and Colleen Ganey have done to get this book in shape and to the market. I suspect that any sales will be due more to their work than to mine.

Acknowledgment is also due to members of my family and special friends, not because they actively encourage my passion for state legislatures, but rather because they provide a support system that permits such a passion to flourish. I not only love but also truly appreciate all my children—John, Kai, Tony, and Lisa; their spouses—Lisa, Garrison, and Kathleen; all my grandchildren—Patrick, Kelly, Chas, Dylan, Tori, Mason, Ian, and Emily; and even my ex—Vinnie. As if I were not lucky enough to have such a wonderful family, recently I was both blindsided and blessed by the appearance of Lynda, who has diverted much of my thinking away from legislatures and toward her. Without the intervention of our good friends Hex and Monica, Lynda and I would never have met—so I owe the two arrangers much more than thanks.

All of these people had something to do with this book, whether they realize it or not. And whether they read it or not, I only hope that it is worthy of them.

1 LOOKING AT WHAT LEGISLATURES DO

Richard Finan, president of the Ohio senate, took time from his leadership responsibilities during the 2001 legislative session to meet with a group of about twenty fifth graders who were visiting the capitol building in Columbus. Finan enjoyed chatting with youngsters, asking them questions, answering any they might have, and trying to convey an upbeat message about government. "How long does it take to make a law?" one of the children asked. "Six to nine months," Finan replied, although he might have said that it depends on the nature of the issue, and so much else. The senate president asked how many of the young visitors would want to become politicians when they grew up. Not a single child raised a hand. How many, he then asked, would want to make laws when they grew up. About half the children raised their hands.

How people respond to a question depends both on how it is framed and on the stereotypes people carry in their heads. Like these fifth graders, Americans know that legislatures make law, but they do not know how they do it. Nevertheless, as public opinion shows, they do not like the way they do it. Americans are too busy to watch legislatures, whether from near or far. However, they do not like what they see, even when they are not looking. Nowadays, the public is especially unhappy with politics, politicians, and political institutions. Legislatures and legislators are probably hit hardest of all by public cynicism and disdain for things political in American life.

What Legislatures Look Like

Appearance means a lot today—probably because it is as close as we come to the object or behavior being examined. With respect to appearance, legislatures are at a distinct disadvantage. They can and do look bad to the American public because they are naturally inefficient, unpredictable, and messy—none of which are appealing characteristics to most people.

Even proximity and involvement do not make a legislature appear more attractive. Undergraduate and graduate students who intern in the legislature, with few exceptions, look askance at what goes on under capitol domes. True, they develop respect for legislators themselves, and they acknowledge the hard work they do; but the process is something else entirely. One of the legislative interns in the Vermont legislature, a man in his fifties, was attending law school at the time. He had already had a successful career as a surgeon on a university medical school facility. For him, being in the legislature was culture shock. He

1

was accustomed to the precision of surgery, with the surgeon and a support team operating on one patient, and with no outside interference. The legislature, of course, was an entirely different experience. Everything seemed to be going on at once—not precisely, as in the operating room, but rather sloppily.

Legislatures also look bad in part because they are made to look bad. They are the whipping boys (and girls, perhaps) of the political system. The executive and judiciary have their critics, but they do not suffer nearly as much abuse as does the first branch of government. The legislature offers a very convenient target for criticism from all quarters.[1]

Take legislators themselves. When newly elected lawmakers arrive at the capitol, they encounter obstacles they had never imagined. It takes them years to overcome feelings of frustration and really appreciate the nature of the process. If they are in the minority party, they feel a sense of powerlessness because the majority pretty much controls the agenda. Even if they are in the majority party, they usually have trouble doing what they want to do—getting their bills enacted and funding projects for their constituencies—and find that there are not enough resources available to satisfy everyone. There are too many other legislators with too many other constituencies. Unless they are from Nebraska, with its unicameral legislature, legislators feel that the legislature has one house too many—the other house. If their bill has a fiscal impact, they feel that their own house has one committee too many—appropriations, ways and means, or finance—to which their bill has been given a second referral. It is a daunting business, but who or what is at fault? Where can blame be placed? On the *system*—the legislature, that is.

Just as legislators are left wanting, so too are advocacy groups that pursue special interests of one type or another. Perhaps a half-century ago, these groups did not expect as much and could be satisfied with the proverbial "half loaf." That is no longer the case. However savvy a group's leadership may be with regard to what it can reasonably expect to achieve, it is necessary nowadays to make sure the rank and file is mobilizable for grassroots campaigns. The troops have to be kept fired up. The message communicated to the rank and file is that the group did not get from the legislature what it deserved. Something is in the way; the system has to be overcome.

Political campaigns for legislative seats also tend to put the legislature in a bad light. The legislative minority party may run against the legislature, since the institution is under the opposition's stewardship. It is common, moreover, for candidates who challenge incumbents to run against the legislative system. "Elect me, I'll change things in [the name of the state capital]," is a popular campaign pledge. Even incumbents run against the institution in which they serve, because such a stance has appeal to the voters. Beyond this, negative and attack campaigns influence how people regard their politicians and political institutions. Over time the negatives have serious consequences.

Add to the mix the nature of media coverage of the legislature, which has tended over time also to feed the negative. Television today barely covers the legislature, unless the print press has led the way. Legislative coverage is the job of the daily newspaper, which in many respects does good work, with both penetrating and insightful reporting and analysis. For example, the *New York Times* does a first-rate job in Albany and the *Sacramento Bee* does fine work in Sacramento. The *Baltimore Sun* provides a running account of the legislative session in Annapolis, while the *Columbus Dispatch* and both the *Star Tribune* and *St. Paul Pioneer Press* do good jobs covering Ohio and Minnesota, respectively. All of these newspapers and others in state capitals across the country are important sources of information about issues being contested in the nation's legislatures.

But the contemporary media also have a negative bias, one that gets through to their readers. "If it bleeds, it leads," the journalistic saying goes, demonstrating the unfortunate reality of how today's news is defined: If it's positive, it's not news; if it's negative, it is. Alan Ehrenhalt, a journalist by training and trade (but a political scientist by nature), puts it more subtly: In comparing political scientists and journalists, he notes that while political scientists are interested in institutions and institutional stability, journalists only take a serious interest in governmental bodies when they start to break down. The former are essentially students of order, the latter are students of disorder.[2]

Conflict is newsworthy, so the media look for it. When they find conflict, they attribute it to partisan politics, campaign contributions, and political ambitions. Rarely do they portray it as simply legitimate disagreement over the merits of an issue; there is not much interest in such a story. The more negative, the more newsworthy. The positive is not news, and it is either not reported or is underreported. But the more sensational or scandalous the material, the more newsworthy it is. The media's incentives are understandable. In a competitive struggle for an audience, the media give people what they believe people want—the interesting, the negative.

The incentives for journalists—which can be referred to as the three Ps—run in the same direction. If they want their stories to have good *placement*, if they want to be *promoted* to the Washington, D.C., bureau, and if they want to win the *Pulitzer* Prize, members of the state house press corps are well advised to investigate aggressively and then take no prisoners. To add to these incentives, skepticism and distrust are probably part of journalists' genetic makeup. "What journalists can't see, they don't believe," is the way a student of journalism put it. Most of the legislative process, as we shall see (or not see) is going on in many places simultaneously—so it cannot be viewed by one pair of eyes, journalistic or otherwise.

Finally, there is the public experience of the legislature. Although the legislature is not really on the radar screen of the overwhelming majority of citizens, the public's overall perception of it is negative. Public disapproval is a consequence of the factors noted above, but especially the highlighting by the media of the public officeholders who do wrong and the public transactions that go wrong. People tend to generalize from these worst cases to everything about legislatures. (Curiously, they neglect to do the same regarding their own legislators, whom they regard positively and whom they regularly return to office.)

Even in a benign environment, Americans would find it difficult to appreciate legislatures and the legislative process. John Mueller captures the essence of the public's attitude:

> When politicians respond to what they think their constituents want they are routinely accused of "pandering to public opinion" and of "doing anything to be elected." When they go in a direction different from what public opinion seems to dictate, they are accused of "ignoring the will of the people" and "pandering to special interests." If they have sharp differences, they are accused of polarizing the situation, encouraging an "either/or" politics based on ideological preconceptions rather then a "both/and" politics based on ideas that broadly unite us. If they manage to agree, they are accused of selling out principle for a Tweedledum and Tweedledee me-tooism. It's a tough racket.[3]

More fundamentally, as awful as it may sound, people do not like legislatures because they do not care for democracy in action. They may appreciate it in principle, but they do not care for the nitty-gritty of democracy at work.

"Why," people wonder, "is there so much conflict?" They think—wrongly—that most Americans agree on policies and priorities.[4] People with whom other people associate face to face normally are in agreement. But within larger entities—the nation, state, and even legislative districts—disagreement is common. Americans see eye to eye only at the most general level—on the need for better education, a cleaner environment, improved health care, and the like. But they do not agree on how to achieve these goals; nor do they concur on abortion, carrying concealed weapons, capital punishment, or a number of other heated issues.

"Why," people ask, "do legislators pay so little attention to what regular citizens think and so much attention to what special interests want?" A recent survey conducted by the National Conference of State Legislatures (NCSL),[5] for example, indicated that one-third of Americans felt that elected public officials were indifferent to what people like themselves thought. Only slightly more felt that they did care about what their constituents thought. Despite the fact that legislators spend so much time and effort relating to their constituents, people felt that they were not accessible. And despite the fact that seven out of ten Americans are members of at least one political interest group, people decry the special interests (although not the particular special interests to which they belong). When asked in the NCSL survey whether they thought special interest groups represented people's opinions or special interest groups did more harm than good, only 24 percent responded the former while 40 percent responded the latter (and 36 percent had no opinion or did not know). Evidently, people feel that their own group espouses the public interest, while everyone else's espouses a "special interest."

And people question the legislative process itself: "Why all the bickering?" they ask. Indeed, one-third of the respondents in the NCSL survey believed that legislators spent too much time arguing, while half acknowledged that disagreement and compromise were necessary parts of lawmaking. People do not realize that what they refer to as bickering is actually deliberation. "Why all the compromise?" they question, when compromise is not selling out as is popularly thought, but rather the way in which consensus is built and settlements reached. Whether or not Americans really like *representative* democracy is in doubt. Many of them presumably would prefer direct democracy, or at the very least the possibility of the initiative and referendum, which enables citizens to end-run or overrule their legislature. When the NCSL survey offered respondents the choice between "Making laws is a job best left to elected representatives" and "The public should decide issues directly by voting on them," 30 percent chose the former, while 47 percent preferred the latter (with 23 percent registering "Don't know" or "No opinion").

Add to all of this just what a legislature would look like if people actually took time to observe it. If the legislature were not in session, it would look all right. But when it is at work, the legislature is extremely difficult to comprehend. It is neither neat nor linear, and too much is happening at once.

What Legislatures Do and How Well They Do It

Political scientists have shed much light on what legislators do and how they function. The past twenty-five years have witnessed an upsurge in the attention paid to state legislatures by the political science profession. Thanks in large part to the work of Malcolm E. Jewell and his students, the study of legislators and legislatures is in an especially healthy state nowadays. Anyone who delves into the research reported in the *Legislative Studies Quarterly* can attest to that. Among the subjects that have been gainfully explored are recruitment, determinants of voting behavior, legislative parties, standing committees, professionalization, development and reform, turnover, staffing, leadership, and the legislature's budgetary role. Currently, the effects of term limits are being studied by, among others, a consortium of scholars working with the NCSL, the Council of State Governments, and the State Legislative Leaders Foundation.

Thanks to the efforts of political scientists, we have a far better idea of what legislatures are all about. But one question eludes us, in part because political science has not addressed it: "What is a good legislature?" The exploration of this subject has been left to others—to journalists, advocates, and reformers. Much of the discussion has been quite uninformed. Indeed, it has been dominated by what is "bad" about legislatures: the members; their motives and ethics; the process and procedures; and the products, which are insufficient or misdirected. The objective of this book is not to answer that question, but certainly to shed light on it by providing readers with a better grasp of what makes a legislature "good." The destination toward which we are heading is important, but even more so is the trip itself and what can be learned by looking closely at how legislatures work.

Standards for Assessment

At the outset, it is necessary to have some notion of what is meant by a "good" legislature. Whether a legislature qualifies depends on the standards used in assessing it. Different standards will yield different results. The standard that is used for judging a baseball team is pretty straightforward. It is not whether the players have the highest batting average or receive the highest salaries; nor is it the number of pitchers who have won twenty games. It is whether the team has won more games than others during the season and whether it wins the divisional playoffs and the World Series. The "goodness" of a corporation or business is not as easy to assess, but earnings and valuation would make the bottom line.

Assessment is even more difficult with regard to a legislature. The way to begin is to review the standards that are commonly, albeit implicitly, used in judging these institutions. Each has its adherents, but we shall dispense with them one by one before offering the standard that will be employed in the study at hand.

Product is an obvious standard. What is a legislature for if not to improve life for people in the state? The public cares more about what comes out of the legislature than what goes on inside it. The better the policies, the better the legislature. This makes intuitive sense. Political interest groups do not have much trouble assessing a legislature. A business organization, teachers' association, or environmental group—any such entity judges a legislature in terms of what it does for or against it. Is a "good" legislature one that has given much and denied little to the particular group? But, of course, one group's "good" legislature is another's "bad" legislature. An interest group's success rate cannot be an indicator of a legislature's quality, but only of a legislature's policy preferences. You may or may not agree with such preferences.

No one has succeeded in adequately measuring a legislature's overall product, although from time to time political scientists have come perilously close to equating the quantity of output with the quality of output. One measure of legislative "goodness" might be the number of bills enacted into law (or possibly the percentage of bill introductions that become bill enactments). This assumes that the more law, the better the legislature. But is one enactment equal to another? Anyone familiar with the legislative process will agree that this is not the case. The variation in the substance and significance of laws enacted is tremendous.

What about isolating those measures that are significant, and putting the others aside? Take the budget, for example. Is a "good" legislature one that grows the state budget? Republicans—and many Democrats—might disagree. Is it one that increases funding for higher education or for elementary and secondary education? Senior citizens might not think so. Or is a "good" legislature one that makes laws that protect the environment? That protect animals? That deregulate economic enterprise? That take away the licenses of drunk drivers?

It is probably not possible to agree on a product that is indispensable for a "good" legislature. It may not even be worth the search. Product as a standard rests on the assumption that the legislature is a means to an end, the end being what it produces. But suppose the legislature is not primarily a means to another end, but rather an end in itself. The legislature does furnish the mechanism by which public policy ends are reached. But the legislature is also the end in that the institution and the process allow for settlements among the different values, interests, and priorities that people have. If such differences did not exist, there would be no need for settlements, and legislatures would not be necessary. Administration and implementation could be left to the executive. Given the existence of diverse and conflicting public views, however, a legislature of representatives elected by citizens provides a way of working things out—deciding on priorities, allocating resources, and inflicting burdens. Democracy is largely about process, and the legislature—not the executive or the judiciary—is the engine that drives democratic processes. The legislature is the place where the people's representatives assemble, where individual citizens and organized groups have ready access, and where differences come into conflict. If the institution and the process are what matter most, then any assessment has to focus on the legislature itself.

Such a focus ordinarily has led to an assessment tied to the legislature's *structure*. By structure, we mean the way these institutions are set up to do their job. Structural features range widely, and they include elements that might also be categorized as capacity. One house or two houses, the number and size of standing committees, the salaries of members, the facilities available, the amount and organization of staff, and the laws and rules pertaining to the integrity of members and the process—all are structural elements that are thought by some to be the defining elements of a good legislature.

Structure as a principal standard came into prominence during the legislative reform movement of the late 1960s, the 1970s, and the early 1980s. Led by legislative leaders, rank-and-file members, national legislative organizations, the Eagleton Institute of Politics at Rutgers University, and the Citizens Conference on State Legislatures (CCSL), the reform movement represented a sustained national effort to modernize state legislatures, which political scientist Alexander Heard in 1966 referred to as "our most extreme examples of institutional lag." [6] In their efforts to modernize their structure and increase their capacity, state legislatures used as models the U.S. Congress and the California legislature, both of which were highly developed institutions.[7] Over the years the reform movement achieved notable success; almost everywhere structural change and capacity enhancement was achieved.

A major assessment of the fifty state legislatures was a key part of the reform movement. In 1969 the CCSL, with a large grant from the Ford Foundation, conducted an evaluation of legislatures in the fifty states. A political objective underlay the evaluation enterprise. In ranking the states from 1 to 50, the CCSL wanted to persuade the lower-ranked states to adopt reforms that the higher-ranked states had already implemented and to persuade the higher-ranked states to go even further.

The evaluation was published in both popular and scholarly versions.[8] The overall scores given to each of the states were based on five sub-rankings, with states scored on each. The FAIIR rankings, as they were called for short, were functionality, accountability, informedness, independence, and representativeness. Scores for each of these sub-rankings were based on hundreds of factors. For example, legislatures scored higher if they had, among other things, limitations on their sessions; deadlines for filing bills, introducing bills, etc.; adequate circulation patterns in the chambers; superior offices for leaders; joint rules for house and senate; fewer than eighty members in the house; exactly seventeen committees in the house and twelve in the senate; and private offices for each member. What was the justification for each of these standards in assessing a legislature? The only one that comes to mind is that this was how the California legislature did it.

The specific criteria and scoring are arbitrary, at best. Essentially, the states that ranked at the top—California, New York, and Illinois—were those that devoted the most resources to the legislature. In these places, salaries, staff, and facilities were relatively plentiful. The assumption of the CCSL evaluation, moreover, was fairly linear: the more capacity a legislature has, the better it is. While the criteria and the scoring could not be justified, the approach was dictated by two very different considerations. First, social science methodology had little use for anything but quantitative indicators that were susceptible to statistical manipulation. Second, political objectives required that each state receive a numerical ranking, its own number and not a place in a quartile, quintile, or even decile. In practical terms, the methodology worked; hundreds of items were totaled and numerous scores were calculated. The political objective was accomplished; legislatures took their numerical ranking seriously, and they started to make changes to improve where they stood relative to others—mainly in terms of their capacity.

But a number of legislative leaders (some of whom served in states with lower rankings) pointed out publicly that the CCSL rankings made little sense. Evaluating a legislature in this manner, they charged, is like evaluating a football team by the condition of its uniforms, locker rooms, and training facilities rather than by its performance on the field. Legislative structure, they said, is not indicative of how a legislature functions. At best, structure furnishes a legislature with the wherewithal to do its job; but there is no guarantee that the legislature will exploit that structure to do its job. At worst, wherewithal has little or nothing to do with how well the legislature goes about its business. Higher salaries, more staff, fewer committees, member offices, and so forth may be nice for legislators, but they may not be necessary for the performance of the legislature.

The Job of the Legislature

Neither products nor structural features a "good" legislature make. What matters is how the legislature functions, how it performs. What, then, is the job of the legislature? Legislatures have many tasks and do a variety of things. For example, they advise and consent to a governor's appointments, they serve as training grounds for politicians who go on to higher office, and they conduct oversight with regard to executive departments and agencies. But mainly the legislature's job consists of three principal functions: *representing, lawmaking,* and *balancing the power of the executive.* These components, as we shall see, are not independent of one another. Like just about everything else involving legislatures, they overlap. Indeed, lawmaking and balancing executive power are not distinguishable in practice, though they can be assessed from distinct perspectives. And representation is part and parcel of the other two.

Whether legislatures can be considered "good" or not depends on how they handle these three functions. Yet there is very little in the literature of political science that takes on all three as elements of legislative performance. If, for example, one examines the *Encyclopedia of the American Legislative System,*[9] only a half-dozen of its ninety-one chapters relate to two of the specified functions, representing and balancing the power of the executive. Not one of these chapters is on the processes by which laws are made. This omission has not gone unnoticed in the profession. Charles O. Jones, a former president of the American Political Science Association, observed that scholars rarely study lawmaking itself; instead, they research institutional arrangements and legislative behavior.[10] This is the place, then, where the performance by legislatures of these jobs will be scrutinized.

Representing constituencies and constituents is obviously one of the principal jobs of the legislature in a representative democracy such as ours. James Madison, in *Federalist* No. 10, extolled the virtues of a system of representation whereby the views of the public were refined and enlarged "by passing them through the medium of a chosen body of citizens." Representation, as practiced by those elected to represent, has come to mean more than the moderating of public views that Madison had in mind. It now encompasses hands-on activities as well. As it is examined here, the job of representing deals primarily with the work done district by district by individual legislators and then aggregated into the whole. The examination undertaken here does not attempt to correlate the legislature's public policy outputs with the views of a statewide public. That is not the best measure of representation, in our judgment. Instead, it is preferable to focus on the relationships of individual legislators to their constituencies.

Chapters 2 and 3 do just that—first, from the standpoint of how legislators *serve* their districts' interests, and second, from the standpoint of how legislators *express* their constituencies' views. The former chapter pays attention to just how representatives and districts are linked, as well as to communications and the securing of benefits for individuals and groups. The latter chapter wrestles with the issue of whether, to what extent, and how representatives reflect what constituents want by way of public policy. It examines, as virtually every discussion of representation does, the classic tension between constituency on the one hand and conviction on the other—the "delegate"/"trustee" distinction. The chapter concludes with an attempt to deal with representation at an institutional level, as well as at the aggregated individual level.

For most legislators, making law is the job they chiefly associate with being members of the legislature. Their representational duties are important, but when the legislature is in session the transformation of bills into laws is their main occupation. A former Wisconsin lawmaker put it succinctly: "The raison d'etre of a legislative body is to pass laws." [11] Not only are individual legislators motivated to make law, but the legislature itself is an arena in which individuals, parties, and interest groups battle with one another to get their values, interests, and priorities reflected in statute. Law is the means by which it is decided who gets what, and who does not.

Lawmaking is, indisputably, one of the principal jobs of the legislature. It has been studied in a variety of ways, but perhaps the most popular model is that tracking the stages by which a bill becomes a law—from introduction to committee referral to action on the floor in one house and on through similar stages in the other. The approach taken here is entirely different. Lawmaking for us is complex and convoluted and by no means as simple and direct as the "bill-becomes-a-law" model would suggest. Lawmaking is the subject of chapters 4, 5, 6, and 7, in which the focus is no longer mainly on the individual but rather on elements of the process and looked at from an institutional perspective.

The aim here is not to pursue a sponsor with a bill that he or she wants passed. Rather, it is to take various cuts of the process—different photographs, as it were—in order to try to capture what appears to be most important about lawmaking in the states.

Chapter 4 looks at legislatures' large workload and the limited time available to handle it. Chapter 5 highlights the obstacles lawmakers have to overcome—disagreement by participants, jurisdictional disputes, intercameral rivalry, and the scarcity of resources. Then, with the ground laid, the question in chapter 6 is: "How does it all get put together?" Of interest here are the deliberative aspects of the process, as arguments are heard, problems are studied, and contestants debate the merits of their positions. Support for a measure is being fashioned, or thwarted. Successive majorities have to be won over in both houses, not just one. How that is accomplished and how settlements are achieved is the topic of chapter 7. Inside and outside strategies come into play here, and disputes are finally worked out; legislation is enacted.

In considering the third principal part of the legislative job, the institutional perspective has to be the dominant one. Legislators individually can represent their constituencies, but it takes the legislature to balance the power of the executive. In creating a new governmental system, the framers of the Constitution wanted the three branches of government to share power, with neither the executive, legislative, nor judicial branch having substantial power over the others. Consequently, they demanded a system of separated powers—one in which checks and balances operate but there is still sharing. Initially, legislatures were the dominant institutions, but that is no longer the case. Putting the courts to one side, it is the executive that has dominated for the past fifty years or so. The executive dominates today, and legislatures have to work hard to maintain parity.

Chapters 8 and 9 examine how and how effectively legislatures balance the power of executives. Chapter 8 discusses the advantages governors generally possess vis-à-vis their legislatures. The main one, possessed by every governor, is that of unity. The governor is one, the legislature is two houses (except in Nebraska), two parties (except in Nebraska), and usually one hundred or more individuals (although there are fewer than one hundred members in Nebraska and seven other states). Other things being equal, governors have the upper hand; but other things are seldom equal. Whether a balance is achieved between the executive and legislature depends on how the governor confronts the legislature and how the legislature responds to gubernatorial leadership or lack thereof. That is the focus of chapter 9.

What becomes very clear in chapters 4 through 9 is that legislative leaders are central figures in the process. How and how well legislatures do their lawmaking and balancing, and even to some degree how they do their representational work, depends substantially on legislative leadership—the top leaders of the majority party. Therefore, chapter 10 undertakes an examination of the role of leadership in the functioning of the legislature. It is difficult to see how a legislature can perform well without effective leadership. At this point, the case is implicitly made that a "good" legislature requires such leadership.

Chapter 11, by way of conclusion, addresses the question that largely motivated the present study. What is a "good" legislature, given the performance standards adopted here? What requirements have to be met for a legislature to pass a "goodness" test?

Figuring Out How They Do What They Do

This study of the legislature's job draws on a variety of source materials, each of which serves to illuminate the subject, at least to some extent. Together, these varied materials should cast substantial light on how legislatures go about their business of representing, lawmaking, and balancing.

First, this study draws on work already published by political scientists on legislatures, some of which have proved vital to the present endeavor. Joseph M. Bessette's wonderful theoretical treatment of deliberation in Congress was invaluable. Of an entirely different nature, John A. Straayer's insightful analysis of the Colorado General Assembly helped make sense of one state legislature. Laura A. Van Assendelft's splendid portraits of southern governors made a significant contribution to the chapters on the legislature and the executive. The present study also relied on my own research and writing.[12]

Second, memoirs, biographies, and first-hand accounts are drawn upon to flesh out the people and the process. Tom Loftus, the former speaker of the Wisconsin assembly, offers legislative wisdom that nicely buttresses some of the arguments made herein. Ralph Wright, the former speaker of the Vermont house, offers candor and humor, which is happily incorporated into the narrative of this study. John E. McDonough's war stories from his days in the Massachusetts legislature illustrate important points and, besides, are much too good to ignore. Harriet Keyserling's memoirs of her experience in the South Carolina house also are valuable, as is James Richardson's fascinating biography of Willie Brown, the former speaker of the California assembly.[13] It would be foolish for anyone writing about the job of the legislature to overlook such rich materials.

During the 2000 session of the Minnesota legislature, Sen. Ember Reichgott Junge took advantage of her insider's knowledge to write an account of Gov. Jesse Ventura and the legislature. Her work has not been published, but with her permission parts of it are used here. All references to her work are cited in the endnotes as "Ember Reichgott Junge, unpublished manuscript, 2000." Along similar lines, I made use of a diary kept by Del. Sandy Rosenberg of the Maryland house, also cited when reference is made to it.

Third, the coverage of the legislature by the capital press corps in a number of the states is extremely useful to the current study. The comments of participants in lawmaking, which are quoted in daily newspapers, are gratefully borrowed and noted in this study. Also useful for present purposes are a number of case examples reported in the press. Coverage by the following dailies has been of special help: *Baltimore Sun, Columbus Dispatch, Minneapolis Star Tribune, New York Times,* and *St. Paul Pioneer Press.*

Fourth, the bulk of this study relies on newly conducted research—interviews, a survey, and observation—I conducted in Maryland, Minnesota, Ohio, Vermont, and Washington. Are these five states representative of all fifty? The answer to that question is a resounding "no." It is not possible to choose states or legislatures that are representative of other states or legislatures. Every state and every legislature differs from every other, at least in some important respects. Indeed, the same legislature differs from session to session, and sometimes even more frequently than that—depending on partisan control, member composition, political circumstances, and environmental factors. It may, therefore, be assumed that different legislatures employ a somewhat different mix of means in pursuing their work of representing, lawmaking, and balancing; and that mix is never constant.

Why these states? Although not representative *per se,* the five states under special scrutiny here are in different regions of the nation: Minnesota and Ohio are in the Midwest, Washington is in the West, Vermont is in the Northeast, and Maryland (at least according to the regional groupings of the Council of State Governments) is in the South. More important than whether the five represent other states is the fact that they represent different patterns of control of state government, which is critical to the examination of lawmaking and to executive-legislative balance.

At the time of my observations in 2001–2002 the patterns of control were as follows: In Maryland Democrats were firmly in control of both houses of the legislature, as well as the office of governor. In Ohio the reverse was the case; Republicans were firmly in control of both houses of the legislature, as well as the office of governor. In Washington Democrats controlled, but the margins were extremely narrow, one seat in the senate and two in the house; the governor was also a Democrat. Vermont was divided, with a Democratic governor and senate and a Republican house. Minnesota was even more divided; the legislature was tripartisan, with the senate in the hands of the Democratic-Farmer-Labor (DFL) Party, the equivalent of Democrats everywhere else, the house in the hands of Republicans, and the governor, Jesse Ventura, a member of the newly formed Independence Party.

These five legislatures varied in several institutional respects. The size of legislative districts ranged widely, as did the capacity of the legislatures, in terms of staff, facilities, and the like. Ohio's legislature was the most "professional," while Vermont's was the least (and thus the most "citizen legislature") of the five. The legislatures in Maryland, Minnesota, and Washington were in between, but much nearer to Ohio than Vermont. These factors will be revisited in the chapters on representation and lawmaking.

An important criterion in selecting these five legislatures was my likely access to leadership and, through leadership, to the inner workings of the lawmaking processes. In three of the states access was excellent and in another it was very good. In the fifth, Washington, less time was spent on first-hand observations, partly because the end-of-the-session visit did not allow for direct observation.

In each of these states I conducted a number of interviews and, more casually, engaged in conversations about the process. Among those interviewed were legislators, lobbyists, journalists, executive officials, and a governor. But the principal method of investigation was my observation of the process. I spent two weeks in the Maryland, Minnesota, Ohio, and Vermont legislatures during their 2001 sessions. These visits were conducted midway through the Maryland and Vermont sessions, just before the deadline for the budget in Ohio and toward the end of the session in Minnesota. The journey to Washington occurred the following year but was limited to four days.

Only a small slice of the lawmaking process could be observed. I had to choose where to be—in the house or senate, in one committee or another, at a floor session, or somewhere else. And I had to choose when I would be in each of the states. A lot is going on at any one time. To the extent possible, I observed the process looking over the shoulder of a legislative leader—especially the house speaker in Maryland, the senate president in Ohio, and the senate majority leader in Minnesota. But work in committee, especially in Vermont, and in caucus and on the floor also was closely observed. In each chamber the focus was on the majority party, which is responsible for the legislature's agenda and enjoys the initiative in making law.

Another way to observe lawmaking would have been to track a particular issue or to follow the efforts of a legislator trying to get a bill enacted. The former would not have been possible because of the limited amount of time I could spend in each legislature. One never knows much in advance what will be happening when, except for the budget. So, selecting an issue and tracking it would be out of the question. For much the same reason, monitoring a member's efforts would not pay off in an exploration of the job of the legislature.

It was decided, therefore, to look at those issues that came up during the time span during which I as observer was scheduled to be in the state. Most of the issues observed in some depth were on the agendas of the majority leadership, especially the budget, school finance, guns, and gay rights. Obviously, this approach leaves something to be desired; only a small part of the proceedings could be viewed first hand. But these proceedings were critical parts of the process, and not ordinarily open to outsiders. At a senate DFL caucus meeting in Minnesota, one senator welcomed me to the discussion of strategy that was about to begin: "You're in the huddle," he said. And that was the way it felt, although there was no risk that I would be asked to carry the ball.

Proximity is important, but so is coverage. Snapshots capture only a small part of what is going on, which is impossible to see at any one time, anyway. But one can make better sense of the job of the legislature by watching the institution at work, extracting illustrations, and trying to get at what seems most generalizable. That can best be done when such observations are supplemented by other materials. The manner of inquiry pursued here is far from science, but it can be extremely informative. Observation is not the only approach, but it is one that probably should be used more often than it is in the study of legislatures.[14]

The representational job of the legislature is best approached differently. Although lawmaking in the state house illuminates aspects of representation, major reliance here is on a survey I mailed to all the members of the Maryland, Minnesota, Ohio, Vermont, and Washington legislatures. The surveys were sent to legislators in four states in May 2001 and then to legislators in Washington in April 2002. Of the 848 legislators sent surveys, 364 completed and returned them, a response rate of about 43 percent. Among states the response rate varied as follows: Maryland, 51 percent; Minnesota, 45 percent; Ohio, 33 percent; Vermont, 48 percent; and Washington, 32 percent. Subgroups—such as senate or house, Democrat or Republican, majority or minority party, male or female, and years of experience in the legislature—were appropriately represented in the total sample. The responses of legislators to the questions asked are cited in the text as the "five-state survey" and referred to mainly in chapters 2 and 3.

This book is about legislatures generally and how they go about doing their jobs. Yet most of its observations are based on only five of the fifty state legislatures. Admittedly, even these observations are highly selective. They were made during only one session, and only a short part of it, and only of a few of the many transactions going on then. They are offered here, with these caveats. But even with such limitations, it ought to be possible to get nearer than we have been to how legislatures perform. And nearer, also, to understanding what "good" legislatures are.

NOTES

1. See Alan Rosenthal, "Democracy Works," *State Legislatures,* February 2003, 22–25.

2. Alan Ehrenhalt, "Political Science and Journalism: Bridging the Gap," *Perspectives* 1 (March 2003): 128.

3. John Mueller, *Capitalism, Democracy, and Ralph's Pretty Good Grocery* (Princeton, N.J.: Princeton University Press, 1999), 177.

4. John Hibbing and Elizabeth Theiss-Morse, *Stealth Democracy* (New York: Cambridge University Press, 2002).

5. Karl T. Kurtz, Alan Rosenthal, and Cliff Zukin, "Citizenship: A Challenge for All Generations" (Denver: National Conference of State Legislatures, September 2003), 9.

6. Alexander Heard, ed., *State Legislatures in American Politics* (Englewood Cliffs, N.J.: Prentice Hall, 1966), 3.

7. See Nelson W. Polsby, "The Institutionalization of the U.S. House of Representatives," *American Political Science Review* 62 (March 1968): 144–168; Peverill Squire, "The Theory of Legislative Institutionalization and the California Assembly," *Journal of Politics* 54 (November 1992): 1026–1054; and Alan Rosenthal, "State Legislative Development: Observations from Three Perspectives," *Legislative Studies Quarterly* 21 (May 1996): 169–197.

8. Citizens Conference on State Legislatures, *The Sometime Governments* (New York: Bantam Books, 1971), and *State Legislatures: An Evaluation of Their Effectiveness* (New York: Praeger, 1971).

9. Joel H. Silbey, ed., *Encyclopedia of the American Legislative System* (New York: Scribner's Sons, 1994).

10. Charles O. Jones, "A Way of Life and Law," *American Political Science Review* 89 (March 1995): 1–9.

11. Mordecai Lee, "Looking at the Politics Administration Dichotomy from the Other Direction: Participant Observation by a State Senator," *International Journal of Public Administration,* vol. 24, no. 4 (2001): 377.

12. Joseph M. Bessette, *The Mild Voice of Reason* (Chicago: University of Chicago Press, 1994); John A. Straayer, *The Colorado General Assembly* (Niwat: University Press of Colorado, 1990); Laura A. Van Assendelft, *Governors, Agenda Setting, and Divided Government* (Lanham, Md.: University Press of America, 1997); and Alan Rosenthal, *The Decline of Representative Democracy* (Washington, D.C.: CQ Press, 1998).

13. Tom Loftus, *The Art of Legislative Politics* (Washington, D.C.: CQ Press, 1994); Ralph Wright, *All Politics Is Personal* (Manchester Center, Vt.: Marshall Jones Co., 1996); Harriet Keyserling, *Against the Tide* (Columbia: University of South Carolina Press, 1998); John E. McDonough, *Experiencing Politics* (Berkeley: University of California Press, 2000); and James Richardson, *Willie Brown* (Berkeley: University of California Press, 1996).

14. Richard F. Fenno Jr. has, of course, relied heavily on observation in his studies of the U.S. Congress and its members. See, especially, his explanation of observation as a methodology in the appendix of his *Home Style: House Members in Their Districts* (Boston: Little, Brown, 1978).

2 REPRESENTATION: SERVING THE DISTRICT'S INTERESTS

A brochure published and distributed by the Ohio senate informs citizens: "You elect members of the Ohio senate to represent you. As your employees, they seek your input on pending legislation and want to help you with personal matters involving state agencies." Representative democracy in the nation and states is based upon a connection existing between representatives and their districts. When they are elected to state senates, these representatives are called "senators." Otherwise, with the exception of six states where they are known as "assemblypersons" or "delegates," they are called "representatives."

Representation is one of the major functions legislatures perform. Indeed, it may be the paramount one as far as legislators themselves are concerned. Individual legislators can make a distinction between representing and lawmaking, although in practice the two are not exclusive. For example, in a survey conducted some years ago, when asked what they should do in order to be most effective, Ohio legislators responded generally as follows: 56 percent of representatives and 62 percent of senators referred to representational activities, such as working with constituents and representing groups; and 44 percent of representatives and 38 percent of senators referred to lawmaking activities, such as introducing legislation, engaging in committee work, and dealing with major issues.[1]

For many scholars representation has revolved around the question of whether the legislator pursued policies that conformed to the preferences of voters in the legislator's district. As we shall see in the following chapter, and as Jane Mansbridge has demonstrated, this is a very limited approach.[2] Representation certainly entails that constituency views and interests be taken into account as part of the lawmaking process. But it also involves processes by which individual legislators provide service of various sorts and also connect constituents with government. And it requires, moreover, that constituents have access to their senators and their representatives to ask for help and to express their views. Representation works at two levels: the individual level, in which legislators relate to the districts from which they are elected, and the collective level, in which the legislature itself serves and reflects statewide interests and preferences. This chapter will focus on the way in which legislators and the legislature *serve* their district's interests, while chapter 3 will deal with how legislators and the legislature *express* constituency views.

Legislators and Their Districts

The nature of representation depends on three factors: the district, the representative, and the legislature. What this means, of course, is that there is enormous variety in just how representation gets played out from place to place.

Districts vary in size, with the larger states having more populous districts and the smaller states less populous ones. Table 2-1 presents the number of seats and the district populations of the senates and houses of the fifty states. On the senate side, California's 40 members each represent 846,791 people at one extreme and North Dakota's 49 members each have 13,106 constituents at the other. On the house side, California's 80 members each represent 423,396 people and New Hampshire's 400 members each have 3,089 constituents.

The five legislatures under special examination here also vary greatly, as is indicated in Table 2-2. In two of the states the districts are all represented by single members. But in house districts in Washington State each have two members, which are nested in the senate district. In Maryland, with the exception of a few cases, each senate district includes three house districts. In Vermont the house has some single-member and some double-member districts. In the Vermont senate the lines of the fourteen counties are kept intact as the state constitution prescribes, so all but two of thirty senators are in multimember districts, with six representing Chittenden County, where Burlington is located. While Burlington is the largest city in Vermont, its population is less than 40,000. Ohio's senate and house districts are large. The senate districts of Maryland and Washington are smaller, but still sizeable, while those of Minnesota are smaller still and Vermont's are among the smallest in the country.

Imagine the difference between representing house districts in Ohio and Vermont. In the former, it is difficult to campaign personally, whether house to house or farm to farm. Tough enough to accomplish in a district of 100,000, it is nearly impossible to do in one of 350,000. In a district of 4,000 (or even double or triple that number), door to door is the custom. Ralph Wright, a former speaker of the Vermont house, recalls a visit with William Bulger, president of the Massachusetts senate. After hearing that Wright's district at the time contained only 3,700 constituents, Bulger, who had almost fifty times as many constituents, remarked: "My God, I could take that many to lunch." [3]

In a state like Vermont legislators lead significantly different lives than do their counterparts in most other places. In such a small state constituencies are more likely to be relatively homogenous. Officials can get to know a large proportion of their constituents and interact with them face to face. The nature of representation is also affected by geographical size and shape. In this respect, there is considerable variation within states, with urban districts more geographically concentrated, rural districts more dispersed, and suburban districts in the middle. One set of estimates of intrastate variation shows that California's districts range from 18 square miles to 28,991 square miles; New York's range

Table 2-1   Legislative Districts

State	Senates		Houses	
	Seats	District population	Seats	District population
Alabama	35	127,060	105	42,353
Alaska	20	31,347	40	15,673
Arizona	30	171,021	60	171,021[a]
Arkansas	35	76,383	100	26,734
California	40	846,791	80	423,396
Colorado	35	122,893	65	66,173
Connecticut	36	94,599	151	22,553
Delaware	21	37,314	41	19,112
Florida	40	399,559	120	133,186
Georgia	56	146,187	180	45,480
Hawaii	25	48,461	51	23,756
Idaho	35	36,970	70	36,970[a]
Illinois	59	210,496	118	105,248
Indiana	50	121,610	100	60,805
Iowa	50	58,526	100	29,263
Kansas	40	67,210	125	21,507
Kentucky	38	106,362	100	40,418
Louisiana	39	114,589	105	42,562
Maine	35	36,426	151	8,443
Maryland	47	112,691	141	112,691[b]
Massachusetts	40	158,727	160	39,682
Michigan	38	261,538	110	90,349
Minnesota	67	73,425	134	36,713
Mississippi	52	54,705	122	23,317
Missouri	34	164,565	163	34,326
Montana	50	18,044	100	9,022
Nebraska	49	34,924	NA[c]	
Nevada	21	95,155	42	47,578
New Hampshire	24	51,491	400	3,089
New Jersey	40	210,359	80	210,359[a]
New Mexico	42	43,311	70	25,986
New York	61	311,089	150	126,510
North Carolina	50	160,986	120	67,078
North Dakota	49	13,106	98	13,106[a]
Ohio	33	344,035	99	114,678
Oklahoma	48	71,889	101	34,165
Oregon	30	114,047	60	57,023
Pennsylvania	50	245,621	203	60,498
Rhode Island	50	20,966	100	10,483
South Carolina	46	87,218	124	32,355
South Dakota	35	21,567	70	21,567[a]
Tennessee	33	172,403	99	57,468
Texas	31	672,639	150	139,012
Utah	29	77,086	75	29,776
Vermont	30	20,294	150	4,059
Virginia	40	176,963	100	70,785
Washington	49	120,288	98	120,288[a]
West Virginia	34	53,187	100	18,083
Wisconsin	33	162,536	99	51,179
Wyoming	30	16,459	60	8,230

Source: National Conference of State Legislatures, 2003.

Note: District size is calculated by dividing the number of seats into the total 2000 population.

[a] Two-member districts.

[b] Three-member districts, except in about a half-dozen cases where delegates have single-number districts.

[c] Unicameral legislature.

Table 2-2 Legislative Districts in Five States

State	Senates		Houses	
	Member seats	District population	Member seats	District population
Maryland	47	112,691	141	112,691[a]
Minnesota	67	73,425	134	36,713
Ohio	33	344,035	99	114,678
Vermont	30	20,294	150	4,059
Washington	49	120,288	98	120,288[b]

Source: Data compiled by the author.

[a] Three delegates are elected at large in senate districts, except in about a half-dozen cases where delegates have single-member districts.

[b] Two delegates are elected at large in senate districts.

from 1 square mile to 4,731 square miles; and Colorado's range from 6 square miles to 12,916 square miles.[4] The larger the territory the more difficult it is for representatives to get around and meet face to face with constituents. Imagine representing a district in Maine consisting only of 8,433 people, but all of whom live on a number of islands off the coast; or one in Colorado that spans the Rocky Mountains. Although neither district has many constituents, reaching them must be quite the task.

However many people and however difficult the terrain, legislators do manage to represent their constituencies. One reason that they do so is that they identify with their constituents—as one of them and not simply as their agents. They have spent considerable time living in their districts, although not necessarily their entire lives. One-third of the nation's state legislators, in fact, were not born in the states they represent. In Arizona, Florida, and Nevada majorities of the members had moved in from elsewhere.[5] But others, like Tom Loftus of Sun Prairie, Wisconsin, were born in the districts they were elected to represent. Loftus describes what his upbringing meant in terms of identifying with people in the district:

> Like many of those represented, I was raised a Lutheran and married a Catholic, can eat lutefisk with a smile, speak some Norwegian and some German, know how to play euchre, and with the help of beer, can dance the polka. Like most of those I represented, I understand everything Garrison Keillor has to say.[6]

Even if they are new to their districts, members are quick studies when it comes to identifying with their districts.

As is shown in Table 2-3, the "five-state survey" indicates that 27 percent of the legislators have lived their entire lives in the districts they now represent. Another 40 percent have lived in their districts twenty-five years or more. All but 17 percent have twenty or more years of residence. The variation is not great among the states: while 75 percent of Maryland legislators have lived in their districts twenty-five years or more, 59 percent of Washington legislators have done so. At the other end of the spectrum, on average only 5 percent are

Table 2-3   Number of Years Legislators Have Lived in Districts They Represent (in percentages)

Length of time	Total	State				
		Maryland	Minnesota	Ohio	Vermont	Washington
Less than five years	1	1	0	5	1	2
Five to nine years	4	1	3	11	6	0
Ten to nineteen years	12	12	13	9	12	11
Twenty to twenty-four years	16	11	19	5	17	28
Twenty-five years or more	40	46	36	27	41	48
All their lives	27	29	29	43	23	11
Total	100	100	100	100	100	100

Source: Data compiled by the author.

relative newcomers, with nine or fewer years of residency. In Ohio, however, 16 percent are in that category. Change may be underway, as residency "requirements" appear to be relaxing. Of those legislators with ten or more years in the legislature, 36 percent have spent all of their lives in the district. Out of those with less than ten years of service, only 23 percent have lived only in their districts.

The people who are elected to the state legislature have to *represent* their constituencies, but they do not have to *mirror* them. Collectively, the legislature looks different than the public. Members are older, better educated, and higher incomed than the population they represent. Most important, they have chosen politics and public service as careers—or partial careers, for those who plan on short-term service. For almost half of the respondents in the "five-state survey" the legislature is not their first elected office. Serving in these legislatures are former mayors, members of municipal councils, county commissioners, school board members, and a few who have been elected statewide. The variations among the five states in terms of elective-office experience is significant—67 percent in Vermont, 52 percent in Ohio, 36 percent in Washington, 31 percent in Minnesota, and 29 percent in Maryland. In Vermont, for example, many of the legislators had had experience either on local councils or school boards. The route to the legislature differs from state to state.

Legislators are people who are deeply interested in politics and government. Even though they may not have held prior office, they either participated in politics or followed politics closely. In his study of Ohio legislators, Samuel C. Patterson found that some said they had been fascinated by politics for as long as they could remember and others became so either through personal experience or by working on a campaign. Some even acquired the political urge from studying politics in school. Others were motivated by a sense of civic duty.[7]

Legislators in the states are "citizen legislators." Unlike their counterparts in the U.S. Congress, members of every state legislature are permitted to earn outside income. Only in a few states are legislators paid substantial salaries. In California they receive base pay of $99,000 per year, in New York $79,500, and in Pennsylvania $61,900. In New Mexico they are paid nothing and in New Hampshire $200 for their two-year term. In the five states under special study here, the pay is not much for people with families. Ohio legislators, who meet year round, receive $53,700. Leaders earn somewhat more than the rank and file. Maryland, Minnesota, and Washington legislators earn $31,000–$32,000. In Vermont legislators are paid $536 a week, which means that if they put in twenty weeks at a session they will earn just under $11,000 for the year.

In states such as California, Illinois, Massachusetts, Michigan, Ohio, and Pennsylvania legislators serve essentially full time, although a good number work somewhat at other occupations as well. In about fifteen states including North Dakota, Wyoming, and Vermont legislators are more part time, and those who are not retired or otherwise financially secure hold additional jobs. It is very tough financially for a legislator with a family in Vermont. The salary is low but the time commitment is high. To get by, one has to be single and willing to live frugally, be comfortably retired, or just plain rich. According to the National Conference of State Legislatures, taking into account session time, interim work, constituent service, and political work, the amount of time legislative service requires is roughly three-quarters to full time in ten states, one-third to three-quarters time in thirty states, and less than one-third time in ten states.

Clearly, members spend more time on their legislative work when the legislature is in session and less in the interim periods between sessions. According to the "five-state survey," during the session 46 percent of the legislators spend sixty or more hours a week and another 29 percent spend from fifty to fifty-nine hours a week at their legislative jobs. During the interim periods, the percentages working such long hours are lower, with 58 percent spending fewer than twenty-five hours doing legislative work of one kind or another. The hours per week during the session and interim for the five states surveyed are shown in Table 2-4. Just about everyone puts in at least the normal forty-hour workweek, while majorities put in sixty hours or more in Maryland, Minnesota, and Washington, all at so-called part-time jobs. Legislators spend somewhat less time in Vermont, the only complete citizen legislature of the five. Here not many grind away more than sixty hours a week during the session. In Maryland the session lasts for ninety calendar days, in Minnesota 120 legislative days (over the biennium), in Ohio roughly 130 days a year, in Vermont four or five months, and in Washington 105 calendar days in odd-numbered years and sixty calendar days in even-numbered years. When legislators are not in session they still have work to do, as is indicated by the time they spend during the interim, shown in Table 2-4. They are no longer full-time legislators; thus, in these months they can ply their other trades. Even so, 71 percent in Ohio, 63 percent in Washington, and 53 percent in Maryland put in twenty-five hours a week or more on constituency, political, and legislative study work. Only 35 percent in Minnesota and 10 percent in Vermont spend that much time. Two-thirds of Vermont's legislators are at their jobs during the

Table 2-4   Hours per Week on the Job during the Session and the Interim
(in percentages)

Hours per week	Total	State				
		Maryland	Minnesota	Ohio	Vermont	Washington
Session						
Thirty-nine or less	5	3	0	11	11	1
Forty to forty-nine	20	14	18	20	38	0
Fifty to fifty-nine	29	20	31	44	35	19
Sixty or more	46	63	51	25	16	80
Total	100	100	100	100	100	100
Interim						
Fourteen or less	30	16	30	6	66	9
Fifteen to twenty-four	28	31	35	23	24	28
Twenty-five to thirty-four	22	31	21	28	10	26
Thirty-five or more	20	22	14	43	0	37
Total	100	100	100	100	100	100

Source: Data compiled by the author.

interim for fourteen hours a week or less. They have citizen status, and they behave accordingly.

In terms of time spent at the job during the session, it does not matter whether the legislator is in the majority or minority party, or whether he or she is a Democrat or a Republican. But when it comes to gender, it does. Female legislators tend to spend more time at work than their male colleagues, in part because they are less likely to have other occupational commitments. Of most significance is the length of service. Of those with ten or more years' service, 61 percent spend sixty or more hours a week, but of those with four years' or less, only 29 percent spend that much time at their jobs. With tenure comes responsibility. In terms of time spent at the job during the interim, gender again makes a difference. Among women, 31 percent spend thirty-five hours a week at work or more; among men, only 13 percent do. Here is where outside occupations require time from people who have not been able to give it during the session. Veteran legislators spend more interim time on the job, just as they spend more session time. Among those with ten or more years of service, 27 percent devote thirty-five hours or more per week, but among those with four years or less, only 15 percent work thirty-five hours or more.

Legislators in these states and elsewhere understandably feel that they do not have enough time to do their jobs. "If only I had more time in the day" wished a Minnesota house member. "There isn't enough time, if you want to live a reasonable normal life," echoed a Vermont house member. A member of the Minnesota house bemoaned the fact that "There is a lack of time to meet with constituents. Working and keeping in touch is difficult and takes a lot of time." Legislators also feel the need for more staff to help them with constituency work.

They would also like to have district offices, which among the five states sur-veyed were luxuries known only to Maryland legislators. Nor do rank-and-file legislators have much staff at their disposal at their capitol offices. Take Min-nesota, for example. Here, senators each have one full-time staff member, while three representatives have to share one legislative assistant. If legislators lack resources in most states, in Vermont they are virtually nonexistent. Members have no staff whatsoever for constituency work and no capitol—let alone dis-trict—office. Legislators feel the lack, but they have adjusted to it. One Vermont senator explained: "As a citizen legislator, I personally am limited as to the serv-ices I can provide my constituents. Having some staff assistance would be invalu-able, but it won't happen. So I (we) do the best we can."

Constituency Service

Limited or not in the support they get, legislators service their constituents and constituencies in many ways. Just how legislators provide service depends on the district's population, on the legislature, and how active and imaginative the representative chooses to be. At the *individual* level good service to con-stituents involves communicating with them, acknowledging them, educating them, and helping them with their government-related problems. At the *symbolic* level good service requires being at one with constituencies so that people feel represented. And at the *district* level good service means "bringing home the bacon"—that is, providing funds for local projects, defending the district, and even occasionally getting involved in community activities.

Being One of Them

As discussed earlier, some lawmakers have been born and raised in their dis-tricts, while others have been in residence for years when they get to the legis-lature. Even recent arrivals put down roots rather quickly, if they have any thought of entering politics. Most have organizational or political affiliations and a number have already been elected to public office before coming to the legis-lature. And outside of politics, legislators work at jobs just like their constituents do. The "five-state survey" found that overall only 11 percent admitted to being full-time legislators, while another 13 percent said that they were retired. Thus, three out of four have other jobs (including the 5 percent who are homemak-ers). The largest bloc, 13 percent, is made up of attorneys; about 25 percent are in business-related occupations; and 11 percent are educators. With 39 percent, Ohio has more full-time legislators—including the retired as well as those who report no other occupation—than any of the other four states. Washington fol-lows with 26 percent; then Vermont, with 25 percent (nearly all of whom are retired); Maryland with 24 percent; and Minnesota with 17 percent. Women are much more likely than men to declare no occupation other than legislator, with 20 percent as opposed to 6 percent (in addition to 12 percent as opposed to 14 percent retirees).

Because most legislators have to supplement their legislative salaries with other employment, they feel that they do not have sufficient time to do their legislature job as well as they would like. "The requirement to be one of them," John E. McDonough writes, "is onerous, draining, time-consuming, and relentless. There are always far more events, meetings, and conferences to attend than one human can accomplish. The act of representing is complex and varied, and can't be reduced to a single dimension or act." [8] Legislators, as representatives, have to be constantly available to one and all. They have to communicate in a way that says they understand the pressures in the lives of their constituents. They need to have pictures of themselves with members of the communities they represent, so called "photo actualities." [9] It helps if the district is small enough that the representative can knock on every door during an election campaign. Indeed, in Vermont if house members do not go door to door, constituents will feel slighted by the neglect. It does not take many votes to win a district in that state. Wright recounts that a district is only 3,700 people, which includes children and not just voters. Eligible voters might number about 2,200. If the turnout were unusually high, a victory could be achieved by appealing to as few as 900 voters.[10] If the district is too large for door to door, legislators go where constituents are to meet with them—the library, shopping malls, and local meetings. The election campaign is important, even if the district is not competitive. It enables legislators to reach out and ask their constituents for their support, their votes. It provides legislators with an opportunity to educate voters, at least a bit. Just as critical, the campaign educates the candidate about his or her district. Loftus writes, "All the handshaking, all the pleasantries exchanged, help make a politician representative." [11]

Attending meetings with people in the district allows legislators to communicate their linkage to the people in their district. In the "five-state survey" legislators were asked to rate the importance of attending meetings with people in the district on a scale from 1, not important, to 5, very important. Of the total, 83 percent rated the activity 5 or 4, with no substantial differences among the five states. Only 3 percent of the respondents rated the activity as 1, or not important.

Legislators spend as much time as they can attending events and meetings with their constituents and/or constituency groups. Such functions take place in their districts or in the capital city. Those who travel weekly back and forth to their districts have fewer nights available back home, while those living within driving distance of the capital have more nights available. For example, Brad Benson, a member of the Washington legislature from Spokane, moves to Olympia for the session, bringing his family with him. He still returns to his district four or five weekends during the course of the legislative session. When the session is over, he opens up shop in Spokane practically full time, meeting with people and listening to them. Other legislators, who live a considerable distance from the capital, leave their families in the district and during the session return to pursue their occupations and their constituents (and see their families) over an extended weekend. In addition, receptions for legislators, hosted by statewide interest groups in the capital, allow legislators additional opportunities to get together with some of their constituents. During the course of a legislative session, legislators manage an average of 2.35 nights a week meeting with constituents or constituency groups, ranging from an average of 1.64 in Vermont to 3.05 in Ohio. During interim periods, when they are in their districts nearly full time but also engaged in their other employment, legislators average 2.16 nights a week, ranging from 2.98 in Ohio to 1.2 in Vermont.

Few legislators grow too big for their districts. No matter what their lawmaking positions and responsibilities, they stay in close touch. Thomas Finneran, for example, has been a member of the Massachusetts house since 1979 and speaker since 1996. He represents the Twelfth Suffolk District, which includes sections of Dorchester, Mattapan, and Milton. The district's composition has changed over the years, but Finneran's presence has been constant. He is described as a man who continues to care deeply about people, one who responds to phone calls and shows up at local events. He has a reputation for being accessible, despite the responsibilities he bears on Beacon Hill.[12]

Lawmakers everywhere resemble Finneran in his representational behavior—they identify *with* their constituencies and are connected *to* their constituencies. And it pays off. "They don't really care how I vote," says Maryland senator Norman Stone Jr., "as long as I get around." And he does, to every event and every meeting back home. If these public officials make the rounds and pay their respects, chances are they will be positively viewed. "People don't care how you vote," says Speaker Walter Freed of Vermont. "If they like you, that's what counts."

Communicating

One veteran Maryland lawmaker offered the following advice to the newly elected: "Above all else, answer your constituent mail and phone calls first. This is more important than being schmoozed by the governor or anyone else." [13] Few legislators need such counsel. When asked to rate the importance of communicating with constituents on a scale of 1 to 5, from least to most important, legislators in the "five-state survey" overwhelmingly agreed it was very important. The average score was 4.61, with little variation among the states or by party, seniority, or gender.

A member of the Maryland house expressed a view held generally: "I wish constituents contacted me more often. I am constantly trying to find more ways to contact them." A Vermont house member echoed the sentiment: "I wish I could find more ways to communicate, both face to face, in groups, and in the media." Legislators manage well face to face, but they still cannot contact as many people as they would like. Some send notes of congratulations to families celebrating a child's high school graduation or letters of condolence to those mourning a loved one, sometimes managing to get thank-you notes in return. An increasing number of members have Internet sites, to which they refer constituents. In Ohio and Washington they find newsletters especially useful, but the numbers of pieces that can be mailed are limited and prohibited in the period before elections.

Legislators would like to be able to communicate to constituents through the media, but they get precious little coverage. If they are in metropolitan areas, neither electronic nor print media care much about what they are doing, unless they are involved in sensational or highly controversial issues. There is little interest in them as individuals plodding away for their constituents. If they are in more rural areas, they do better in getting space, at least in local weeklies. A number can get regular columns they write printed in local newspapers. But many local publications will not run such columns because they are "not local enough" or "too political." Without the help of local media outlets, and with strict limitations on the number of pieces of mail that can be sent, one Ohio house member wondered, "How are we supposed to keep 115,000 people informed on issues?"

Legislators in the "five-state survey" believed overwhelmingly, scoring a mean of 4.19, that it was very important for them to educate their constituents about issues in the legislature. Women felt somewhat more strongly on this respect than men, but otherwise there were no differences by state or legislative status. One house member in Ohio went as far as to say, "As a new legislator I hope to teach my constituents about the votes of their political leaders and encourage them to become more active in the political process and proactive on issues that affect them." Most of them take their communications responsibility very seriously.

Helping People and Groups

Beyond talk, legislators are eager to give people whatever help they can. They consider that to be a central part of their representational function, and one which they are happy to perform (and would do even better, they believe, if only they had more time and staff!). Moreover, retail service to constituents and constituency groups brings dividends. Legislators recruit support and campaign contributions from the people they help, and they expect them at least to proffer their votes.

Indeed, most legislators seek out constituent requests, so that they (or their offices) can be of help. And constituent requests seek out legislators, in all but the most citizen of legislatures. There may not be many such requests on average, but there are enough to keep legislators in touch with problems of constituents. In the "five-state survey" members were asked to estimate the number of constituent requests for help they handled per week. A majority of members overall handled fewer than ten, but 10 percent of them handled fifty or more. The work distribution among the states is shown in Table 2-5. Other than Vermont, with its very small house districts, legislatures are not terribly dissimilar in the numbers of constituent requests that are generated, although Ohio's workload is somewhat greater than those of Maryland, Minnesota, and Washington. As expected, because senate districts are larger than house districts, senators

Table 2-5 Number of Constituent Requests for Help Handled per Week (in percentages)

Number of requests	Total	State				
		Maryland	Minnesota	Ohio	Vermont	Washington
Four or fewer	26	11	22	7	62	14
Five to nine	25	23	30	19	24	28
Ten to twenty-four	30	41	28	40	11	35
Twenty-five to forty-nine	9	12	9	19	1	7
Fifty or more	10	13	11	15	2	16
Total	100	100	100	100	100	100

Source: Data compiled by the author.

receive more requests than representatives typically do. What really makes a difference, however, is seniority. Of legislators serving ten or more years, 19 percent receive fifty or more requests per week; of those serving five to nine years, 11 percent receive fifty or more requests per week; and of those serving four years or fewer, only 4 percent get fifty or more. With years of service, legislators build up a clientele. Some of these requests require substantial effort, but many can be handled with relative dispatch. It does not have to be a big deal; legislators know that "people really appreciate the little things," as one Maryland senator put it. One of these little things is just listening. For example, West Virginia delegate James Manchin recounted how one constituent telephoned him to complain that the dogs in his neighborhood were barking frequently and loudly. "What do you want me to do?" the legislator asked. "Nothing," was the reply. "I just want to talk to someone about it."

Another one of these little things is acknowledgment. One way representatives acknowledge the folks in their districts is by showing up at events and meetings back home. If invited, they attend—if they possibly can. In delivering their remarks at luncheons, dinners, and the like they are sure to say something nice about the community, the group, and the individuals associated with the function. When constituents travel to the capitol building their representatives are there to welcome them and give them whatever time they can. During the legislative session members will be visited by any number of groups, from sixth graders to automobile dealers. Between floor sessions, caucuses, and committee meetings, legislators will go from one place to the next in the building to meet and greet individual constituents or delegations. Or they will meet with them in their offices.

Legislators in Maryland, Minnesota, Ohio, and Washington have or share office space in which to meet with delegations from their districts. In Vermont, however, it is an entirely different story. Instead of offices, legislators make do with file cabinets in the rooms of the committees on which they serve. Even Peter Shumlin, the president pro tem of the senate—who does have an office—is quite limited in the size of the delegation he can invite to visit. His office is about 12 x 15 feet and is shared with an assistant and a desk. All he has is a couch that seats three people, but not very comfortably, and a desk chair. Folding chairs, however, are available and can be set up to seat two or three more visitors. When a dozen or so people want to see him, he takes them to the senate floor—that is, if the senate is not in session at the time. Ordinarily, legislators meet with constituents, lobbyists, and anybody else in the state house cafeteria. When the senate or house is not in session and standing committees are not at work, the cafeteria is where just about everyone can be found, and it is where much business is transacted.

Legislators not only acknowledge constituents in the cafeteria or in their offices, they also convey acknowledgment more formally. Following the call to order, the prayer or devotional exercise, and the pledge of allegiance, and before the calendar of legislative business is addressed on the floor, a senate or a house normally will recognize visitors in the gallery or near the podium. The Ohio senate, for instance, has no gallery so visitors are seated on both sides and at the rear of the chamber. On May 22, 2001, the Ohio senate welcomed the Graham High School wrestling team, which had just won the division wrestling championship. The senator who represented the district introduced the seventeen young men on the team. "I congratulate you," she said, "as a mama who had two wrestlers." On April 3, 2001, in St. Paul, the University of Minnesota at Duluth women's ice hockey team was applauded by the members assembled in the senate chamber, while in recess. It had won the National Collegiate Athletic Association (NCAA) Division I women's hockey championship. Since the team's players had to be in class, they were not able to be there to watch both the Minnesota senate and house pass resolutions commending them, so the team coach and university administrators had to represent the players who were being honored.

On April 6, 2001, members of the University of Maryland Terrapins basketball team were honored for their success in the NCAA tournament. They were commended in a resolution passed by the senate for being a "source of pride" for the state. Earlier in that same legislative session, on March 14, the Maryland house recognized a group of citizens from Allegheny County. A delegate from Western Maryland introduced the visitors, who stood in the gallery while legislators rose at their desks on the floor and applauded. On March 21 the Snow Hill Eagles boys' basketball team was commended for its 22–5 record, and team members had their picture taken with the speaker.

In each of these states hundreds and hundreds of resolutions are passed at each legislative session to acknowledge youngsters and adults alike. In a small state like Vermont about two hundred resolutions are passed at each session, similar to the J.R.S. 49, on April 10, 2001, in which Sen. Gerry Gossens congratulated a high school field hockey team. The resolution gave a capsule description of the Mount Abraham Eagles' championship game against the team's rivals from Champlain Valley Union High School. In a scoreless tie at halftime, the team rallied in the second half, thanks to the goal-scoring duo of Miranda Jones and Michaela Casey and another goal by Alexis Butler. Mentioning the entire team by name in one *"Whereas"* clause and the coaching staff in another, the resolution concluded: "Resolved by the Senate and House of Representatives: That the General Assembly congratulates the 2000 Division II championship Mount Abraham High School field hockey team. . . ."

Reinforcing the connection of representative to constituency is the form of address used on the floor of the senate or house. Sometimes legislators are referred to as being from specific numbered districts, sometimes from particular counties. Occasionally, the nameplates on their desks also have local designations. The localism of the Vermont legislature, for instance, is evident in how members of the house are addressed by the presiding officer. Each is referred to by the town he or she represents, whether it is Brattleboro, Burlington, Jericho, Winooski, or wherever.

Casework

Less symbolically, legislators assist constituents with casework and appointments. The latter involves getting them named to boards and commissions and helping them find jobs on the public payroll. The former relates to helping constituents with problems they may have regarding welfare benefits, health and hospital benefits, unemployment compensation, traffic conditions, nursing-home care, driver's licenses, insurance costs, taxes—almost anything under the sun.

Years ago legislators appeared to be much less involved in the service function than they are today. Of the 474 members in California, New Jersey, Ohio, and Tennessee interviewed almost four decades ago by John Wahlke and his associates, only about one-quarter spontaneously mentioned service as an important aspect of the job. Depending on the state, anywhere from one-third to two-thirds would now cite constituency service as an important, or even *the* most important, part of the job of being a legislator. Research conducted several years ago by Malcolm Jewell shows that constituency service looms extremely large in California, Massachusetts, Ohio, and Texas; less so in Indiana, Kentucky, and Tennessee; and hardly at all in Colorado and North Carolina. The differences are attributable, at least in part, to the availability of staff to take on constituency service tasks in some places but not in others. Take Michigan, for example, where legislators have staff assistance. As described by William P. Browne and Kenneth Ver Burg, legislators are asked to intervene with bureaucracies on behalf of constituents to get them a waterway dredging permit, or even to find them temporary lodging. Satisfying constituents is a major task of their staffs, taking up more than two-thirds of their office time.[14]

Without resources at their disposal, legislators in states like Vermont do less casework than those in states like Ohio (and, certainly, states such as California, New Jersey, and New York). Yet legislators in each of the five states surveyed felt that casework was very important. On a scale of 1 (not important) to 5 (very important), overall they rated its importance at 4.46, with little variation among the legislatures. It is just as important for Republicans as for Democrats, minority members as majority members, veterans as newcomers, and male as female legislators. And few ignore doing it.

Pork and Projects

Bringing home the bacon—that is, pork barrel projects—is also on the service agenda of legislators, although it does not rank as high as casework. Overall, legislators in the "five-state survey" rate the importance of getting projects for their districts at 3.53. This activity is more important for Maryland and Ohio legislators, less so in Minnesota, Vermont, and Washington, and substantially less so for Republican than for Democratic legislators, but it ranks about the same for veterans and newer members, majority and minority members, and men and women.

In their representational capacity, legislators seek projects that range from the prominent (such as courthouses) to the paltry (such as funds for boys' choirs and high-school bands). Some spare no efforts to bring home bacon. Minnesota's freshman senator Michele Bachmann is a case in point. After the Minnesota Department of Transportation canceled her efforts to get a new four-lane bridge over the St. Croix River in Stillwater because of insufficient funding, she tried to offer an amendment in the Senate Tax Committee that would have provided the additional $18 million necessary to complete the project. The chair, however, refused to call for a vote on her proposal. Bachmann tried again on the senate floor, but once again the majority party did not allow it to come to a vote. Undeterred, the senator tried to convince the department not to cancel the project and solicited the member of Congress from the area for help. She was not about to abandon her efforts on behalf of her district.[15]

Bringing home the bacon was difficult for a minority member like Bachmann. But it was a problem even for her majority Democratic-Farmer-Labor (DFL) colleagues. Gov. Jesse Ventura had taken a position against adding local projects to an emergency bonding bill. Already included in the bill were funds for the University of Minnesota, flood hazard mitigation, conservation, digital television conversion, and wastewater treatment, totaling $213.5 million. But the DFL anticipated a rash of amendments for local projects that would never survive a conference committee. Members of the DFL caucus were asked by their majority leader, Roger Moe, to stick together and be disciplined. "What do we do about amendments on local projects when they come up?" asked one senator. "What about the balance between metro and rural?" questioned another. DFL members were committed to getting as much as they could for their individual districts, and they were competing for a limited pie, so the caucus discussion of local projects became pretty contentious.

In Maryland the process of constructing the capital budget—which includes local projects—commands the undivided attention of legislators, who feel strongly about bringing something home. It is up to legislative leaders to figure out how to divvy up the limited amount of funding for capital projects. Speaker Cas Taylor wanted a one-time expenditure for his district, Allegheny County, included in the capital budget. The subcommittee chair handling the capital budget was concerned: "My only problem is that I open the door to twenty-three other counties." As the process proceeded, requests were whittled down. At a hearing of the Senate Budget and Taxation Committee, at which constituent groups were advocating their projects, Sen. Barbara Hoffman, the chair, questioned: "How much do you need for Healthy Neighborhoods?" When she was told $2 million, Hoffman responded: "You've got to be kidding. How about $1 million?" That amount would have to do. Other requests were eliminated. All told, members of the Maryland senate and house had asked for $39.1 million for projects such as museums, recreation centers, theaters, hospitals, and so forth. The capital budget finally included less than half of what was requested, amounting to $18.8 million for legislators' bond bills.

State Aid

Service also entails getting as much state aid for the district as possible. Critical here are school aid formulas that allocate a large share of the funding for K–12 education. Legislators responding to the "five-state survey" consider getting local aid formulas that produce dollars for their districts to be important, but not as important, as casework. They rank it about the same as getting projects for people and groups in their constituencies. Overall, they rate the importance of delivering local aid at 3.65, roughly the same in Maryland, Minnesota, Ohio, and Vermont, but slightly lower in Washington. No difference exists between majority and minority members, but Democrats are far more concerned with this task than Republicans.

In Vermont, Sen. Cheryl Rivers, the powerful chair of the Finance Committee, discussed with fiscal staff revision of Act 60 and the variety of very technical indexes that could be used to allocate funds to Vermont towns for their schools. The staff had employed different models and produced numerous computer runs. Amidst the technical comparisons, however, Rivers did not ignore one thing: how her own constituency would fare under successive options. "It's unfair to my little town," she interjected. "They're going to be mad." That is because her constituents felt the state was "sending all the money north," and her district was further south.

Similarly, in the midst of managing the legislative process in the Maryland house, Speaker Taylor turned his attention to HB1 and new money for Allegheny County schools. He had worked with local school boards in fashioning the bill. The new money would be included in the governor's supplemental budget bill and Taylor would make sure of it. In addition, he would ask the governor to issue a press release that would notify his constituents that the district was benefiting. Although the schools had asked for more, the speaker managed to get them about $5 million in additional funding, by no means a bad day's work for a legislator trying to serve his district. At around the same time, Senate Majority Leader Moe had his hands full with what could have become a revolt in the DFL caucus in Minnesota. Just about all the school districts represented by his members were unhappy and fearful that teachers might have to be laid off.

Those who received more state aid, including so-called "equity aid," felt under-funded because their needs were so great. The wealthier districts received less aid and were capped, so they could not raise local tax rates beyond a certain point. These districts objected to being leveled down. "I have to explain to St. Louis Park why they are getting less money than other districts," exclaimed Sen. Steve Kelley from a suburban district. The reason was Minnesota's attempt to narrow spending disparities among the districts. That did not satisfy Kelley or his constituents, who felt that narrowing the gap was not bringing the bottom up but rather bringing the top down.

In dealing with the education part of the budget, the Minnesota legislators were primarily concerned with how well their districts would do under alternative formulas and allocations. One computer run after another was brought to their attention as they spoke in favor of "fairness" to their districts. One DFL senator, relating how education was suffering in his district, almost burst into tears while meeting with the majority leader. During consideration by the Tax Committee of the omnibus K–12 financial bill, another senator complained: "I have five school districts and they don't think it's equal at all." Some DFLers did better than others for their districts. Lawrence Pogemiller was one of them. As chair of the Education Committee for eight years, he had provided aggressive leadership in the field and managed to protect the interests of his Minneapolis district. Meanwhile, his suburban DFL colleagues fared less well.

At a meeting with DFLers on the K–12 budget division (subcommittee), Majority Leader Moe made efforts to bring members together. The conflict was between the inner cities on the one hand and the surrounding suburbs on the other. If they could have freed up additional monies, the districts that felt short-changed could have been given more. But by late April revenues were pretty well locked in so that extra resources were not in the offing. DFLers representing the northern and western suburbs were unhappy with the school finance bill the senate majority appeared to be backing. Moe realized that a number of his party colleagues would be put in a tough position on the floor, and he wanted to figure out how to mitigate their discomfort and the possibility that suburban DFLers would suffer at the polls because of equity funding going to Minneapolis and St. Paul. "If we don't do something, the Republicans will take over," said one senator. They had not been able to reach a consensus in committee, with Republicans participating, so they had to try to do it in caucus. The committee chair, LeRoy Stumpf, indicated, "We need to decide on a strategy we can all stay together on. If not, the Republicans will pick us apart." "Mr. Chairman," the majority leader responded, "when we have a bill on the floor, we can't lose votes."

On the one hand, the DFL stood in principle for equity funding, but on the other hand it was concerned about Republican challenges to members representing the northern and western suburbs. The DFL had a policy position, but members also had constituency positions, with the suburbs squaring off against the cities. Each computer run, in search of a consensus formula, alerted members to exactly how their districts would fare. Suburban members complained that they could not justify what they would get to their constituents. City members argued how their districts had special needs. The majority leader urged them to relax about their districts and find some balance. The discussion among DFL senators was about as parochial as it could be, with representation of their districts by far the strongest value expressed.

And More

Constituency service involves a multiplicity of representational activities, legislative and otherwise. A proposal that would financially assist people who have high levels of radium in their well water was of special help to residents of Pasadena, Maryland. A bill specifying that a county transfer station could not be built within two miles of Bowie State University was of special benefit to the African American institution that suggested that an industrial site be found for a station where garbage would be taken in and compacted before being shipped off.[16] The senate president, in defense of his district, pushed legislation that would block construction of a supermarket and a strip mall.

John E. McDonough, who had represented Jamaica Plain, a Boston neighborhood, in the Massachusetts house, recounts just how far constituency service could extend. Every Saturday morning one of his colleagues, Steve Angelo, helped constituents unload newspapers and bottles from their cars for the recycling program in Saugus. That was service. McDonough himself writes of his efforts to resolve differences between the Egleston Square community in his district and a local street gang, and of his work to develop an economic development master plan for the area. According to him, for an urban legislator representation means acting as a social worker, preacher, negotiator, salesperson, coach, and street worker. He especially likes "plumber" as a metaphor for representative: "I fixed problems and tried to improve systems using my special box of tools," [17] he says.

How Service Counts

Legislators believe that constituency service contributes to their reelections, since virtually all incumbents are reelected. Therefore, this is an activity that deserves their time and energy. Good service is good politics and good politics means additional votes. What explains the fact, however, that even the many members in relatively safe districts work diligently at service? The truth is that good service is more than votes; it conveys other benefits to people who run for and are elected to public office. Legislators believe that an important part of representation is looking out for their district and running errands for and intervening with government on behalf of their constituents. That is an ingrained belief. Moreover, legislators want to have a sense of fulfillment in the jobs they do, and taking care of their constituents is a fulfilling activity.

The results of providing service tend to be tangible—information supplied and errands run, projects authorized, and funding allocated. By contrast, the process of lawmaking tends to be less tangible, more indeterminate. What one wants by way of legislation is seldom what one gets; legislators have to settle for far less than they ask for. Individual satisfaction is harder to come by in lawmaking. Providing service does require time, but not stress. And there are always benefits of one sort or another. Recall that legislators in the "five-state survey" expressed their belief that doing casework is more important than getting projects and funding formulas that benefit their districts. This is because casework depends mainly on their individual efforts. Whether they succeed or not, they leave the constituents they serve with a positive feeling. People feel that their representatives went to bat for them. And legislators themselves have a sense of accomplishment. By contrast, projects and funding formulas are part of lawmaking, a process in which legislators' agendas compete and in which legislators have to depend on one another to achieve anything at all. Accomplishment and gratification are in shorter supply, while frustration is in greater supply. No wonder, then, that being an ombudsman is considered to be so important. In legislative life the rewards of connecting to the constituency are handsome. No wonder, also, that legislators are so good at this part of the job.

NOTES

1. Samuel C. Patterson, "Legislative Politics in Ohio," in Alexander Lamis, ed., *Ohio Politics* (Kent: Ohio State University Press, 1994), 240, note 12.

2. Jane Mansbridge, "Rethinking Representation," *American Political Science Review* 97 (November 2003): 515–528.

3. Ralph Wright, *All Politics Is Personal* (Manchester Center, Vt.: Marshall Jones Company, 1996), 20.

4. Anthony Gierzynski, "Elections to the State Legislatures," in Joel H. Silbey, ed., *Encyclopedia of the American Legislative System* (New York: Scribner's, 1994), 441.

5. Joel A. Thompson and Gary F. Moncrief, "Nativity, Mobility, and State Legislators," in Moncrief and Thompson, eds., *Changing Patterns in State Legislative Careers* (Ann Arbor: University of Michigan Press, 1992), 26–27.

6. Tom Loftus, *The Art of Legislative Politics* (Washington, D.C.: CQ Press, 1994), 7.

7. Patterson, "Legislative Politics in Ohio," 238–239.

8. John E. McDonough, *Experiencing Politics* (Berkeley: University of California Press, 2000), 163.

9. Remarks of David Dixon, a political consultant, to senate Democratic caucus in Maryland, March 13, 2001.

10. Wright, *All Politics Is Personal*, 233.

11. Loftus, *The Art of Legislative Politics*, 16.

12. *Boston Sunday Globe*, February 23, 2003.

13. Howard A. Denis, "To a Young Legislator," *Baltimore Sun*, January 10, 1995.

14. John C. Wahlke et al., *The Legislature System* (New York: Wiley, 1962), 267–286; Malcolm E. Jewell, *Representation in State Legislatures* (Lexington: University Press of Kentucky, 1982); and William P. Browne and Kenneth Ver Burg, *Michigan Politics and Government* (Lincoln: University of Nebraska Press, 1995), 110.

15. Sen. Michele Bachmann, *Stillwater Gazette*, May 3, 2001.

16. *Prince George's Journal*, March 30, 2001.

17. McDonough, *Experiencing Politics*, 59, 61, 144.

3 REPRESENTATION: EXPRESSING CONSTITUENCY VIEWS

Service is relatively easy to figure out, as far as representatives themselves are concerned. They may not have the wherewithal to achieve their objectives fully, but they know what they have to do in this area of their work: as much as possible and get as much as possible for the constituency and constituents. From time to time intervening on behalf of constituents may raise questions about the legitimacy of people's claims, but rarely does this complicate the life of the representative. When it comes to casework, the claims are passed on and it is usually up to executive branch officials to decide on the case's merits. The problem with pork and projects is that on occasion a representative has to choose among various competing projects within the district, since there are many worthy claims and only so much to go around. Enacting funding formulas is important to members, but it is one of the most collective endeavors of any legislature. Putting a majority together is daunting, so everyone's demands for local funds have to be scaled down. In all of this, legislators cannot accomplish everything they want to, but they pretty well know what to do and they rarely come home empty handed.

The other part of representation has to do with mirroring or at least giving expression to the policy views of the district and the people in it. This is more difficult for representatives to figure out and, thus, is more difficult for them to do. What views exist and whose views ought to be expressed? At what level of specificity? How do constituency views square with constituency interests? What role should the intensity, organization, and affiliation of district views play in the representative's decision? And what role should the representative's own views play? All of these questions confound the notion of representation as the simple expression of constituency views.

Who They Hear From

How do legislators know what their constituents think about issues on which they have to decide? During the session they find out when they return home and make the rounds in their districts. They find out when constituents visit them or when they attend receptions sponsored by interest groups in the capital. They learn from mail, e-mail, and telephone communications by constituents. If a national sample of respondents in an Internet survey is to be believed, many Americans contact their state senators and state representatives (although substantially more report contacting their U.S. senators and

U.S. representatives). Of nineteen thousand respondents in the fifty-state survey, 7 percent said they contacted their state representatives and 5 percent their state senators in the last twelve months, with about half reporting more than one contact. About 3 to 5 percent said they were expressing an opinion on a bill or on a policy issue.[1]

Just how much legislators hear from their constituencies depends on the nature of the issue and the extent to which grassroots support or opposition is being mobilized. That is to say, much of the communications on issues that legislators receive are organized, not spontaneous. Grassroots lobbying is becoming the norm, at least on substantial and contested issues.[2] As one Maryland delegate commented at a meeting of the house senior leadership, "I have tons of doctors. They're beating on me like a tom tom." One of his senate colleagues, Leo Green, had gotten 450 letters and calls from constituents on a gay rights bill—more than he had received on any previous bill. Both sides targeted Green. Free State Justice, a gay rights organization, organized phone banks and got the senator's friends and associates to visit, call, or write to him. A priest from his parish was sent to talk to him. "Our goal was to have one of his constituents in his office talking about this bill every week of the session," said the organization's executive director. Even one of Green's daughters lobbied him. In Minnesota, during the fight over the budget in the 2001 legislative session, the Republican Party aired radio ads pointing out that the Democratic-Farmer-Labor (DFL) senate majority leader, Roger Moe, was blocking action on property tax cuts. More than six thousand people called legislators in response to television ads run by the teachers' association. Moe's office received on average about 50 budget-related calls a day—a number members thought high, but not as high as the 300–400 calls a day when issues involving guns, abortion, or a sports stadium were being considered by the legislature.[3]

Constituents also show up at the capitol as part of demonstrations organized by interest groups. Hundreds and sometimes thousands of people will rally on the steps of the capitol on an issue or on the state budget. And then members of the crowd fan out to visit the legislators in whose districts they reside. The numbers can be impressive, and the representatives take the one-on-one visits seriously.

There are many issues, however, about which representatives hear little or nothing from the public. They are simply not on the local radar screen, and interested groups have not tried to mobilize constituents, or have not succeeded in doing so. John E. McDonough recalls that despite the importance of campaign finance as an issue to Common Cause and attempts by the Massachusetts legislature to deal with the subject, constituents were unengaged. McDonough never had a single call or letter from a constituent on the issue. He concluded that:

> When it mattered to them, the people spoke. When the discourse became too technical and complex, they tuned out, as long as no one felt the need to reawaken their interest. Such is the reality of much of representation, American style.[4]

If they do not hear from their districts, legislators make efforts to seek out constituency views, especially on contentious issues. They are expected by legislative leaders to use weekends home during the course of a legislative session to check the pulse of their constituency. In Minnesota, for instance, during the 2001 session legislators left Wednesday evening for a five-day Easter weekend during which they could run budget basics by some of their constituents to test the political viability back home of the DFL plan.

In Vermont the process in the house during the same year focused on revision of Act 60, the education finance law that had been passed in the previous legislature. The job of the Republican majority was twofold: first, to educate members on the subject; and second, to have members check possible revisions in their constituencies. "As leadership," the Republican house majority leader addressed his caucus, "I want to build consensus. We want you to be able to talk it over back home." Members of the House Ways and Means Committee, which had the job of fashioning a revision of Act 60, also checked constantly with their constituents. One member reported the people were happy because of the proposed provision for property-tax relief. Another reported that local officials opposed what the committee had been putting together. Many constituents, according to members, were confused by the complexities of the issue. The committee's vice chair indicated, "I go back to the district and speak to people constantly." A Republican caucus member had had early reservations about what was emerging from the committee. After trips to his district, he told the chair, Rep. Richard Marron, that when he talked to people about the proposed lowering of property taxes, even with a rise in sales taxes, he got support. "I'm eating crow here," he said. "You read the state correctly, so I'm leaning your way." His constituents had relieved him of his earlier anxiety.

Legislators are used to hearing the expression of views from organized interests. They are on the receiving end of such input all the time. But what those responding to the "five-state survey" would have liked, as a representative from Washington volunteered, is "more direct communication with a true cross section of the constituency, not just those with an ax to grind." There is an assumption here that those without an ax to grind care enough to actually have opinions and then to advance them, which may not be the case. Several Minnesota legislators added their own frustrations. One wanted a way to determine constituent opinions on the bills that crop up each year, since "orchestrated lobbying efforts aren't particularly representative." Another felt the great need for increasing people's awareness, so they could express themselves like interest groups do. A third would have liked "to have a better mechanism for understanding the views of the uninvolved." That is what a Vermont representative was seeking. "My district mate and I make lots of efforts," he indicated, "but still hear from only a few, except on civil unions." Face-to-face discussions with small groups of constituents might help during the session, but there is no time for that. "What about community meetings attended by constituents? We hold them and few attend," volunteered a Minnesota senator. "Those that attend are cranks, very special interests, or just like to bitch and hear themselves talk."

A Maryland house member came close to advocating some type of referendum or public opinion poll. Since "you only hear from those who are personally affected or care on subjects," he wrote, "it is impossible to really know what the constituency thinks without a total vote of all." Did it occur to these legislators that constituents might not have views on particular public policy issues, but expected their representatives to act on their behalf anyway? In Washington the legislature proposed a gas-tax increase, but the house insisted on putting it on the ballot for approval by the electorate. Legislators did not want to run the political risk of raising a tax on their own; rather let the electorate decide. On a weekend back home, a Washington legislator was confronted by her hairdresser. "I get paid to cut your hair," the hairdresser said, "you get paid to make gas-tax decisions." Some constituents feel that way, but others do not. Most would want to have the power, through the initiative and referendum, to decide on issues even though they do not feel competent to do so.[5]

How They Figure Out Where People Stand

Legislators in the "five-state survey" were asked to rate the importance of eight sources of information in helping them figure out where their constituents stood on issues. The mean scores for each source of information, ranging from 1, "not important," to 5, "very important," are shown in Table 3-1. Legislators regard their political supporters as the most important source of information on constituency views, rating the source 3.92 overall. Political supporters rank highest in each state. Next comes hearing from friends and associates at 3.81. Local political leaders rank lower.

Table 3-1   Importance of Sources of Information on the Views Held by Constituents

Sources of information[a]	Mean Importance[b]					
	Total	Maryland	Minnesota	Ohio	Vermont	Washington
Political supporters in district	3.92	3.92	3.91	4.02	3.94	3.83
Friends and associates	3.81	3.81	3.70	3.89	3.91	3.79
Positions taken by organized groups in district	3.59	3.74	3.52	3.95	3.29	3.62
Political leaders in districts	3.38	3.07	3.38	3.66	3.42	3.62
Public opinion polls	3.08	2.96	3.09	3.20	3.08	3.15
Information from lobbyists	2.99	2.68	3.15	3.41	2.80	3.29
Legislative staff	2.94	3.19	2.81	3.45	2.41	3.02
Local media	2.91	2.84	2.90	3.32	2.68	3.07

Source: Data compiled by the author.

[a] Listed in order of overall importance.

[b] Scores range from 1, "not important," to 5, "very important."

The people from whom they hear most, organized groups in the district, are rated 3.59, ranking third. This source is highest in Ohio, where the district size is largest, and lowest in Vermont, where the district size is smallest. Lobbyists are ranked much lower, probably because the information they provide tends to be statewide and not district by district. Or possibly because legislators do not believe that lobbyists convey accurate information about what ordinary people think and want. In Ohio, however, with its professional legislature, members tend to rely on lobbyists, as well as on political leaders, somewhat more than in other states. Curiously, legislators do not dismiss public opinion polls as sources of information, despite the fact that virtually no polling (outside of polls that may be included in legislators' newsletters) is done at the district level. Legislative staff is not regarded as a very important source of information on constituents' views, probably because staff is so limited and tends to be based in the capital, not in the district. But staff counts more in Ohio, where the legislature is most professionalized. Lowest ranked of the eight sources are the local media, which give legislators in their opinion a better indication of the views of editors than the views of rank-and-file constituents.

Despite the legislative feeling that they do not have adequate information on constituents' opinions and preferences, legislators probably do much better at figuring out their constituencies than they give themselves credit for doing. On many issues, however, the "constituency" as such may not exist as far as rank-and-file opinions are concerned, although interest groups within the constituency do feel strongly and do express their concerns.

In their striving to find out what their constituents think about issues before the legislature, representatives today put faith in classical democratic theory, despite evidence that such theory does not apply in practice. According to this theory, for a democracy to function properly people should be interested in, pay attention to, and participate in politics. Political science research since the 1950s has shown that these requirements are seldom satisfied. Few Americans are engaged in politics and few are familiar with the issues on which their representatives have to act.

As Hanna F. Pitkin noted in her book on representation, a constituency is not a single unit with an opinion on every topic. A representative thus cannot reflect what is not there to be reflected.[6] One Florida legislator pointed out several years ago that there was virtually no opinion in her district on 95 percent of the issues on which she had to vote. She recalled that one of her early votes affected the disposition of the Florida stamp on a beer can. Why should constituents have an opinion on such a subject? "It is rare," she commented, "that I have a sense of really what my district feels on any issue, except the most major questions."[7] A public opinion poll on most issues a legislature faces would not be helpful, since the very term "public opinion" implies the existence of developed public attitudes. Yet as Joseph Bessette, among others, points out, when attitudes are measured by an opinion poll, they may constitute little more than the aggregate of off-hand, unreflective responses to a pollster's questions.[8]

Legislators responding to the "five-state survey" appreciated that not all of their constituents had views on every issue, but some did on each of a small number of issues. Lawmakers were asked to take into account all the bills on which they had to cast a vote (during the biennium ending in 2001). On what percentage of them, respondents were asked to estimate, did a substantial number of their constituents have an opinion one way or the other? Their responses are shown in Table 3-2. Just about half of the total think that a substantial number of their constituents have an opinion on no more than one out of twenty bills on which legislators vote. The percentage of low estimates range from 57 percent of legislators in Minnesota to 37 percent in Washington. Perhaps, because of the initiative activity in Washington, legislators in that state sense a somewhat greater interest on the part of their constituents. In Ohio, the large districts and relatively few bill introductions help explain why 37 percent of the legislators think constituents have an opinion on about one-quarter or more of the bills. Relatively few lawmakers, however, believe that their constituents have opinions one way or the other on many of the issues with which they engage. For the most part, as far as constituency opinion is concerned, legislators are on their own.

Opinions on issues held by constituents are in very short supply. Moreover, belief and opinions are different among the numbers holding opinions. Some could be on one side of an issue and others on the opposite side, balancing out support and opposition. The challenge for legislators is to figure out whether or not something approaching a mandate exists. Legislators in the "five-state survey," therefore, were asked on how many bills that they had voted on during the last two years did their *constituency* have a *clear* position; that is, a large number of constituents were on one side of the issue, while substantially fewer constituents were on the opposite side. The distribution of legislator responses is reported in Table 3-3. Of the total legislators, about half report a clear constituency position on five or fewer bills over a two-year period. Roughly two out of three legislators in Ohio and Vermont report five or fewer bills with clear constituency positions. By contrast, only 17 percent of the total legislators perceive a clear constituency position on more than twenty bills, with about one-quarter of Maryland and

Table 3-2   Percentage of Bills on Which Constituents Had an Opinion

Percentage of bills	Percentage of legislators					
	Total	Maryland	Minnesota	Ohio	Vermont	Washington
About 5 percent or fewer	48	52	57	45	46	37
About 10 percent	26	26	20	18	31	33
About 25 percent	18	16	13	23	16	26
About 50 percent or more	8	6	10	14	7	4
Total	100	100	100	100	100	100

Source: Data compiled by the author.

Table 3-3 Number of Bills on Which Constituency Had a Clear Position

Number of bills	Percentage of legislators reporting					
	Total	Maryland	Minnesota	Ohio	Vermont	Washington
Two or fewer	19	10	11	35	30	13
Three to five	30	30	33	26	36	23
Six to ten	23	22	27	25	20	21
Eleven to twenty	11	12	11	9	10	15
Over twenty	17	26	18	5	4	28
Total	100	100	100	100	100	100

Source: Data compiled by the author.

Washington legislators among this group. Interestingly, the more senior the legislator, the more likely he or she perceives a clear constituency position. Some of the issues had been around for a while, and repeated experience tends to suggest where the constituency stands (or where the legislator believes the constituency stands) and such a suggestion is reinforced over time.

In view of the hundreds and hundreds of bills on which they vote, not to mention the many amendments to bills, legislators seldom have much of an inkling of where their constituents as such stand on the overwhelming majority of them. In every session, however, a number of issues arise about which constituents do have views. But their views do not always run in the same direction; often they are split, with a sizeable number on each side of the issue. A clear constituency position is a rarity. Where, as is most often the case, such a position is absent, legislators have to—and do—decide on the basis of other factors, ranging from their own beliefs and past records to the committee's and their party's position. In these cases constituency is not a factor. But on those issues where constituents do have views and especially where legislators perceive a clear constituency position one way or the other, it is an entirely different matter. Constituency weighs heavily in what legislators decide to do.

Delegate versus Trustee

No discussion of representation would be complete without reference to the classic dichotomy between "delegate" on the one hand and "trustee" on the other. In her book on representation Pitkin posits a continuum, ranging from a "mandate" theory of representation, where legislators assume delegate roles, to an "independence" theory, where they assume trustee roles. At the mandate/delegate end of the continuum, the representative acts on explicit instructions from constituents. Here the representative as delegate is an agent of the constituency, a tool or instrument by which the constituency acts. Further along the continuum, the representative exercises some discretion but is required to consult on controversial issues and then do as the constituency wishes, or else resign. Toward the middle of the continuum a representative acts as he or she thinks constituents would want, unless they give instructions to the contrary, which the representative must obey. Proceeding further toward the independence/trustee position, the representative acts in the way that he or she thinks is in the interests of constituents, unless constituents give instructions to the contrary, which then have to be obeyed. Near the independence/trustee position, the representative must do as he or she thinks best, except insofar as the representative is bound by campaign promises. At the very end of the continuum the representative, once elected, is entirely free to use his or her own judgment as trustee, no matter what he or she promised or what the constituents want.[9]

Legislators are aware of the possibility of being pulled in different directions by conscience and constituency. As part of a legislative orientation program of the Florida house (held in December 2000), several former legislators were asked to render advice to the sixty-three new members who had just been sworn in. Dale Patchett, who had served in the house from 1976 to 1990, had this to say on the subject: "You each came here with your own personal philosophy, underlying beliefs and opinions. . . . Notwithstanding who you are or why you chose to run, you were elected by your peers to be their voice in Tallahassee. Never forget that they elected you to represent their views as well as your own." Richard Longley, who served in the house from 1972 to 1978 and in the senate from 1984 to 1986, put it this way: "When you seek office your platform should identify your beliefs on certain issues. When elected, you should continue to hold, and be guided by, those beliefs. . . . I voted my conscience and beliefs, and eventually a majority of my district disagreed with me. So be it." Such advice comes in various forms and shapes, but much of it relates to what we think of as delegate and trustee models and of representation.[10]

Where do legislators generally position themselves? Do they consider themselves to be delegates or trustees? Political scientists have been exploring this question for over forty years. In 1962 John Wahlke and his associates analyzed the representational role orientations of legislators in California, New Jersey, Ohio, and Tennessee. On the basis of responses to an open-ended survey question, which was later coded, the investigators found that the trustee role predominated in each of the legislatures. More recently a survey of Minnesota legislators found that 85 percent viewed their role mainly as that of trustee, while only one out of ten saw their role mainly as that of delegate. An Ohio study produced somewhat different results. Only 13 percent reported a delegate orientation, while 47 percent reported the trustee orientation. But 40 percent were classified as "politicos," because they insisted that both the delegate and trustee orientations were important to them.[11] Apparently, these politicos saw their role as a mixture of expressing constituency views and using their own expert judgment, depending on the issue. There are a number of reasons why the trustee orientation is more widely held than the delegate orientation. First is the philosophical justification that is expounded by British statesman Edmund Burke in his speech to the electors of Bristol in 1774:

> Their [constituents'] wishes ought to have great weight with him; their opinions high respect; their business unremitted attention. It is his duty to sacrifice his repose, his pleasures, his satisfactions, to theirs—and above all, ever, and in all cases, to prefer their interest to his own. But his unbiased opinion, his mature judgment, his enlightened conscience, he ought not to sacrifice to you. . . . Your representative owes you, not his industry only, but his judgment; and he betrays, instead of serving you, if he sacrifices it to your opinion.

The representative extolled by Burke is a free agent, left unfettered to do his work in the legislature. Burke, in fact, did not think that the act of representing even required that the represented be consulted. If the interests of a constituency are objective and unattached to individual constituents, as Burke believed, it is possible for the representative to promote the interests of constituents without consulting their wishes. The representative simply should know what is in the constituents' best interests.[12] Second, a rationale for the Burkean position is the belief that representatives not only have better judgment but also greater knowledge about the issues and the process. Legislators are exposed to more information and a different perspective than their constituents. Moreover, they have to deal with the details of legislation, which require day-to-day decision making that cannot be directed by the district. The third reason is that the very nature of the constituency and constituents' views precludes a delegate role on the overwhelming majority of issues. If constituents have views on only a few of the many issues the legislature is called upon to decide, then legislators cannot look to their districts for instructions, for no instructions exist.

The "five-state survey" posed two questions that bear on the delegate-trustee choice.[13] Legislators were asked, first, to rate the importance of voting on legislation the way people in the district want. On a scale of 1, "not important," to 5, "very important," the overall mean score was 3.95. No legislators chose the lowest rating, while 71 percent rated the activity as 4 or 5. There was little variation among the states, but Republicans were somewhat more concerned with voting the way constituents wanted than were Democrats. This assumed that the issue was one on which constituents had a relatively clear preference as to how their representative should vote. Not surprisingly, legislators took constituency preferences seriously.

Legislators were also asked: "If a constituency position on a bill were to come into conflict with your own views or judgments, which would generally prevail when you cast your vote?" They were provided with a continuum with "vote constituency position" at the left end and "vote according to own judgment" at the right. The values 1, 2, 3, 4, and 5 ran from left to right. Thus, 1 accorded with voting the constituency position, 5 accorded with voting according to one's own judgment, and 3 was square in the middle. The results are shown in Figure 3-1. The distribution of responses corresponds with the Pitkin formulation mentioned above and the delegate-trustee questions that customarily have been asked. The modal response is at point 4, toward the own-judgment end of the continuum. Of the total legislators surveyed, 59 percent opt for their own

Figure 3-1   Constituency Position versus Legislator's Own View or Judgment: Legislators from Five States

Vote constituency position	1	2	3	4	5	Vote according to own judgment
	6%	14%	21%	44%	15%	

Source: Data compiled by the author.

judgment, points 4 and 5, while only 20 percent select the constituency position, points 1 and 2. The other 21 percent are right in the middle, at point 3. The mean score for all legislators is 3.47. The states vary depending mainly on district size. In Ohio, with large districts, legislators come closest to saying they vote their own judgment (3.73). In Vermont, with tiny districts, legislators come closest to saying they vote their constituency's position (3.20). The larger the district, the likelier it is to be more heterogeneous; the more heterogeneous, the likelier it is to have conflicting views. The smaller the district, the greater the pressure legislators feel to express people's views. As might be expected, members of the senate (whose terms in Minnesota, Ohio, and Washington are longer than those of representatives) tend to vote their own judgment more than members of the house. That may be because the pressure of elections is a little less intense for them. Years of service work in the same direction, with veterans feeling freer than juniors to vote according to their own judgment.

Constituency versus Conviction

Every legislator can recall an occasion or two when one's constituency and one's convictions ran in opposite directions. In his reflections on serving in the Massachusetts legislature McDonough points to several issues that placed "legislators in a serious personal conflict between reflecting their districts and fulfilling their sense of public duty." But, in view of the fact that the constituency is not aroused on many issues and has a clear position on even fewer, there are only a handful of occasions where the constituency's position and the legislator's judgment can conflict.

It is useful to look at particular issues, ones on which constituents are likely to hold views and a constituency is likely to have a position. Among such are what are often referred to as hot-button issues: capital punishment, abortion, taxes, gun control, gambling, and gay rights. During the 2001 sessions, several of these issues were high on legislative lawmaking agendas: capital punishment in Maryland; abortion in Minnesota and Vermont; taxes in Maryland, Minnesota, Ohio, Vermont, and Washington; concealed weapons or other gun legislation in Maryland, Minnesota, and Ohio; and gay rights in Maryland and Vermont. Only gambling was not a major concern in these five states, although it did come up in several instances.

In the "five-state survey" legislators were asked with respect to each of the six issues whether their constituencies had a predominant view on each, and whether their own views were basically the same or substantially different from those of their constituencies.

The distributions appear in Table 3-4. As the first column of percentages indicates, except on the issue of gambling, majorities of legislators believe that their own views and those of their constituencies are basically the same.

The correspondence between the two sets of views is especially true on taxes, presumably because most legislators believe that their constituents want to keep taxes down just as they themselves do. Correspondence is also high on abortion and gun control. This is probably the case for several reasons. First, representatives may truly agree with a majority of constituents on these emotional and recurring issues. After all, they are products of their constituencies and have been elected to office by constituency voters. It is not strange that they share constituency views. Second, representatives may have moved closer to what they deem to be the majority view in their districts. They have adapted over time, in order to reduce cognitive and political dissonance. Third, representatives define their constituencies—at least in terms of some issues—as their supporters, that is, those upon whom they depend for votes in general and primary elections. Constituents holding pro or con views with respect to abortion and gun control are more likely to turn out to vote. Thus, the possibility of conflict between legislator views and constituency views is diminished. Even on gay rights and capital punishment correspondence is substantial, although on these issues a sizeable proportion of legislators believe that no predominant constituency view exists. Gambling poses the greatest uncertainty for legislators. While 42 percent believe that their own views and their constituents' views on gambling are similar, an equal percentage do not believe that a pro- or antigambling view predominates in their constituency, and the remaining 16 percent see a conflict between their own and the constituency views on the subject.

From a different perspective, what is notable about responses to this question is that on these six major issues relatively few legislators perceive differences

Table 3-4 Correspondence of Constituency and Legislator Views

	Percentage of legislators reporting		
Issue	Own views and constituency views are basically the same	No known predominant constituency view	Own views and constituency views are different
Capital punishment	56	29	15
Abortion	75	14	11
Taxes	87	6	7
Gun control	78	12	10
Gambling	42	42	16
Gay rights	66	20	14

Source: Data compiled by the author.

between what their constituents think and what they themselves think. On capital punishment and gay rights, 15 percent and 14 percent may find themselves between a rock and a hard place, having to decide between constituency and conviction. On abortion and gun control, only 11 percent and 10 percent respectively might find themselves in that position. On taxes as few as 7 percent see a conflict between constituency and conviction (although, as we shall see in later chapters, many more may wind up voting against what both they and their constituents ideally would want). And when it comes to voting on taxes, there are ways for legislators to hedge their bets between conscience or necessity on the one hand and constituency on the other.[14]

Incidence of the legislator's conscience clashing with the legislator's constituency is not high, at least not in the five states that were surveyed. Of the total legislators responding with respect to these salient issues, 58 percent reported no conflict at all. Another 23 percent had a conscience-constituency conflict on only one of the issues, 13 percent on two, and 5 percent on three or more. Vermont, with its small and homogeneous districts, had the fewest legislators feeling cross-pressure by conscience on the one hand and constituency on the other.

However, every legislator has probably given passing thought to how he or she would behave in a constituency-conscience crunch. They may not be crunched often, but no legislators can enjoy finding themselves in such a position. It is psychologically and politically preferable to be on the same side of the issue as one's constituency. Tom Loftus, the former speaker of the Wisconsin assembly, a man who was usually sure of his own views, writes of the boundary members drew where right or wrong, in their eyes, was at stake: "Every member I served with had a boundary in his or her mind—a line the member would not cross regardless of the political consequences." Bills on abortion, obscenity, civil rights, and due process tended to be issues where representatives drew a line. Another issue on which Loftus stood firm as a matter of principle was gambling. He opposed gambling, and especially gambling sanctioned and promoted by the state in order to raise revenues. "This was un-Wisconsin, un-Lutheran, un-Progressive, and I didn't care if I was unenlightened and unrepresentative about what the voters wanted."[15]

Sometimes members have convictions but back off because they are not as strongly held. In Loftus's case, he had a position on the mandatory seat belt law that differed from the views of most of his constituents. He opposed such a law on the basis of the principle of federalism. He objected to the federal government trying to force states to pass such bills or lose highway aid. But because of personal experience Loftus changed his mind and supported mandatory seat belts even though the federal government had violated the principle of federalism.[16] McDonough of Massachusetts also made a distinction among issues:

> Some issues relate closely to personal values, such as a woman's right to choose to have an abortion, capital punishment, and civil rights. On those issues, I always

would vote my conscience as best I could (the trustee model), hoping I was in sync with my district's views. But if not, they had the choice to get rid of me because I would not change my vote.

On other issues, however, McDonough did not really care. He chose trolleys over buses on a public transportation line called Arborway. That is because two-thirds of his district supported trolleys. "To me," he writes, "it was a choice between vanilla and chocolate ice cream, not one of principle, and I respected the expressed view of my constituents on the matter, whatever my personal feelings." [17]

"Trolleys versus buses" are typical issues about which legislators can go either way. Many such issues come before them; in fact, they comprise the overwhelming majority that land on their desks. Then there are also principles that legislators hold firmly—principles they might put in abeyance and follow the views of their constituency if they and their district appear to come into conflict. Legislators responding to the "five-state survey" were asked, with regard to each of the six issues mentioned above, how they would likely vote if their own views and those of their constituency were to come into conflict. The responses of the total number of legislators are presented in Table 3-5. One house member from Ohio took a trustee-like position: "My constituency's views and my views are very similar," he said. "On matters of difference, I subscribe to Edmund Burke's philosophy that the voters picked me to use my judgment on issues." For many of his colleagues it is by no means so simple. On some issues their own views would trump their constituency's, and on others their constituency's would override their own.

As a matter of principle, from which legislators are least likely to deviate, nothing quite compares to the legislator's position on abortion. All but 5 percent take a position here, with 82 percent inclined to vote their own view, not the constituency's, if the two were in conflict. Capital punishment and gay rights find almost as great adherence to principle: 71 percent would vote their own view while fewer than a third of that number would vote the constituency's view. Gun control is another issue on which the large majority of

Table 3-5   How Legislators Would Probably Vote If Their Views and Constituency Views Were in Conflict

Issue	Percentage would probably vote		
	Own view	Constituency's view	Don't know
Capital punishment	71	19	10
Abortion	82	13	5
Taxes	48	40	12
Gun control	65	27	8
Gambling	46	39	15
Gay rights	71	20	9

Source: Data compiled by the author.

legislators—65 percent—would abide by conscience, but 27 percent would go with their constituents'.

Taxes and gambling are quite different. The former is probably a mandate issue, at least at the general level. Constituents do not want their taxes to be raised; they might prefer to cut services, if that were the choice. Even though most legislators agree with their constituents on taxes, if there were disagreement almost as many say they would vote the constituency view as say they would vote their own. If mandate opposes principle on taxes, it is practically a toss-up. A legislator's support for or, more likely, opposition to gambling also would be challenged by an opposing constituency view. A plurality of legislators—46 percent—would bow to the wishes of their constituencies.[18]

The real, rough-and-tumble world of legislative politics differs, at least somewhat, from the academic domain of survey research. A recent example may show conscience bowing to constituents. It is the vote in the New York senate in 2003 to override Gov. George Pataki's veto of a tax increase the legislature had voted in order to balance the budget. Republican legislators were not in favor of raising taxes, but the alternative was cutting aid to local schools. Such a cut would have necessitated large increases in town and county taxes. New York's legislators heard from their constituents on the issue, and both Republicans and Democrats concluded that constituents were more concerned about rising property taxes than a temporary income tax surcharge on the wealthy or a small sales tax increase. Both Democrats and Republicans in the senate overrode Pataki's veto, by a unanimous vote. Constituency counted more than the legislator's own preferences and more than the Republican governor's strong feelings on the matter.

The Electoral Connection

When legislators are asked about their constituency, one can never be absolutely sure what constituency they mean when they respond. In his study of representatives and their districts, Richard F. Fenno Jr. distinguished among constituencies, which could be diagramed as four concentric circles, with the larger circle or constituency including the other three, the next largest the other two, and so on. The largest constituency for legislators is the geographical one; the next largest, the reelection constituency, or the supporters; then the primary constituency, or the strongest support; and finally, the personal constituency, or the intimates.[19] When it comes to service, legislators probably think of their constituency as the district. They are happy to help out everyone. However, when their thoughts turn to issues their most relevant constituencies are likely to be their supporters of various kinds.

On issues that matter in their districts and to their constituents, individual representatives are certainly responsive. In most cases they and their constituents, or those constituents they count on for support, generally agree on issues. At least, that is how legislators see it, and how they see it is what influences how they behave. On certain issues, however, there is divergence between representatives and their constituencies. It is here that legislators face the test of constituency versus conviction, and it is here, depending on what happens in the legislative process, that legislators may run considerable risk if they put their convictions before constituency views.

On most issues constituency is not a major factor. Few people are directly affected; only those in organized groups are attentive and care. Legislators have a significant degree of freedom as they participate in the highly complex process of lawmaking. But still, the district is the bottom line. As a Washington legislator put it, "I always ask what's better for most people in my district?" Legislators constantly calculate, consciously or otherwise, how their actions would *help or hurt their districts and their constituents,* and particularly those constituents who are not firmly in the opposition camp. Connected to that calculation is another: how would their actions *help or hurt them in their districts and with their constituents.*

By "help or hurt them," we mean would they gain, solidify, or lose support at the polls? As Fenno points out, "there is no way that the act of representing can be separated from the act of getting elected." [20] The next election is what keeps representatives as constituency oriented as they are. Yes, they identify with their constituency. Yes, they feel that it is their job to be of help to their district and their constituents. Yes, they get gratification from serving district needs. Yes, most of them see eye to eye with their constituents on major issues. But the forthcoming election is what nails it all down. In his book on the California legislature, which in the 1970s was considered a model for all other legislatures, William Muir Jr. maintained the critical importance of the discipline imposed by elections:

> Without the threat posed by the constituent's vote, it was inconceivable that legislators would have labored so long and so promptly over constituent matters. Without the prospect of possible political defeats, legislators would have been unlikely to go back to the district every weekend and sacrifice their personal lives to one more Kiwanis luncheon. The need for votes was sufficient explanation of why they sought to keep their constituents happy.[21]

The election provides parameters for what legislators do by way of policy as well. Bessette posits that the chief mechanism for ensuring a reliable link between what representatives do and the interests and desires of those they represent is the electoral connection. Richard A. Posner recognizes that, even with the electoral connection, legislators have considerable independence of constituency. Representatives, in his view, are no more agents of the voters than actors are the agents of their audience. Nevertheless, he writes, "the electoral process does tend to align the representatives' interest with those of the voters—to keep the representatives on a tether, though a long one." [22]

A few legislators here and there do not worry much about their next election. The electoral connection may not bind those like a member of the Maryland house, whose view of his district afforded him considerable freedom to do what he thought right. "My constituents have no idea how I vote, what I do as a legislator, or what the legislature does to them or for them." But for most legislators reelection is seldom far from their minds.[23] "The thought of reelection may not occur to a first-term legislator within the first five minutes after winning the election," writes a Michigan lawmaker, "but I would not count on that." Why do legislators worry, since so many of them appear to be electorally secure? Depending on the state, anywhere from two-fifths to four-fifths of legislative districts are reasonably safe for one party or the other and for the incumbent. The probability is high that incumbents who run will be returned to office.

Yet for legislators running for reelection, subjective—not objective—standards are the ones that count. Incumbents are not impressed by statistics regarding their electoral success rates. They feel vulnerable. There is no such thing as a "safe" district for them; losing is always a possibility, whatever the statistical history of a district. Primary opposition is always possible. Lightning can always strike in a general election, and it does strike on occasion. It is the lightning that legislators remember. They have seen colleagues relax their efforts and subsequently lose their seats. They have seen incumbents swept out by a national tide, an unpopular candidate at the top of their ticket, or a scandal. They have seen colleagues lose after being pummeled by the press. They have seen seemingly entrenched legislators go down in defeat because they cast a vote that upset their constituency or caused a key group to mobilize against them. They have witnessed successful challenges to incumbents by members of their own party who attacked them from the right or from the left. No legislators want any of this to happen to them, so they attend assiduously to their constituencies—on policy as well as service.

Even though they would appear to have freedom on most issues, constituency is always a lingering factor. Some people do care, albeit they may be organized into so-called special interest groups. Often one group that is organized in the district opposes another group that is also organized in the district. The district, or at least the interest-group district, is divided. One Florida legislator called these "coin flip" issues: concerns that find as many people feeling one way as the other. Frequently, these are issues legislators would prefer to avoid, sensing they can make enemies either way—unless, of course, they have already chosen sides and one side is part of their support base and the other is not.

The political task of legislators in their lawmaking endeavor is damage control as much as anything else. They deal in electoral margins or increments and are never certain how many disgruntled people are too many, electorally that is. Nor do they want to find out. Retaliation by an interest group, resulting in a net loss of support, is always possible. Reprisal by the voters, because of legislators' behavior on any issue, is more remote. One reason is that there are few such issues. Another is that representatives manage to align themselves with their constituencies, or with the predominant positions there.

Legislators are particularly sensitive to district "mandates," although such are few and far between. When they exist, they vary by district, but representatives have a pretty good idea of what the mandates are where they live. "There are some issues where it is so overwhelming," said a member of the Florida house, "you hear it from so many people in so many different walks of life that it is clear." This particular representative, like others, was able to derive what he called "guiding principles" from his district. One was, "be tough on crime." For a colleague of his, it was support for bingo.[24] Nowadays, reducing or holding down taxes—at least sales and income taxes—seems to constitute a mandate from most districts to their representatives. That is why, when it comes to their own convictions being out of line with constituency views, legislators are just as likely as not to set the former aside and promote the latter. Sometimes, because of the complexities of politics and the distaste people have for alternatives, constituents and legislators both will shift views and give support—however grudgingly—to a tax increase.

Nonetheless, there are times when legislators not only say they would stick with conviction, they actually do so. McDonough writes about several of his Democratic colleagues, who represented Republican districts but cast repeated votes to increase taxes and cut spending, "fully understanding that their actions placed their careers in dire jeopardy." Their explanations were that their consciences dictated their actions, regardless of the political cost. They paid the price soon after when they were defeated for reelection.[25]

A politically wrong move may cost a legislator his or her seat, as it did Cas Taylor, speaker of the House of Delegates in Maryland. In the 2000 legislative session, Taylor, a Democrat from a conservative Western Maryland district, supported a gun-control initiative of Democratic governor Parris Glendening. He tried to recoup political ground at home by sponsoring a gun-safety education bill in the following session of the legislature and working with the National Rifle Association to get it passed. Nevertheless, Taylor was targeted by the Republican Party and defeated in a close race in the 2002 elections. No one expected that the speaker would lose his election, but he did. His vote on guns contributed to his defeat.

Vermont illustrates the broader costs that may be incurred when conscience confronts constituency. In December 1999 the Vermont Supreme Court, in the case of *Baker v. State of Vermont*, issued a ruling that required the legislature to either legalize gay marriage or create a "parallel institution," a domestic partnership.[26] The chief justice's opinion required that the legislature act on behalf of the ultimate source of constitutional authority, the people of Vermont. The legislature had little choice. Subsequently, a civil unions bill providing for domestic partnership worked itself through the Vermont legislature in 2000. The question of whether legislators should follow their conscience or heed the views of constituents became central to the deliberations that took place. Polls showed that a slight majority of Vermonters opposed the proposal, while legislators favoring civil unions argued that they would have to vote according to the dictates of their conscience. The legislature finally passed a civil unions law.

A number of legislators knew that their votes in favor of civil unions put their careers at risk. But, as journalist David Moats writes, "those who brought the civil unions bill along its tortuous path toward passage believed it was their finest hour." These included the speaker, who understood that his speakership was imperiled, and legislators who already felt the anger of opponents. Subsequently seven senators and twenty-nine representatives who supported the law retired or were defeated in the election of 2002. As a result, the Republicans gained control of the house from the Democrats (although they did not win the governor's office or gain control of the senate). In the 2001 session of the legislature, repeal or modification of civil unions was high on the agenda of the Republican house.

Collective Representation

Although complex enough, it is much simpler to see how individual legislators represent their districts than it is to see how the legislature as a whole represents the state. Is the latter simply the sum of the former? Probably not. Even if all legislators were to perfectly represent the districts that elect them, they collectively might not perfectly represent the state as a whole. Such representation requires more. Ideally, for the state interest to emerge, legislators must think in terms of the whole, and not just the part that elects them. Whether they do or not, the process serves somehow to fashion out of district representation policies that generally fit the state. Getting to that, as we shall see in chapters 4, 5, 6, and 7, is what lawmaking is about. It combines the policy views and preferences of legislators themselves, along with those of their districts, and supplements them with the positions espoused by organized groups, legislative parties, the governor, and sometimes the courts and the federal government. Add to all this the deliberations and the negotiations, as well as the strategies designed to build majorities at various stages in order to enact law. All of this goes on with the forthcoming election in the back or further toward the front of legislators' minds, in what Jane Mansbridge refers to as "anticipatory representation." [27] Shake well in the legislative process and you have the not-so-simple formula for making law.

Representation of district policy concerns begins with general policy preferences, which both guide and limit legislators in the process. But the specifics of public policy have to be worked out by the participants—that is, by legislators, executives, and representatives of organized groups, as they struggle to reach agreement during the course of the legislative session. To get an idea of the parameters set by constituency, legislators in the "five-state survey" were asked to list the top five issues during the current legislative sessions, and the positions of their constituency on each. They reported whether their constituency overall was in support of or in opposition to the issue as it was generally posed in the legislature. The issues, state by state, are listed in Table 3-6. Even though individual legislators may perceive a clear constituency position, collectively constituency positions can come into conflict. At the top of the table are the issues on which different constituencies appear to come into conflict; below are the issues where all (or nearly all) the constituencies represented by respondents appear to be in agreement.

Table 3-6   Issues in the 2001 Legislative Sessions (as reported by legislators)

Issues on which constituency positions conflict				
Maryland	Minnesota	Ohio	Vermont	Washington
Private school textbook aid (33)	Right to know/ informed consent/ abortion (40)	School funding (23)	School funding/ Act 60 (63)	Transportation (22)
Gay rights (41)	Concealed weapons (39)	Budget (16)	Civil unions repeal (70)	School funding (15)
Death penalty moratorium (27)	Baseball stadium (29)		Parental notification/ abortion (35)	Taxes (10)
Issues on which constituency positions agree				
School funding (33)	School funding (62)	Concealed weapons (16)	Growth/Act 50 (32)	Budget (14)
Prescription drugs (24)	Tax reform (45)	Uninsured motorists (14)	Prescription drugs (28)	

Source: Data compiled by the author.

Note: The number of legislators mentioning the issue is indicated within the parentheses.

Five issues were mentioned with some frequency by Maryland respondents. On three of them constituencies in the state disagreed. Some wanted state aid for textbooks to private schools, but some did not. Constituencies were also split on gay rights and the death penalty moratorium.[28] On each of these issues, constituencies represented by Democrats generally took a different position than those represented by Republicans. On two issues—school funding and prescription drugs—there seemed to be consensus. People, no doubt, favored more money for schools and a prescription drug program for senior citizens. As is often the case with benefits, the problem was not one of much popular opposition. Rather, the problem for the legislature was how to find the money for more school aid and a new benefits program and then how *exactly* to spend it.

The divisive issues in Minnesota, as far as constituencies were concerned, involved parental notification in the case of abortion, concealed weapons, and a state subsidy for a new baseball stadium. Here, too, the partisan identification of legislators related to whether their constituency was on one side of the issue or the other. Interestingly, the informed consent issue was supported by the constituencies of both Democrats and Republicans, but more by the latter.[29] Minnesota legislators saw their constituencies on the same side when it came to school funding and tax reform. They were apparently in favor of more school aid and lower property taxes. But, of course, that begged the important questions of where the money would come from, who would pay more and who less, and how the funds would be allocated.

The major issues in Ohio were school funding and the biennial budget. The school funding and budget issues were intertwined, involving tax increases and/or budget cuts. Legislative districts were perceived to be divided on these matters. According to the responses of Democratic and Republican legislators, their districts were on opposite sides on these issues. On two issues Ohio legislators perceived overall consensus. The ones who thought concealed weapons legislation was an issue mainly represented districts that favored the change.[30] All of those who thought uninsured motorists were a concern said their constituents favored legislation to solve that problem.

In Vermont, modification of Act 60 relating to school funding, change in or repeal of civil unions, and parental notification were the divisive issues. Most legislators saw their districts as favorable to modification of Act 60, and perhaps two-thirds of Vermont citizens wanted change. The problem, of course, was to change Act 60 to what? And how to get agreement? Most saw their constituencies as opposed to actual repeal of civil unions, but a substantial number wanted to undo the act. The chair of the House Judiciary Committee, Peg Flory, said that the legislature ought to look "at all possible alternatives." It might be difficult to agree on anything, she said, but "There are an awful lot of constituents who sent their representatives here to do something about Civil Unions." [31] Constituencies, according to their representatives, split sharply on parental notification. By contrast, there was little disagreement in the state on the growth act or a program for prescription drugs. Not at the general level at any rate; the only real issues were details and costs.

In Washington transportation, school funding, and taxes all divided the legislature as far as constituency positions were concerned. There was unity, however, on the budget; nearly all the constituencies seemed to find fault with it.

Representing one's district in terms of policy, as well as service, is possible for legislators. But it is only a first step. Much depends on building majorities and working out the details of the legislation or finding revenue sources to pay for programs that most people would like to have. When values clash, settlements are contingent on the numbers on each side, the course of the process, and the skills of participants. On most issues with which legislators deal, few constituents have views apart from those who are organized in advocacy and interest groups in support of and opposition to any measure. One could not declare a dominant constituency position in these cases, even though one group may have more members in the district than another. The only reference for the representative on such issues are the groups in the constituency, not the constituency itself. The lawmaking process, however, brings a myriad of other factors into play. Representation is first and probably foremost; the constituency is usually in the minds of legislators, and it continues to thread its way through the deliberations, negotiations, and strategizing that take place in lawmaking. But there is so much else that enters into the process as well. In a close contest, just about everything counts.

NOTES

1. Richard G. Niemi and Lynda W. Powell, "United Citizenship? Knowing and Contacting Legislators after Term Limits," in Rick Farmer et al., eds., *The Test of Time* (Lanham, Md.: Lexington Books, 2001), 197–200.

2. See Alan Rosenthal, *The Third House,* 2nd ed. (Washington, D.C.: CQ Press, 2001).

3. *St. Paul Pioneer Press,* May 6 and June 21, 2001.

4. John E. McDonough, *Experiencing Politics* (Berkeley: University of California Press, 2000), 195.

5. See John Hibbing and Elizabeth Theiss-Morse, *Stealth Democracy* (New York: Cambridge University Press, 2002).

6. Hanna F. Pitkin, *The Concept of Representation* (Berkeley: University of California Press, 1967), 147.

7. Quoted in Alan Rosenthal, *The Decline of Representative Democracy* (Washington, D.C.: CQ Press, 1998), 20.

8. Joseph Bessette, *The Mild Voice of Reason* (Chicago: University of Chicago Press, 1994), 212–213.

9. Pitkin, *The Concept of Representation,* 125, 145–146. Jane Mansbridge offers different normative models of representation, all of which fit various realities in one way or another. "Rethinking Representation," *American Political Science Review* 97 (November 2003): 515–528.

10. Alan Rosenthal, John Hibbing, Burdette Loomis, and Karl Kurtz, *Republic on Trial* (Washington, D.C.: CQ Press, 2003), 112.

11. John C. Wahlke et al., *The Legislative System* (New York: Wiley, 1962), 267–286; Royce Hanson, *Tribune of the People* (Minneapolis: University of Minnesota Press, 1989), 232; and Samuel C. Patterson, "Legislative Politics in Ohio," in Alexander P. Lamis, ed., *Ohio Politics* (Kent: Kent State University Press, 1994), 24.

12. Rosenthal, *Decline of Representative Democracy,* 8.

13. It intentionally omitted any question asking legislators whether they thought of themselves as trustees or delegates. Although commonly asked, such questions are too general to learn what we need to know about representation.

14. The five legislatures vary substantially in the percentage of members who believe that they and their constituencies shared views on the six issues. Such variation might have depended on the salience of each issue in each state at the time the survey was conducted. The more salient the issue, the more likely legislators would see themselves and their constituencies in alignment.

15. Tom Loftus, *The Art of Legislative Politics* (Washington, D.C.: CQ Press, 1994), 93, 153.

16. Ibid., 4.

17. McDonough, *Experiencing Politics,* 161–162.

18. There are very few legislators in the category whose own views differ from those of their constituencies (as reported in Table 3-4, page 45), ranging from 57 in the case of gambling to 25 in the case of taxes. Therefore, we have not analyzed how legislators would probably vote *when* (not if) their own views and constituency views come into conflict.

19. Richard F. Fenno Jr., *Home Style: House Members in Their Districts* (Boston: Little Brown, 1978), 1–30.

20. Ibid., 233.

21. William Muir Jr., *Legislature* (Chicago: University of Chicago Press, 1982), 106.

22. Bessette, *The Mild Voice of Reason,* 36; and Richard A. Posner, *Law, Pragmatism, and Democracy* (Cambridge: Harvard University Press, 2003), 167.

23. The next few paragraphs draw on Rosenthal, *The Decline of Representative Democracy,* 169–171.

24. Ibid., 24, and note 37.

25. McDonough, *Experiencing Politics,* 156–157.

26. This account is based on David Moats, *Civil Wars: A Battle for Gay Marriage* (New York: Harcourt, 2004), 241.

27. Mansbridge, "Rethinking Representation," 516–520.

28.The *Baltimore Sun* (March 22, 2001) poll found that people in Maryland were split on the death penalty moratorium, with 44 percent in favor, 49 percent opposed, and the rest undecided.

29. The Minnesota poll found that 61 percent of the people supported an "informed consent" bill, while 32 percent were opposed.

30. Probably those legislators who would have been in opposition to concealed weapons did not regard it as a major issue of the session. It had not yet surfaced, and virtually all the attention during the first five months of the session was on school finance and the budget.

31. *Burlington Free Press,* April 4, 2001.

4 LAWMAKING: CHALLENGES OF THE LEGISLATIVE PROCESS

In the introduction to his book on the Colorado legislature, John A. Straayer writes that "amidst all the sightseeing, touring, demonstrating, hustling, vote-seeking, and deal-making, serious business is being conducted." [1] Legislators are making decisions as to what policies are being adopted, what taxes are being levied, and what monies are being allocated; who is paying, who is being paid, and what services are being provided to whom.

The objective of legislators and others who participate or have stakes in the process is to pass law. Passing a law sounds a lot simpler than it actually is. In this chapter we shall examine what is entailed in the making of law. The bedrock requirement is to get the agreement of majorities of members. That has to be done in the context of a large legislative workload of bills that they must handle. This is because the legislature provides the opportunity for almost anyone to propose an idea for a bill to become a law. And all of the sifting, screening, and processing have to be done in a limited period of time, with more items on the overall agenda than can be handled. The legislative process, by which laws are fashioned, can be uncomplicated in the case of noncontroversial matters or extraordinarily complicated in the case of controversial ones. Most of the attention in this chapter will focus on the latter processes.

What Is Required

What the enactment of law demands is one agreement after another, with a succession of individuals, agencies, and institutions endorsing and re-endorsing the measure in question. Examine the multiple requirements, each entailing agreement by a majority, for a bill to become law:

1. *Gubernatorial acquiescence.* To begin at the end of the process, there must be a gubernatorial majority, a majority of one. The governor must say yes, or at least not say no, to a measure that the legislature passes. If the governor vetoes a bill passed by both houses of the legislature, there is still a chance for a law to be enacted. But both houses have to override the veto. That requires an extraordinary majority—either three-fifths or two-thirds—voting to override in each chamber. In most states a bill becomes law unless a governor vetoes it, although in a number of states a bill dies unless it is signed. In the case of appropriation bills, governors do not have to veto the entire measure but can veto particular items instead. If the governor does

not go along, chances are the measure is dead. So ordinarily the governor's opposition is sufficient to kill a measure.

2. *House and senate agreement.* The bill that the governor receives must pass both legislative bodies in the same form. This means that if bills are not identical after enactment by each chamber, differing house and senate bills have to be reconciled through negotiation. This requires a vote in one or both bodies, with a majority recorded in favor. If a second house makes changes in a bill, it will seek concurrence from the first house. If a majority concurs, the bill goes to the governor. If not, the second house may recede from its amendments, or it can request a committee of conference, whose recommendations have to be endorsed in each chamber.

3. *Conference committees.* Ordinarily a conference committee is the means by which the house and senate resolve differences on major matters of legislation. The budget is usually the most important and contentious bill to be dealt with by a conference committee. A conference committee may consist of three members from each house, as in Ohio, or either three or five members from each house, as in Minnesota, or some other ratio depending on the state. Whatever the numbers, however, a majority of conferees from each chamber must agree on the conference committee report that is transmitted for adoption to the house and senate. Each chamber must ratify the conference report, if a law is to be enacted.

4. *Passage on floor of each house.* To have made it to conference, a bill must have won majority votes in each house on two occasions. The first occasion, often called "second reading," customarily permits amendments to the bill. The second occasion, often called "third reading," may limit the amendatory process. In either case, a majority of those present and voting (as required in about three-fifths of the states) is required for the bill to pass. Amendments also are subject to majorities of those present and voting. A constitutional majority (a majority of all members elected to the chamber) is required in some places. It is a significant hurdle, since at least a few members will be absent on a vote or on a session day. For example, in New Jersey even if only sixty of the eighty members of the assembly vote on a measure, 41 affirmative votes are needed. The same is true in Maryland, where 71 out of 141 votes are required in the House of Delegates. In Minnesota a majority of all members, an "absolute" majority, is required on "third reading."

5. *Leadership or rules committee clearance.* To get to the floor for consideration, a bill must be put on the session calendar in one form or another. Except in the few places where bills reported from committee automatically are put in line for floor consideration, legislative leaders or their designees exercise discretion. In houses, scheduling authority usually resides with the speaker, who can facilitate or impede a bill's progress. In this particular case, a majority of one decides. Leadership staff often perform the function on behalf of the leader. In senates, usually a rules committee or its equiva-

lent has to act before a bill goes to the floor. A motion is made, seconded, then discussion ensues, and finally a vote is taken. In such cases, a majority of the committee decides.

6. *Committee and subcommittee decisions*. The initial screening of a measure is undertaken by standing committees and sometimes by subcommittees beforehand. Again, a majority vote is required to keep a bill alive and move it along to the next stage of the process. The product of house action may go directly to the senate floor, or vice versa, but often a measure must undergo screening by committees, and perhaps subcommittees as well, in both bodies. At the committee level decisions thus are made at a number of points. The committee or subcommittee chair normally has discretion over what bills receive consideration. Once a bill makes it onto the committee agenda, a majority decides whether or not to report it favorably and with or without amendment.

Many major items—those that overlap committee jurisdictions and those that leaders would prefer to see given special scrutiny or be buried in committee—are referred to more than one standing committee in the same house. Generally, measures that are likely to entail expenditures are reviewed by the appropriations committee as well as by the committee with jurisdiction over the policy area. Each of these bodies must vote favorably if the bill is to move forward on its way to passage.

To complicate matters, at the committee, floor, and conference committee stages decisions are not simply made in terms of support or opposition to a bill. Motions can be made to report a bill back to committee, postpone debate, lay it over until a later date, and take other action. Amendments can be introduced that weaken a bill, strengthen it, or change it substantially. So-called "killer" or "poison pill" amendments are designed to add a provision that virtually guarantees that a bill will not be able to command a majority. Furthermore, "substitutes"—measures that replace one bill with an entirely different or somewhat different one—are also in order along the way.

Take the budget bill or bills that every legislature enacts either annually or biennially. Enacting a budget requires one majority after another at every step from introduction to enactment. The budget bill is often an omnibus bill, with policy proposals included among financial allocations. In order to get them passed, bills extraneous to the budget are rolled into the budget bill in states such as Minnesota, Ohio, and New York. The budget bill is usually the most hotly contested bill of the session, subject to more amendments and more votes than any other legislation. For example, during the 2001 session in Ohio the budget bill ran 2,140 pages, while a 277-page omnibus amendment, combining 86 separate amendments, was also introduced. Unlike any other legislation, however, a budget for the state has to be enacted. The original bill might be changed substantially, but one way or another a budget for the state would be enacted.

It takes not one or several majorities to make a law, but a succession of majorities. At any one of more than a dozen formal decision points, a measure may be defeated or damaged irreparably. To traverse the legislative process, proponents have to build, maintain, and rebuild majorities in support of their measure while trying to ensure that neither the presiding officers in the house and senate nor the governor will oppose their measure. It is not surprising, then, that lawmaking has been likened to an obstacle course that advantages those who want to defeat something. Opponents can derail a measure at any stage of the process, while supporters have to keep it on track. But neither passing nor killing a bill is easily accomplished. Those who are pro and those who are con must constantly seek support for their positions, either to get a bill enacted or to defeat it along the way.

Handling the Workload

The sheer volume of bills introduced in many state legislatures is staggering. Looking at the regular 2001 session of legislatures in the forty-nine states for which data are available, the total number of bills was about 115,000. During this period the range in the numbers of bills introduced, as is indicated in Table 4-1, was tremendous. At one end is New York with 16,892 introductions, followed by Massachusetts with 7,924. At the other end is South Dakota with 553, followed by Maine with 388. Among the states explored here, Minnesota had 4,972 introductions; Washington 2,439; Maryland 2,365; Vermont 711; and Ohio 668.

The numbers of bill introductions, it should be pointed out, are not strictly comparable from state to state. They may be inflated by the introduction of duplicates, companions, and cross-filed bills in both the house and senate. Sometimes, however, only one of these bills moves through the process, while the others languish. But often both house and senate bills move forward. In some places, such as New York, multiple introductions of the same bill are permitted, and in some, such as Arkansas, the budget is broken down into several hundred separate measures. In Massachusetts, the total is inflated by a constitutional provision, the right of free petition, which allows any citizen to submit a bill to a legislator for introduction. Omnibus bills are the norm in some places but not in others. In twenty-one chambers the numbers of introductions are constrained, because members are limited in how many bills they may each introduce.

Legislation runs the gamut, in terms of the problems that are addressed and the issues raised. Just about any idea that can be justified or has some support and would benefit from governmental sanction winds up as a bill. And some that are downright silly also get introduced. Almost anything imaginable is grist for the lawmaking process, and the range in terms of scope and importance is tremendous. In Maryland's 2001 session, for example, the legislature dealt with bills ranging from establishing collective bargaining in state higher education and

Table 4-1 Bill Introductions, 2001 Regular Session

State	No. of bills	State	No. of bills
Alabama	1,589	Montana	1,172
Alaska	830	Nebraska	939
Arizona	1,221	Nevada	1,262
Arkansas	2,643	New Hampshire	920
California[a]	2,500	New Jersey	1,927
Colorado	652	New Mexico	1,788
Connecticut	NA	New York[b]	16,892
Delaware	624	North Carolina	2,587
Florida	2,148	North Dakota	934
Georgia	1,290	Ohio	668
Hawaii	3,331	Oklahoma	814
Idaho	662	Oregon	3,106
Illinois	5,153	Pennsylvania[a]	2,150
Indiana	1,756	Rhode Island[b]	2,767
Iowa	1,302	South Carolina	1,386
Kansas	969	South Dakota	553
Kentucky	579	Tennessee	2,044
Louisiana	3,185	Texas	5,544
Maine[b]	388	Utah	664
Maryland	2,365	Vermont	711
Massachusetts[b]	7,924	Virginia	1,965
Michigan	2,553	Washington	2,439
Minnesota	4,972	West Virginia[b]	2,052
Mississippi	2,926	Wisconsin	1,030
Missouri	1,657	Wyoming	522

Source: Council of State Governments, *Book of the States,* vol. 34 (Lexington, Ky.: The Council, 2002), 111–112, and vol. 35 (Lexington, Ky.: The Council, 2003), 152–153.

[a] Estimate.

[b] 2001 data not available; 2002 data provided.

abolishing the death penalty on the one hand to repealing the Maryland state song and increasing the annual salary of the Howard County sheriff on the other.

Although the trivial as well as the substantial make the legislative agenda, legislatures do confront major issues facing the state and its people. The 2001 session in Minnesota illustrates the number of ways in which lawmaking affects the people living in the state.[2]

The Minnesota legislature dealt with the following issues:

- Taxes, including a variety of health care, property, income, and sales taxes, as well as a proposed state constitutional amendment to require a two-thirds vote in the legislature to increase taxes.
- Transportation, including a proposal to allow cities to use cameras to photograph and ticket cars that run red lights, a gas tax, opening up reserved highway lanes, bus service, and busways.
- Elections, including redistricting, campaign finance to regulate independent expenditures, and a requirement for voters to show photo identification.

- Corrections and public safety, including concealed weapons, racial profiling, repeat drunken driving, seat belts, and a statewide criminal justice information system.
- Health and human services, including suicide prevention, prescription drugs, a waiting period for abortions, specialty license plates reading "choose life," family planning, and benefits for same-sex partners.
- The environment, including agriculture and natural resources, banning of mercury thermometers, frog research, land conservation, and game and fishing limits.
- K–12 education, including high school graduation standards, teacher contracts, accountability reporting, new teacher pay schedules, the Pledge of Allegiance requirement, and tests for seventh graders.
- Jobs and economic development, including the merger of two state departments and use of tobacco settlement funds.
- Higher education, with tuition pacts with neighboring states and accountability—along with the budget—constituting the main items on the legislature's agenda.

The Minnesota legislature also dealt with the governor's security and the disclosure of his outside income, a requirement of a state energy plan, the restriction of cell phones in cars, pay toilets, the abuse of pets, the registration of beer kegs, fire-retardant cigarettes, banning the sale of soda pop in schools, building a ballpark for the Minnesota Twins, and studying the stadium needs of the Minnesota Vikings and the University of Minnesota.

Given the numbers of bills introduced, it is not surprising that only a minority—on average one out of three—are enacted into law. The rest fail to receive action, are voted down at some point, or just do not get brought up at each and every stage of the process. Despite all the bills that fall by the wayside, a lot of law is made. According to a compilation by the Council of State Governments, in 2001 about 22,500 measures were signed into law. Even in a state like Minnesota, where only a small proportion of the bills introduced are finally passed, in that one-year session 208 new laws came into being, by no means an insignificant amount. Reflecting the increase in law, in the past thirty years Minnesota's statute books have grown from two to fifteen volumes.[3]

Where Does It Come From?

Legislation comes from many sources. Every bill has an origin or origins and a distinctive history. Some bills have been around for years but have not made it into law. Their sponsors, however, keep trying session after session. One such example is the bill to build a new stadium for the Minnesota Twins. In a special session in 1997, the bill could not get through. It lay dormant but was resurrected four years later, when it gathered some steam but still did not make it to a vote. Or take collective bargaining for state employees in Washington, which had passed several times in the Democratic senate but had not gotten to the floor of the Republican house. In 2002, with both chambers controlled by the Democrats, the bill finally passed.

Constitutionally Required Legislation

While the legislature has discretion as to whether or not it will act on most bill introductions, a few items demand the legislature's response because of the state constitution. The budget is one of them. In most states a budget is adopted annually; in the rest it is adopted biennially. Maryland, Washington, and Vermont budget every year, while Minnesota and Ohio budget every other year. The budget allocates resources for the agencies and programs of state government in areas such as education, higher education, health, transportation, and corrections. The largest portion of the budget is considered the base, which supports core functions and services and is undisturbed from one year to another. "It's in the base" is an expression used, most often successfully, to defend an expenditure from cuts. Normally, less than 5 to 10 percent of the budget is up for grabs. It is on this part of the budget that the legislature can make a difference and that conflict is most likely to occur.

Whether the budget is encompassed by one bill or by several, it seldom fails to command attention. In states like Maryland and Vermont, the budget for operations is within a single bill, while that for capital construction is in another bill. In Ohio several budget bills—a general appropriations budget, a capital appropriations budget, and a transportation budget—go through the process relatively independently of one another. In Minnesota the budget is ordinarily divided into half a dozen or more budget bills; the 2001–2002 fiscal year biennial budget for that state was parceled out in eight omnibus budget bills.

At the congressional level, legislation that addresses numerous and not necessarily related subjects, issues, and programs is referred to as omnibus legislation, although there is no consensus technical definition of what constitutes an omnibus bill. At the state legislative level, omnibus bills normally are budget bills, which may serve as vehicles for policy issues as well as expenditures by the state. In 2001, for example, Minnesota's eight budget bills had a number of policy issues included. So did the budget bills in Ohio and Vermont. Maryland's budget bill, however, cannot amend existing law, so policy is excluded from the budget. With or without policy issues, budget bills are probably the most important and among the most contentious items on the legislature's agenda.

Budgets have to be enacted in one form or another. Sometimes the fiscal year ends before a budget is adopted. This has been the pattern in New York for twenty consecutive years through 2004. But even when the budget is late the legislature and governor agree to an interim arrangement, whereby state spending continues at the past year's level. It serves until a regular budget agreement can be reached. Sometimes the legislative session ends before a budget gets worked out. This happened in Minnesota, where the governor called a special session in 2001 and a budget was enacted and signed into law just before the end of the fiscal year.

Because of constitutional provisions, legislation cannot be avoided in other cases as well. Every ten years after the census figures are announced, states enact a redistricting plan for Congress and for the state senate and house. States vary in just how they draw their congressional and/or legislative maps. Normally the legislature has the initiative, although the governor is also a player in the process (only in Maryland does the governor have the initiative). In some states, such as New Jersey, redistricting is done by commission and automatically becomes law. If the legislature fails to act, redistricting has to be done by the courts; and even when the legislature does act, its plan is likely to be challenged in the courts by those who think they have lost out in the process. If the courts overturn a plan, it is usually up to them to replace it.

Judicially Required Legislation

By virtue of its power to review the constitutionality of state law, the judiciary can and sometimes does rule that laws enacted by the legislature are null and void. Courts can also require that the legislature act to meet constitutional obligations. The most frequent example of judicial intervention in this regard is in the area of public education, particularly school finance. About forty states have been sued for failing to provide poor school districts enough money to meet what courts specify to be constitutional standards. In the past quarter-century federal and/or state courts have ruled state formulas unconstitutional in about half of the states. New Jersey's school-finance system, for example, has been challenged repeatedly and overturned on a number of occasions since the first case, *Robinson v. Cahill,* was decided in the 1970s.

In 1997 the New Hampshire Supreme Court ruled that the state's reliance on the local property tax to pay for public schools was unconstitutional. Since then, the governor and the legislature have used money from unspent surpluses to increase education funding, but by 2001 New Hampshire had to face the possibility of considering a broad-based tax. That same year a state judge ruled that New York's school-aid formula short-changed urban students, failing to provide them "a sound, basic education as guaranteed by the State Constitution." The result for the New York legislature was that the most contentious budget issue involved school aid. The assembly Democrats favored increasing education aid by $1.7 billion, while Gov. George Pataki wanted only a $382 million increase, a huge difference that was almost impossible to bridge.[4] Court-mandated school finance reform is a lingering issue in a number of other states as well. The legislature does not always enact subsequent legislation that responds to the satisfaction of plaintiffs, and they do not hesitate to return to court to make their case for greater equity.

School funding in Ohio has been on the state's agenda for more than a decade, since a lawsuit was filed in 1991 by a coalition representing over five hundred Ohio public school districts that claimed they were inadequately funded. In 1997 the Ohio Supreme Court, in a 4–3 decision, agreed with the plaintiff and ruled that the school funding system was unconstitutional. The legislature worked diligently to respond and in 1998 put two questions on the ballot to get public approval for an increased sales tax and to issue general obligation bonds for school facilities. The sales tax failed by 80 to 20 percent and the bonds by 61 to 39 percent. Early in 1999 an Ohio judge ruled that the system continued to be unconstitutional and in 2000 the supreme court again struck down the school-funding system and gave the legislature until June 2001 to comply with the state constitution.

Needless to say, the fashioning of a school finance plan, in conjunction with enactment of a budget, dominated the early part of the Ohio legislature's 2001 session. The legislature accused the court in its two rulings of encroaching on its authority to make law, but it enacted a plan that it hoped would win over one judge of the 4–3 court majority that had struck down the legislature's school funding. According to Senate President Richard Finan, waiting to see whether the supreme court approved of what the legislature had crafted was like playing poker in Jackson County, where the dealer declares which cards are wild only after he picks up his hand. "We don't know what's wild," Finan said. "They write the opinion and we have to fumble around and put together a plan that can beat their three aces." [5] The Ohio legislature during that session managed to craft a funding plan, but the supreme court ordered more state spending for schools.

The Vermont Supreme Court invalidated the state's school-funding system because the sharp differences from town to town in school spending per child "deprive children of an equal educational opportunity in violation of the Vermont Constitution." The legislature had to act, and it responded in 1997 with Act 60, as it is commonly called, which tended to equalize expenditures by means of a statewide property tax. Wealthier towns had to raise taxes by more than they needed for their own schools and contribute the difference to a "sharing pool" from which poorer towns received money for their schools. The requirements effectively transfer money from rich towns to poor towns. Act 60 had many critics, especially representatives from wealthier communities and among Republicans who won control of the house in the 2000 elections. Some wanted to replace Act 60 with something else, others wanted to modify the "sharing pool," and still others wanted to tinker with one provision or formula or another. In any case, a number of legislators, backed by a substantial number of citizens, endeavored to revise Act 60 in the 2001 session. Indeed, along with the budget, educational finance proved to be the major business of that particular legislative session in Vermont.

Judicial intervention extends beyond issues of school finance. Ohio's supreme court also prompted the Ohio legislature in 2001 to take on the subject of automobile insurance. The court, in its decision, expanded the scope of uninsured and underinsured motorists, allowing claims against employers, even if the employees had not been working at the time of accident. The impact on insurers led to the introduction of legislation that would eliminate the mandatory nature of insurance coverage and, in the words of the sponsor, "restore a good insurance market place to Ohio."

Vermont's supreme court also has played a critical role in setting the legislature's agenda in a matter other than school finance. In December 1999 it ruled in *Baker v. State of Vermont* that same-sex couples should receive the equivalent legal benefits to those of heterosexual, married couples. The court left it up to the legislature in its session the following year to figure out just how to comply with the court's ruling. If legislators did nothing, the court would have been compelled to spell out its mandate. The legislature acted by passing a bill legalizing civil unions, which afforded gay and lesbian couples the legal rights of marriage without giving them marriage *per se*. The state was sharply divided on the issue, and the repeal of civil unions also was high on the agenda of many house Republicans the following year. The effects in the legislature of the judiciary's decision were palpable. It was not just up to the legislature to decide whether the civil unions law would stand. Opponents challenged the law in the same court that had prompted its enactment in the first place. In a long-shot appeal to the supreme court to invalidate the law, they argued that fourteen legislators had wagered one dollar each on the law's passage in violation of house rules that prohibit members from voting on an issue in which they have a direct interest.[6]

Sometimes a legislature balks at what a court orders it to do. In Massachusetts, for example, when the legislature refused to fund a public financing law that was passed by a 1998 initiative, the supreme judicial court ordered it either to fund the law or repeal it. The legislature did not fund it, nor did it repeal it right away. It took several years before it repealed it as part of the enactment of a state budget in 2003.

Administration Bills

Other bill introductions may not be as compelling as those demanded by a court decision, but they shape the legislature's agenda as well. Among the most significant are bills that reflect the governor's priorities or program. Not only does the governor have responsibility for formulating the budget in all but a few states, but the chief state executive also has an agenda of items for enactment by the legislature. Some governors offer the legislature a virtual laundry list, but most concentrate on ten to twenty priorities.

Departments and agencies of the executive branch also have items that they need enacted into legislation. A few are important and controversial; many, however, are of an essentially "housekeeping" nature—measures that make changes in previously enacted statutes, accomplish fine-tuning, or are technical rather than substantive. Such a bill, for example, initiated by the State Department of Natural Resources in Maryland, would have required children under seven to wear life jackets while aboard recreational boats—a noncontroversial measure, yet one of some consequence. The Minnesota Department of Human Services sought a law that would permit a few nursing homes to share administrators. A Wisconsin legislator, who chaired the Environmental Resources Committee, explained how a state agency routinely requested that he sponsor legislation it wanted adopted. The Department of Natural Resources would bring him a draft, which he would sign as lead sponsor—his one obligation on the matter. Sometimes the measures codified statutes, updated outmoded laws, or provided for the specifics of agency housekeeping. Others dealt with what executive agencies referred to as "minor policy" changes.[7]

Constituents' Bills

It may appear unlikely, but a number of initiatives just about everywhere come from ordinary constituents, and not necessarily from organized local groups. Take, for instance, New Jersey state senator Joseph Vitale. One bill he introduced came in response to the request of a constituent who had been assaulted and would have imposed penalties on those who abet such crimes. Another asked that the law expand coverage of victims' compensation. The resulting bill also became law. A woman whose HMO was about to change her obstetrician in the middle of her pregnancy also prompted a Vitale bill. One of the senator's aides, visiting a veterans' home on behalf of his boss, was asked by a volunteer that the resident not have to pay the New Jersey sales tax. In response, Vitale introduced a bill exempting from the sales and use tax goods sold at concession stands in state-owned veterans' homes. Several of Vitale's bills passed.[8]

Washington's House Bill 2560 of the 2002 session also illustrates the influence rank-and-file citizens can exercise. The owner of a commercial driving school in the state objected to the fact that both the Office of the Superintendent of Public Instruction and the Department of Licensing regulated his business. He appealed to his representative, who worked with the two agencies to draft a bill with which all parties could live. It passed the house 95–0 and the senate 45–1.

Every now and then a bill of broader scope comes as a result of a constituent's suggestion. A Baltimore developer read about a New York measure, known as the "green buildings" bill, which encouraged developers to incorporate conservation features in new and rehabilitated buildings by offering them tax credits. The developer visited with Del. Sandy Rosenberg, who took on sponsorship of the bill. The first year it did not pass; so the second year Rosenberg persuaded the speaker to sign on as a cosponsor and put the bill in the package of leadership priorities.

When constituents complain legislators try to respond, even if it takes time. In 1964 a number of Baltimore residents complained to their lawmaker that construction vehicles working in their neighborhoods were spilling rocks and sand onto the streets, creating traffic problems and damaging cars. This legislator introduced a bill that required a tarpaulin to be placed over the open portion of sand trucks. Trucking and construction groups opposed the bill because of the costs it would entail. It did not pass in that session or succeeding ones, but it kept being introduced until it passed in 1989.[9]

Local Bills

Legislators just about everywhere feel obliged to pay careful attention to local bills, that is, proposals with only local significance. Minnesota's Senate File No. 1528, for instance, related solely to the city of Edina in authorizing the city to impose additional restrictions on the use of recreational motor vehicles. In Wisconsin, as instruments of the state with no inherent powers, local governments are required to secure legislative permission if they want to engage in a new area of endeavor. Wisconsin representative Mordecai Lee describes how at the beginning of every session

> The lobbyists for my home city and home county would visit with legislators. . . . Each carried a raft of bills that represented changes in state laws requested by municipal and county agencies. Would anyone like to sign on to any of these bills? they asked. It was the legislative version of a bazaar. Usually, each one of us would agree to be the lead sponsor of a few bills, and cosponsor a few more.

The argument in favor of such sponsorship goes like this: These bills are not very controversial. Pushing them will show you are being responsive to local needs. It will also give you experience in the legislative process. They have a good chance of passage, so you can show your constituents how effective you are.[10]

Interest Group Bills

According to William K. Muir Jr., whether a California legislator was an inactive author or a busy one, legislators rarely introduced bills exclusively of their own devising. Typically, bills were thrust upon them by sponsors, many of whom were interest groups and their lobbyists.[11] Indeed, roughly one out of five introductions today is what is often called "special interest" legislation. It is intended to help an organized group that wants to advance the interests of its members or its business. Maryland's independent service station owners got a bill introduced to restrict the predatory pricing of gasoline by large dealers. Raytheon, a Massachusetts-based defense contractor, appealed to the legislature for a tax break, since Massachusetts's taxes were higher than those in other states in which the company also had plants. A similar bill passed in Minnesota. A bill in New York would allow rental-car companies to require customers to bear the cost of insurance for rented cars. A bill in Maryland would help chiropractors caught between old requirements and new ones established the previous year. Another bill provided a funding subsidy for a new baseball stadium for the Minnesota Twins.

Like individuals, interest groups have the constitutional right to petition their government; and they do. These groups have allies in the legislature, who agree to sponsor or author their bills and manage them through the legislatures with the help of group lobbyists and members. Issues like parental notification, concealed weapons, and blood-alcohol levels, which were on the dockets of Maryland, Minnesota, Ohio, and Vermont, are the creations, not so much of legislator sponsors, but of national and state interest groups. For example, Minnesota Citizens Concerned for Life (MCCL) pushes anti-abortion legislation, the National Rifle Association (NRA) favors permitting individuals to carry concealed weapons, and Mothers Against Drunk Driving (MADD) advocates a lower blood-alcohol content to be the threshold for drunken driving. Other bills also are mainly the products of interest groups such as chambers of commerce, labor organizations, teachers' associations, the higher education community, professional and occupational groups, senior citizens, individual companies, environmental groups, municipalities, police chiefs and sheriffs, and many others.

Threat of the Initiative

The introduction of legislation may also be prompted by a popular initiative. Currently, twenty-four states permit citizens to vote on a proposition through an initiative process that bypasses the legislative process. Ohio and Washington have had the initiative since 1912, but of the two only Washington (along with Arizona, California, Colorado, Massachusetts, and Oregon) makes relatively frequent use of it. The very existence of the initiative enables advocates of one measure or another to demand action from the legislature under the threat of putting a more extreme measure on the ballot. This usually prompts legislators to introduce their own bills rather than have something else pass in a popular referendum. Such legislation usually receives serious treatment in the process, since there is general agreement that the alternative is substantively worse and the initiative mechanism allows for neither the deliberation nor negotiation that are possible in legislative lawmaking.

Legislators' Own Ideas

Legislators themselves have their own ideas and their own agendas. Some work on education, others on environmental matters, still others on health, and so forth. They search for bills to sponsor and enact in their areas of interest. It is not unusual for a legislator's bill introductions to stem from personal experience or recent events. In Colorado one legislator, moved by her daughter's ordeal as a victim of domestic violence, sponsored a bill to improve communication among law enforcement officials about restraining orders issued by judges against violent domestic partners. Another lawmaker sponsored a bill that would have required the placement of special zebra-striped auto license plates on the cars of repeat drunken driving offenders.[12] A New York assemblyman, after witnessing an accident caused by a driver talking on the telephone, introduced a bill the next day to ban the use of hand-held cellular phones while on the road. It took six years, but the bill finally passed, becoming the first law in the nation banning the use of hand-held mobile phones while driving.[13]

Former member Harriet Keyserling recalls her experience with legislative initiatives in the South Carolina house. One senator, a perennial sponsor of living-will legislation, had watched his elderly, comatose mother being kept alive for seven years. Keyserling herself championed the bottle bill—an environmental measure—that was a continuation of her interest and experience on a county council. She also made an effort to require contracts to be written in layman's language, inspired by her struggles to read an insurance policy, and thinking: "There ought to be a law." [14]

In Maryland, Sen. Barbara Hoffman sponsored gun-education legislation after a thirteen-year-old was accidentally shot to death by a nine-year-old playmate.

Another Maryland bill, introduced after a nineteen-year-old mother was convicted of attempted murder and sentenced to ten years for abandoning a newborn, would have granted immunity to a parent who leaves an unharmed infant in a "safe haven" such as a hospital or a police station. When a dog was burned viciously, a legislator responded with a bill that made aggravated cruelty to animals a felony instead of a misdemeanor. And the affirmation of a mother's right to breast-feed her baby in public was introduced by two Maryland legislators who heard from a constituent that a manager at a Toys R Us store made her use the restroom when he saw her breast-feeding her child on a bench in the store.

The art of body piercing was regulated in New Hampshire because a legislator's seventeen-year-old daughter had a stainless steel stud pierced into her lower lip. The mother, Rep. Janeen Dalrymple, is a nurse who had seen hundreds of infected navels and upper ears in recent years. She became convinced there had to be a law to regulate the practice, particularly since New Hampshire did not even provide for the maintenance of records at piercing parlors.[15] Personal experience is also at the root of Minnesota senator Pat Pariseau's amendment to a national resources bill. Because her husband had been charged with three misdemeanor trapping violations, the senator tried to do away with the site-tagging requirement that had ensnared him as well as other trappers.[16]

Nationwide Agendas

At any session, a number of items on the legislative agenda of one state are also on the legislative agendas of other states. Legislation is becoming a nationwide phenomenon, mainly because of the requirements of federal law, the efforts of interest groups that are organized across the country, and the easy exchange of information by means of the Internet among legislators and their staffs in the fifty states. Electricity deregulation is an example of legislation that has swept the nation. Made possible by a 1992 change in federal law that required all utilities to share their transmission lines with other electricity-generating companies, it was spurred by the business community and major entities that sought deregulation of electricity pricing. By mid 2001 about half the states had already deregulated and additional legislatures had the issue on their agendas, although the energy crisis in California caused deregulation to slow down in those places where it was about to be taken up.

An excellent example of legislation promoted by federal law and federal incentives is the lowering of the legal limit of the blood alcohol content level from 0.10 to 0.08 percent. If states do not comply by 2004, they will lose 2 percent of their federal highway construction funds, and the penalty will increase in subsequent years. By 2001 legislation to this effect had passed in nearly half the states but had difficulty in both Minnesota and Ohio. A bill to lower the limit to 0.08 percent was introduced in 1991 in Ohio, again in 1997 and 1999, and for a fourth time in 2001, without passing. Similar bills have been considered by the Minnesota legislature since 1997 without becoming law. It did pass in Maryland during the 2001 session, but it would not have passed, according to Sen. Walter

Baker, were it not for the $70 million in federal highway funds at stake. The legislature did not want the money to be withheld.

Abortion and guns are almost constantly on the agendas of many states, in one form or another. In 2001 parental notification was being discussed in Vermont, while requiring a twenty-four hour waiting period for an abortion was one of the most significant issues before the Minnesota legislature. Concealed weapons bills were on the agendas in Minnesota, Ohio, and Vermont, among other places. Also popular was legislation barring cities from suing gun manufacturers, which was enacted by Ohio. Other issues with nationwide currency include legalizing marijuana for medical purposes; outlawing racial profiling by the police; making driving without a seatbelt a primary, instead of a secondary, traffic offense; granting paid family leave; allowing convicted felons the right to vote after serving their terms; and authorizing prescription drug programs for senior citizens.

Controversial and Consensual Bills

Wherever and however they arise, not many of the bills on the legislative agenda are major ones, as far as the state as a whole is concerned. Perhaps fifty to one hundred fall into this category. These bills provide for statewide programs and/or statewide benefits, they advance certain principles, and they regulate behavior. Most of the others either make administrative adjustments or technical changes, affect localities, or advantage certain interest groups (often at the expense of other interest groups).

The overwhelming majority of bills that reach third reading, or final passage, on the floor pass by overwhelming votes, if not unanimously. It is not unusual for a legislative body to take up twenty, thirty, forty, or perhaps fifty bills at a daily session, some of which are on a consent calendar, but others not. Each passes with little debate. Many of them were voted out of standing committees with overwhelming votes in their favor; many of them were noncontroversial to begin with. It is estimated, for instance, that three out of four bills that pass in Minnesota are truly noncontroversial, and the proportions are probably similar, if not higher, in other states.

Some bills that pass by overwhelming majorities are not as consensual, however, as might appear by the votes along the way. By the time a bill is voted on in committee or on the floor, disagreements often have been settled and compromises struck. Thus, the vote is not necessarily an indicator of whether or not a bill has been contested along the way. Bills on unwanted telephone solicitations, abandoned motor vehicles, and mandatory blood tests for persons involved in fatal or serious accidents all passed the Vermont senate easily. But each one had been changed significantly in a senate committee before being voted on at a floor session.

Take, for example, an implement of husbandry bill, which passed by unanimous voice vote on second reading on the floor of the Vermont house. This bill addressed the problem of heavy farm vehicles, in particular manure spreaders that tore up local roads and were costly for localities to repair. The former vehicle weight-limits of 24,000 lbs. were no longer serviceable, so the legislature was asked to come up with a redefinition of the implements of husbandry. The Vermont Department of Motor Vehicles, Department of Agriculture, and several associations testified in favor of a bill that satisfied towns. But those legislators who were themselves farmers or who represented farmers were concerned because of a proposed ban on spreading manure in the winter. For these members, that was too much regulation. The dispute between towns and farmers had to be worked out prior to passage, and it was.

In Minnesota an Omnibus Energy Bill passed in the senate by 59–0 after less than an hour's debate. It would appear to have been noncontroversial, but that was hardly the case. At the start of the 2001 session three different groups submitted energy legislation. The Minnesota Chamber of Commerce backed a bill that called for energy deregulation; the Department of Commerce proposed a bill that would have increased state planning; and a coalition of consumer, environmental, labor, and conservation groups pushed for increased conservation. The chair of the Senate Telecommunications, Energy, and Utilities Committee managed to take bits and pieces of each, forging a supporting coalition of disparate groups. A bill that was controversial at the outset of the process was consensual by its end.

Even seemingly minor legislation can arouse opposition, at least among some people. Wisconsin representative Mordecai Lee recalls that a bill he agreed to sponsor for the state's Department of National Resources would have applied uniform regulations to lakeside boathouses. It was considered minor by just about everybody—but not by the owners of lakeshore homes with boathouses.[17] During her tenure in the South Carolina house, Harriet Keyserling discovered that there was no such thing as a noncontroversial bill: "I learned . . . that when I was working behind the scenes, someone else on the other side was working just as hard, out of my sight."[18] Someone's ox is almost sure to be gored, unless they act to defend their interests.

Nevertheless, many bills go through the legislative process uncontested and unscathed. Nothing has to be worked out. The bill in the 2001 session of the Maryland General Assembly to make the calico the state cat is an example of such a bill. It was sponsored by children in the Westernport Elementary School, who testified on its behalf before the house and senate committees. Since Maryland had a state dog, bird, insect, and even dinosaur, why shouldn't it have a state cat as well? No groups, lobbyists, or other cats emerged to challenge the calico, so it became law. Had there been a bloc for persian, angora, or alley cats, it would not have gone as smoothly; there undoubtedly would have been a cat-fight. In Ohio all did not go as well when the smallmouth bass, the largemouth bass, and the walleye all vied to become the state fish. Who could possibly have cared? But someone apparently had.

Time Constraints

Hundreds or even thousands of bills have to be handled—in the senate and house, in committee, on the floor, and perhaps in conference—during the course of the legislative session. Indeed, one of the major challenges of lawmaking is squeezing everything into a finite calendar. Some legislatures meet throughout the year; others are limited to thirty, sixty, ninety, or however many days. The states that spend the most time in session are California, Illinois, Massachusetts, Michigan, New York, North Carolina, Ohio, Oregon, Pennsylvania, and Wisconsin. New Jersey meets year round, but its members only commute to Trenton once or twice a week and not at all during several recesses. The states that spend the least time—roughly sixty or fewer days—are Alabama, Arkansas, Florida, Georgia, Hawaii, Indiana, Kentucky, Louisiana, Montana, Nevada, New Hampshire, New Mexico, North Dakota, Rhode Island, South Dakota, Utah, Virginia, and West Virginia.

The Pressure Builds

Ohio can work at a more leisurely pace than other states. The legislature does not adjourn until the end of the two-year term, although it does recess. Vermont's legislature can also meet as long as it wants, at least in theory. In practice, however, the legislature tries mightily to get its work done in five or six months, both because members want to return to their regular jobs and professions and because Vermonters simply do not want their legislators continuously in session. The pressures for legislators to go home are great. Washington is limited to 105 days in odd years and sixty days in even years. But in 2001 Washington also had three special sessions called. Minnesota and Maryland are more constrained. Minnesota's legislature is limited by the state constitution to 120 legislative days in a two-year cycle. Thus, if seventy days are used the odd-numbered year, only fifty are left for the even-numbered year. In 2001, under enormous pressure to settle its budget, the legislature ended its regular session at midnight on May 21 and had to return for a special session called by the governor.

Maryland's ninety-day session is illustrative of the time pressures faced by more than half the states with relatively short sessions. As Speaker Cas Taylor emphasized at a meeting of his senior leadership on the seventieth day: "Time is valuable, precious, limited." By the last three or four weeks, time becomes even more important. The holy day of Passover complicates the schedule. As the session proceeds, it becomes more difficult for committee chairs or legislative party leaders to organize informal meetings to work things out between the senate and house, between one committee and another, or among groups. Leaders in particular have virtually no free time in their schedules; finding a place for a bill on the calendar is not guaranteed. "We want it on the floor tomorrow, we're running out of time," Maryland's legislative leaders reiterate as the ninety-day session draws to a close. It is not unusual for the senate or house to run until nearly the last minute, adjourning *sine die* within twenty or thirty minutes of the constitutional deadline.

The pace and metabolism of the session vary. Just about everywhere, the session starts out slowly and quickens as it goes along. In Ohio, where no date is set for adjournment, members ordinarily spend Tuesday, Wednesday, and Thursday in Columbus at tasks of lawmaking and Monday, Friday, and the weekend at home earning a living, attending to constituents, and seeing their families. Until the final weeks of the session, Vermont's legislators normally arrive in Montpelier for a 10:00 A.M. session on Tuesday and return to their districts Friday after a morning floor session. Similarly, legislators in Maryland and Minnesota have Tuesday–Wednesday–Thursday state house schedules, with some sessions on a Monday night and Friday morning in Maryland. During the final week or two, these legislatures are likely to meet six days a week. Washington's legislature also starts out meeting just part of the week and ends up meeting every weekday.

At the start of a session, action takes place in the standing committees. Not many bills have yet been reported out for second and third readings on the house or senate floor. In Ohio, for example, five months into the session out of 264 house bill introductions, only twenty-one had passed the house and only nine had passed the senate as well, and out of 114 senate bill introductions, only twenty-four had passed the senate and only two had passed the house as well. Only five bills had been signed into law by the governor. The pace is slow, the calendar is light, and floor debate—even on seemingly minor issues—increases to fill the time available for it. Since only a few votes are recorded for the first four or five months of the Vermont session, some committees continue to meet while the house is in session. If a roll call is announced, members leave their committee rooms and walk the short distance to the chamber floor. Meanwhile, committees are hearing bills, marking them up, and voting on them. During the early weeks Maryland also operates at a more deliberative pace, with standing committees handling a dozen or so bills a day.

Except for Ohio, legislative deadlines kick in and exert additional pressure. Deadlines for bill introductions, action by the house of origin, and action by the second house are common in the states (seventy-three chambers have them). In Maryland, for instance, bills have to be introduced by the fifty-fifth day; to guarantee that they get a hearing, bills must be introduced by the twenty-fourth day in the senate, the thirty-first day in the house. Even with deadlines, some bills come in too late for committees to give them an adequate screening. Like practically everything else connected with the legislative process, deadlines have strategic implications. Some legislators purposefully hold their bills back, despite deadlines. They do not want to give the opposition time to organize; they are willing to use an extraordinary procedure to move their legislation forward or introduce it as an amendment to another bill. Occasionally deadlines themselves have strategic meaning. In 2000 Minnesota's last two committee deadlines occurred later than in previous years. These late deadlines did not happen by chance; they were intended to leave less time for conference committee and other negotiations and to bring things to a more rapid conclusion.[19]

Standing committees, where much of the deliberation takes place, have to work under the pressure of time. Most start out slowly, but as the workload builds, more bills have to be handled, more hearings held, and more witnesses heard. Each committee chair is conscious of time as the session progresses. "The problem is we're dealing with a two-week time frame at the most," said a committee chair. That was the time allotted her committee of the Vermont senate to fashion a school-funding bill. By the end of the session, there is virtually no time at all. As the work progresses, the schedule is always tight. The chair of the Minnesota Senate Ways and Means Committee, for example, had to complete the committee's voting on amendments so that the majority party caucus meeting could discuss the amendments that same morning. Every committee member knew the issues, but every member also wanted to speak on several proposed amendments. Either the debate or the caucus meeting scheduled afterwards had to give.

As the end of the session approaches, less time is spent in committee while more time is spent on the house and senate floor. "We have three weeks to go—the hardest three weeks to go," the Minnesota senate majority leader told his caucus at the end of April. "The time schedule here is horribly compressed. Everyone who's involved in negotiations is going to realize that there's not time for the customary dance," the Minnesota house majority leader put it the first week in May.[20] About three weeks from *sine die* adjournment, Maryland legislators were working into the evening—and occasionally the very late evening. The crossover deadline was upon them—in forty-seven chambers committee work and action in the first house have to be completed by a set time—and they had to get their bills to the other house quickly.

The state budget brings with it a deadline of its own. It has to be enacted by the end of the fiscal year, no matter how long or short the legislative session itself. Enacting a budget is nearly always a challenge. The Ohio legislature not only had a budget deadline of June 30, but, more important, a deadline of June 15 that was handed down by the supreme court in a school finance decision. Since the budget and school finance were intertwined, the legislature wanted to have the budget on the governor's desk by June 1. That would give the attorney general time to prepare a brief defending the new state school plan. With such a deadline, the first five months of the 2001 session focused on school accountability and finance, as well as the general budget. The senate and house passed the budget bills and the conference committee meetings and leadership negotiations were conducted over the Memorial Day weekend. President George W. Bush was scheduled to visit Cleveland on the Thursday before; nonetheless, the Republican senate leader recognized the need to get the conference underway as soon as possible. "We'll stay here Thursday," he said. "I'll bag the president." The leaders negotiated while conferees sat around waiting to fill out budgetary details of the agreements. On the Wednesday after the holiday weekend the conference committee was scheduled to meet at 9:00 A.M., but the meeting started over twelve hours late because leadership negotiations went on the entire day and did not conclude until 5:00 the next morning.

The Pressure Peaks

Everything either gets settled at the end of the session or it doesn't. But that is when the pressure to get things done is most intense. Although there may be a multitude of bills passing in the New York legislature, according to Assemblyman Alexander B. "Pete" Grannis, "on the big issues, usually the last week of the session is when people make deals and get things done." Or, as a lobbyist for NYPIRG put it, "In Albany, nothing really gets done until everything gets done."[21] Usually adjournment or budget deadlines force contestants to resolve their differences and come to agreement so that everyone can go home. But not always, nor on every issue. There simply may not be time to work everything out. Or, as the Maryland speaker put it: "We're trying to squeeze ten pounds in a five pound bag these last two days."

As mentioned earlier, the New York legislature never meets its budget deadline anymore. But state government remains open, and until the house, senate, and governor work out their differences, state spending continues at the level of the prior year. At some point a new budget becomes law. Minnesota, in contrast to New York, normally manages to enact a budget by its constitutionally mandated adjournment date. But it failed to do so in 2001. The deadline itself did not force the Democratic senate, Republican house, and Independent governor to agree on eight omnibus budget bills by the end of the session. More time was needed. After Gov. Jesse Ventura called the legislature back into a special session on June 11, negotiations resumed and the deadline for the adoption of a 2002–2003 budget began to exert heavy pressure on the negotiators. The two-year budget period ended at midnight on Saturday, June 30. By that time, the budget bills had to be passed by both houses, signed by the governor, and deposited in the secretary of state's office. No one wanted to see government shut down and no one even wanted to rely on a temporary budget. So an agreement was finally reached, only hours before the deadline.

In the final days and hours of a legislative session or special session, while some issues are acted upon, others get left by the wayside. There is simply not enough time, and perhaps not the inclination, i.e., the votes, to deal with them at the end. One such issue in St. Paul was the Minnesota Twins' proposal for a new ballpark. The measure had been lobbied hard, worked over, and approved by six standing committees, but the budget took all the legislature's energies as the regular 2001 session concluded. Even such a high-profile issue as a professional baseball stadium mattered relatively little as compared to state taxes and spending.[22]

When a deadline of any sort is involved, time presses on everyone. Legislative staff is under the gun to proofread and print repeated versions of a bill, and to do it quickly. In Ohio, for example, partisan and nonpartisan staff had to get the budget bill ready for floor action at 1:30 P.M. on Wednesday after the Senate

Finance Committee finished with it at 2:00 that morning. Staff worked through the early morning and into the afternoon. After a typical conference committee in Minnesota, it takes twelve to twenty-four hours to assemble and proofread an omnibus bill and get it to the house and senate floor for debate and a vote. After passage by the two houses, it takes up to three days for the final version to be produced, signed by the legislative leaders, and presented to the governor for signature. It is understandable that some time is needed, since these budget bills may run hundreds of pages.[23] The mechanisms of the process also have to be taken into account, as do computer glitches, staff illnesses, and even power failures. If something can go wrong when the pressure is on, it does.

The Nature of the Enterprise

The legislative process in the states has been described and characterized repeatedly, but never quite satisfactorily. The confusion, humanity, and messiness are difficult to communicate. Probably the most common characterization of the legislative process is that of "a bill becomes a law." It appears in high school and college texts and in a widely distributed cartoon-figure film. It is also the one that is routinely distributed by public information offices of legislatures to citizens and school children who want information. The graphics vary, but the steps by which a bill becomes a law normally include introduction and committee and floor stages in each house, sometimes concurrence, and then action by the governor. As described by John A. Straayer in his book on the Colorado legislature:

> Many people have only vague images of how legislatures work and how bills become law; these mental pictures are often derived from dry textbook descriptions or stick-figure sketches of Mr. Bill walking his way through the legislative process, moving from house to house and landing on the governor's desk.[24]

These several stages certainly exist, but they constitute only the setting for formal action that ratifies a bill's support—at least up to that point in the process. These stages are part of a much more elusive process.

The tip of the iceberg is all that can readily be seen. To see more, one must virtually be engaged in the process—as a member, lobbyist, or journalist. And no one, not even top leaders, can see it all. Even newly elected legislators, however, are not prepared for the complexity and confusion of what takes place. One veteran asked me during my period of observation in Maryland: "Are you making any sense out of the chaos?" Black humor or wisdom, his remark suggests that the legislative process cannot be nailed down.

In perhaps the most often-repeated metaphor about the legislative process, German chancellor Otto von Bismarck advised: "There are two things you don't want to see being made—sausage and legislation." The metaphor no longer holds, even if it did more than one hundred years ago. This is not because the legislative process now is clear, efficient, and easily comprehensible, unlike the making of sausage. Rather, it is the other way around, because sausage making has been rationalized during the past century. In contrast to the legislative process, sausage making is clear, efficient, and comprehensible. The sausage-making process turns out a determinate product; the legislature process deals with less-determinate products.[25]

Other metaphors have also been offered. Muir, in his book on the California legislature, runs through a long list of what he has heard a legislature likened to, in alphabetical order: an arena, assembly, back alley, balance, bawdy house, branch of a tree, brokerage firm, bunch of horse traders, butcher shop, card game, cash register, circus, citadel, club, cockpit, collection agency, decision maker, engine, errand boy, factory, family, forum, group, house, inquisition, judge, jury, linchpin, locus of pressures, machine, magnet, marketplace, medium, mender of the social fabric, mirror, moral midwife, nightclub, organ of the body, porkbarrel, pride of lions, rat race, referee, sausage maker, school, seminar, small town, stage, struggle, theater, and zoo.[26] Straayer contributes two additional metaphors.[27] First, the legislature can be seen as a casino. In a casino there are lots of tables, lots of games. The stakes can be high; cards are held tight; self-interest prevails. There are winners and losers, but the outcome is never final, for there is always a new day and a new game just around the corner. Second, the legislature can be viewed as an arena. In that arena a number of basketball games are progressing, all at once, on the same floor, with games at different stages, and with participants playing on several teams at once, switching at will, opposing each other in some instances and acting as teammates in others.

It is interesting that there are so many different views of lawmaking, each of which accurately portrays one or another aspect of what is entailed. But no metaphor captures everything of importance about the process—perhaps because it is too many faceted for a metaphor. But significant facets of the lawmaking process need to be kept in mind.

First, as discussed above, *the workload is heavy* and time is usually in short supply.

Second, *the participants are many.* They include legislators, most importantly. Leaders, committee members, and rank and file play different roles. Participants also include interest groups and their lobbyists, constituents who may or may not be acting as interest group members, and coalitions of groups and legislators on one or another side of a measure. Finally, the governor and representatives of the administration are important players in the process. Each and every participant is trying to get one or more bills passed and/or defeated. Think about what it is like when 80, 120, or more legislators try to move their own bills forward while attempting to derail someone else's. Everyone angling for his or her bills, and at the same time gunning for those they oppose, makes for what one legislative leader called "a crazy time." Individual members managing their bills, committee chairs managing their jurisdictions, and legislative leaders managing their chamber or caucus agendas—all are engaged in trying to build consensus or keep it from being built. What is that? In the legislative scheme, consensus is

50 percent plus one, although those trying to build it would welcome more than that. Much of what happens is noncontroversial, but on other matters consensus building, or trying to get the votes, goes on among interest groups, within the parties, across the aisle, between the houses, and with the governor.

Third, the process *affords access.* It affords all sorts of interests and views an opportunity to be expressed, and they generally are. Many interests fight for a larger share of the budget, others for a shift in tax burdens. The right clashes with the left; libertarians challenge liberals. Business defends itself against regulation; farmers seek subsidies; teachers question accountability systems. Take animal-rights interests, for example. At the opening of the 2003 year, there were twenty different bills on animals in the New Jersey legislature. Three other bills had become law in 2002.[28] In no other arena than the legislature are so many different and conflicting interests represented. In no other arena—not even a zoo—is there such a cacophony of sound as in a committee meeting room or on the senate or house floor.

Fourth, the process is *ubiquitous.* Representation, lobbying, and negotiation are not confined to committee meeting rooms or the legislative chambers where votes are formally taken. The process of building support cannot be contained; it goes on everywhere. Legislators both are lobbied by and lobby groups and individuals in their districts. They negotiate with colleagues over breakfast, lunch, or dinner. They meet with one another in their offices. They work things out in party caucuses. They deal with legislative leaders in the members' lounge behind the chamber. They are buttonholed by lobbyists in the halls, elevators, or the cafeteria. Discussion goes on and on, wherever two or more participants can be found. And they can be found just about anywhere in the state house or in the capitol when the legislature is in session.

Fifth, *motivations and considerations are many.* Solving problems matters. Getting something through matters. Getting political credit matters. Up close the process comes across as people grappling with tough problems and trying to figure out what can pass, and how, and with what political effects. Legislators do not want to annoy their constituents, and they constantly guard against taking positions that are likely to harm themselves politically. For many legislators, values count; for some, ideology is of prime importance. The more they feel they have at stake, the more they want to win. And winning requires both skill and effort. For many legislators, the game itself—irrespective of the substantive outcomes—is fascinating and consuming. For a few, the game matters most of all.

Sixth, instead of one legislative process, *several legislative processes exist simultaneously,* depending on the controversiality of the issue. If an issue is not controversial, it may proceed on a "smooth track." The legislator manager of the measure only needs to ask for support to get it. The problem, even here, is getting the bill scheduled at all the places where decisions have to be made. In two-party legislative bodies, managing one of these bills is easier for a member of the majority than for a member of the minority. "No opposition" generally is reserved for minor matters, but even an important bill can generate little organized opposition. A bill with such momentum is known as a "speeding train." Everyone has the choice of getting on board or getting out of the way.

More controversial issues, especially but not exclusively when legislative parties hold different positions, move at a different pace. Seldom is the roadbed smooth. Differences often are *worked out,* as on a budget bill. Some issues, however, tap into deeply held ideological, value, or political conflicts. Settlements are almost out of the question, as neither side is willing to compromise on conscience, constituency, or the next election. These issues are *fought out.* One side wins, the other loses, or stalemate results. Either way, the battle is likely to resume in the next session or the one after that.

Seventh, the *number of transactions is great.* On even the easiest issues hundreds of transactions occur and on the tough issues thousands or more are not unusual. Everyone is dealing with just about everyone else, simultaneously, consecutively, and in a variety of arenas. On any issue members converse with one another, lobbyists and members talk, members and staff, committee chairs and committee members, leaders among themselves and with rank and file. On an issue such as prescription drugs for senior citizens, for example, take a legislature with 120 members. Each may meet on average with five lobbyists on two occasions each, as well as with twenty constituents and/or other citizens. Add their discussions with ten colleagues on four occasions and two staff members on three occasions. Conservatively, we have a total of over nine thousand transactions on this issue alone. The metaphor that applies right here is that of the circus, but not the Ringling Brothers/Barnum & Bailey three-ring variety. It is of a circus with hundreds of rings, in each of which at any one time a number of performers are going through their paces. These paces include exchanging information, study, deliberation, offering inducements, and engaging in trades, strategizing, and so forth. Most of this is outside of public view; indeed, it is also outside the sight of those legislators who are not involved in a particular transaction. The legislative process is a fragmentary one, but it is one in which the many little pieces have to come together—and usually they do.

Eighth, the process is *unpredictable.* Exactly how the fragments come together and in which form is never certain. Legislators would have to be able to read tea leaves to be confident of any outcome. Even when everything seems aligned, it can still fall apart. Changes are made continuously. Even when consensus apparently has been fashioned and agreements reached, something can happen to upset things. An inexplicable defection, a surprise amendment, and even an absence can undo what has been wrought. After the Minnesota senate voted 33–30 to reject reducing the drunken driving threshold from 0.10 to 0.08 blood-alcohol concentration, the bill's sponsor commented: "I thought I had the votes. It was a surprise." [29]

Ninth, *it takes time* for an issue to garner support. New issues usually require a gestation period until support coalesces and they can gather a head of steam. The same bills are introduced again and again until they pass. An emergency or scandal, however, can fast-track a measure.

Tenth, even after a measure is passed and signed into law, *the issue lives on.* "There's no such thing as a dead issue" one legislator said of the temporary nature of legislative settlements. Education, the environment, health, gun control, abortion, drunken driving, and other issues return to the legislature year after year in one form or another, and often in very similar form. If one side wins, the other seeks redress. If the two sides split the difference, both seek advantage not long afterward. Once civil unions passed the Vermont legislature in 2000 opponents pushed in the next session for its repeal, while gay-lesbian groups began to gear up to get legislation granting legal marriage. Settlements are reached, with gains made by one side while the other tries to retake territory it lost. The battle continues, and it can be waged anywhere, in the legislature directly or in the courts. The Ohio legislature, for instance, is one of a number that currently has had to respond to state court mandates on educational finance. Ohio's senate president sees no end in sight. "Even if we win in the supreme court, there will be another lawsuit," he said. "If you don't get what you want in the legislature, come on over [to the supreme court] and we'll talk about it." That, anyway, has been the experience in Ohio, as well as in other states. Or proponents, at least in twenty-four states, may resort to an initiative campaign that puts a measure directly on the ballot, thus bypassing the legislature. Whatever the possibilities, the legislative process is truly a work in progress, with no end in sight.

NOTES

1. John A. Straayer, *The Colorado General Assembly,* 2nd ed. (Boulder: University Press of Colorado, 2000), 6.

2. As reported in *St. Paul Pioneer Press,* July 6, 2001.

3. Ibid., May 7, 2001.

4. *New York Times,* June 19, 2001.

5. *Cincinnati Enquirer,* May 27, 2001.

6. *New York Times,* November 30, 2001. For an account of this issue, see David Moats, *Civil Wars: A Battle for Gay Marriage* (New York: Harcourt, 2004).

7. Mordecai Lee, "Looking at the Politics-Administration Dichotomy from the Other Direction: Participant Observation by a State Senator," *International Journal of Public Administration* 24, no. 4 (2001): 375–376.

8. These instances are drawn from an internship paper by Dawn Thomas, Rutgers University, May 3, 2002.

9. Maryland Department of Legislative Services, *Under the Dome: The Maryland General Assembly in the 20th Century* (Annapolis: Department of Legislative Services, 2001).

10. Lee, "Looking at the Politics-Administration Dichotomy," 376–377.

11. William K. Muir Jr., *Legislature: California's School for Politics* (Chicago: University of Chicago Press, 1982), 60.

12. Straayer, *The Colorado General Assembly,* 250.

13. *New York Times,* June 22, 2001.

14. Harriet Keyserling, *Against the Tide* (Columbia: University of South Carolina Press, 1998), 140–141, 145, 151.

15. According to recent surveys 25–50 percent of all college students pierce body parts other than their earlobes. *New York Times,* February 12, 2002.

16. *St. Paul Pioneer Press,* May 26, 2001.

17. Lee, "Looking at the Politics-Administration Dichotomy," 375–376.

18. Keyserling, *Against the Tide,* 153–154.

19. *Politics in Minnesota,* 19 (March 22, 2000).

20. *Minneapolis Star Tribune,* May 6, 2001.

21. *New York Times,* June 18 and 21, 2001.

22. *St. Paul Pioneer Press,* May 22, 2001.

23. Ibid., June 29, 2001.

24. Straayer, *The Colorado General Assembly,* 1.

25. Alan Rosenthal, "The Legislature as Sausage Factory—Isn't It About Time That We Examine This Metaphor?" *State Legislatures* (September 2001): 12–15.

26. Muir, *Legislature: California's School for Politics,* 1.

27. Straayer, *The Colorado General Assembly,* 7.

28. *Newark Star-Ledger,* January 5, 2003.

29. *Minneapolis Star Tribune,* May 11, 2001.

5 LAWMAKING: OBSTACLES TO OVERCOME

The sponsor of the bill promoted it on the Ohio senate floor. "It does absolutely nothing," he claimed. Although it changed the state code somewhat, it had "no substantive effect." His colleagues did not dispute the matter, and the bill was enacted. In Minnesota, the senate spent several sessions in 2001 trying to process noncontroversial items that had been reported by standing committees. Senate File No. 1104 was described by its author, Sen. Dean Johnson, as a housekeeping bill that simply clarified provisions relating to the National Guard. "No one testified in opposition to it," the author pointed out. The Department of Administration's Senate File No. 1894 was described by Sen. Dan Stevens as "a housekeeping bill, it's noncontroversial." That day the Minnesota senate agreed to forty such bills, with virtually no debate and no one in opposition.

Much of what is enacted into law by the legislature arouses no resistance. Everyone agrees and votes in favor. Much of it is noncontroversial, but it may be important nonetheless. Take, for example, a bill enacted unanimously during the Washington legislature's 2002 session that allowed all types of shellfish to be grown on former state tidelands. Without such a law, shellfish growers in the South Sound faced potential enforcement of century-old laws that forbade growing anything other than oysters. These laws, however, were thought to be irrelevant because another old law authorized clam farming and other shellfish growing as well. But the legislature replaced the clam act when it rewrote the state fisheries code, leaving clam and geoduck growers unaware of the change that made their activities illegal. It was only after a citizen complained about geoduck harvesting and a subsequent Department of Natural Resources letter warned about "nonconforming uses" that shellfish growers woke up and appealed to the legislature and their grievance was effectively addressed.[1]

In addition to the so-called housekeeping issues and other matters regarded as noncontroversial are those that require that disagreements be worked out. There may be disagreement as to whether a problem exists, and thus whether legislation is required to do something about it. Even if they agree that there is a problem, its exact nature may be in dispute. And even if legislators see eye to eye on its exact nature, rarely are they in accord on just how to deal with it.

Resolving disagreements and securing majorities at various way stations in the lawmaking process can be daunting. That is because disagreement and conflict are built into the legislative system itself and the resolution of differences has to overcome the several kinds of obstacles described below.

Diversity and Individualism

The legislature is an individualistic institution. Each and every member has a vote and thus the potential to be either someone who is part of a majority or someone who keeps a majority from forming. As Vermont's house minority leader, John Tracy, said: "The easiest thing to do is to find a reason not to vote for a bill." When the vote of a legislator is needed by one side or the other, that legislator has leverage. A colleague, committee chair, legislative leader, or lobbyist has to make a persuasive appeal. Legislators have opportunities to exercise influence throughout the process and their opportunities to do so make things tougher, rather than easier, for anyone trying to get something done. Even when legislation appears to be on a "fast track," with leadership endorsement, a few members can derail it.

The perspectives that legislators bring to the process vary enormously. They have very different constituencies. In just about every state regional rivalries are important: Chittenden County versus the rest of the state in Vermont; Montgomery and Prince George's Counties versus other counties in Maryland or the metro, suburban, rural, and Iron Range districts in Minnesota. Even within regions particular districts vary; no district is exactly like another. And it is the district—the legislator's residential and electoral constituency—to which members feel most obligated.

Most legislators are politically ambitious—they either want to be returned to the legislature or elected to higher office. But pursuit of individual political ambitions impacts on the legislature itself. The gubernatorial ambitions of the senate president, Republican Donald DiFrancesco, and Republican assembly speaker Jack Collins in New Jersey made it more difficult for the two chambers to reach agreement. Years earlier, the gubernatorial ambitions of senate Democratic president John Russo and assembly Republican speaker Chuck Hardwick had similar consequences for the operations of the New Jersey legislature. In Minnesota the Republican house majority leader, Tim Pawlenty, had unsuccessfully sought his party's endorsement for governor in 1998. To win the endorsement for the 2002 gubernatorial race, he had to appeal to a Republican Party with a platform more conservative than his personal image and voting record. That is one reason, explains a senate Democrat, why he took the lead in negotiating a twenty-four-hour waiting period for abortions when the issue had been dormant for years. It is also why he took a key role in the negotiations to repeal Minnesota's education standards that were opposed by conservative Christian groups. On these issues Pawlenty took public and private negotiating positions that were more hard line than those taken by the more conservative house speaker.[2]

Legislators have their own ideas and their own policy agendas, all of which get in the way of quick and easy settlements. Nearly all members, but new members in particular, have bills that they introduce and want to get passed. Some result from campaign promises and others from the legislators' own experiences or beliefs. Some come from constituents, others from interest groups, and still oth-

ers from colleagues and friends. Sponsors or authors do whatever they can to further their own agendas, but they may be less committed to advancing a common agenda. In some places authors never relinquish control of the bill they introduce. They guide it through committee, negotiate necessary compromises, manage it on the floor, arrange for passage in the other house, and try to ensure that the governor will not veto it. In other places authors cannot maintain similar control, but rarely do they leave their bill entirely in the hands of their colleagues.

A legislator's personal agenda can take substantial time and effort. Consider, for instance, a health care bill proposed by John E. McDonough, a member of the Massachusetts house. After months of discussion formulating a bill, McDonough began a time-consuming external sales strategy. He spent three months "moving all over the state, meeting with business, consumer, physicians, senior, and other groups, making presentations to newspaper editors and reporters, using the same pitch and the same lines five to fifteen times per day." [3] Or consider the dedication of a member of the Vermont house to a bill that would require the siting of mobile phone towers, even in residential areas. The representative appeared almost on a crusade to remedy the problem that callers in many areas of the state could not pick up phone signals. Local control, in his view, interfered with effective mobile phone systems and, in the case of an emergency where a phone was needed quickly, was a danger to public safety.

The health care plan and the mobile-phone siting proposal raised problems for some other members, as many bills do. McDonough's plan would have hurt some businesses while being of advantage to others. Opponents of the mobile phone requirement argued that it would destroy local Vermont landscapes and cause distress to property owners and environmentalists. Even legislation that would not appear at first sight to be controversial—for instance, to regulate pedacycles—can arouse opposition. Chris Pracht introduced a bill in the South Carolina house to classify pedacycles as motorcycles and subject them to the same rules because of doctors' reports in his community of accidents that resulted in serious injuries and death. The State Highway Department endorsed the bill and it was approved in the Education Committee. But once it reached the house floor opposition was fierce: people were being licensed to death; drivers with suspended licenses for drunken driving would not have a way to go to work and would not be able to support their families; low-income commuters who rode pedacycles to work because they could not afford cars also could not afford insurance; the mentally retarded who depended on pedacycles would be penalized; and thirteen-year-old newspaper carriers would be deprived of their livelihoods. After each objection, legislators would huddle to work on a compromise. Amendments were passed to exempt drunken drivers and to lower the age of drivers to thirteen, eliminating licensing provisions. The bill that passed did not resemble the one that was introduced.[4]

In committee, in caucus, or on the floor members have different ideas about just what should be included in legislation and what should be left out. In each of these venues members pose questions regarding the substance of a bill, and in each amendments are in order as senators and representatives go about their business of perfecting legislation. Some of the objections voiced and the amendments offered may be devised by organized interests and by executive agencies, but some are the work of members themselves. In either case, most members are sincere in their objections and are looking for ways to make legislation more acceptable. On some issues—but only a minority—members simply want to deep-six a proposal.

Not only do legislators disagree with one another personally on the substantive merits of many issues, but how they regard one another is sometimes important as well. Good relationships count, as far as accomplishing one's objectives in the legislature are concerned. A good legislative leader will try to lay groundwork for the process by encouraging members to get to know one another. Paul Hilligonds, who was then minority leader of the Michigan house, sent his members on a road trip together to get ideas from people throughout the state. Hilligonds, who later became speaker, reflects that "It was really about relationship building, people getting to know each other, understanding each other's perspectives." As understanding developed, consensus could more easily be reached on a number of policies.[5]

No matter what efforts leaders make to build collegiality, some members will simply have it in for others. One Maryland senator, for example, opposed an amendment on the budget because she had served with the sponsor long enough to come to distrust and dislike him. Other legislators, for a host of reasons, will withhold support from colleagues or even undermine their efforts. It is true that in most cases they go along, as legislative norms dictate, expecting reciprocity. But in a few instances they would prefer to even the score, especially if no great risk is involved to themselves.

Interest Group Agendas

In part, the diversity of legislators' views reflects, or certainly parallels, that of group interests. Such interests are represented by lobbyists, on whom legislators rely both for substantive and political information.[6] In any legislative session lobbyists abound, making the case for their organizations, clients, and issues. John A. Straayer describes a typical scene at the Colorado capitol:

> A . . . visit reveals lobbyists milling around and perhaps committees in session, with legislators and lobbyists running in and out for coffee or exchanges with colleagues or staff members. When legislators are on the floor there will be throngs of lobbyists just outside the house and senate doors—in the "lobby." When the chambers recess for the day and members go into committees, the lobby crowd moves with them, to the third-floor Senate committee room area, and to that of the House in the basement. . . .[7]

Although lobbyists play a critical role in the legislative process everywhere, their role is largely contingent on the interests they represent. In each state hundreds of entities are organized and represented at the capitol. These groups seek to advance the economic, professional, financial, ideological, or other interests of their members. Often, however, the interests of one group—as expressed in a bill or appropriation—clash with those of another, or with proposals sponsored by legislators or by the administration. While legislatures deal with many non-controversial matters, scores of bills upset one interest group or another.

Whatever the specific proposal, somebody is sure to make the case that it is not needed, it is unfair, or it will not work. Some interest will be adversely affected by just about anything of substance. A bill in Maryland to lower the cost of prescription drugs for senior citizens would hurt pharmacists. A school finance plan worked out by the Ohio legislature did not provide the funds demanded by a coalition of 550 school districts in the state. In Minnesota the state teachers' organization led the "Keep Minnesota Smart" campaign because it did not think either the governor or the legislature were proposing enough money for schools. In Vermont gas station owners objected to a $7,000 increase in the fee for underground storage tanks, which they could pass on to consumers. One owner appealed to the house committee before which he was testifying: "We collect and pay a lot of taxes (about thirty to forty different ones). By the end of the week, our heads are spinning collecting all these taxes."

Conflict is endemic to the legislative process because legislation that would benefit the interests of one group could be averse to the interests of another. Americans have different values, interests, and views, virtually all of which are represented in one form or another by organized groups. James Madison was concerned with the factional nature of politics and tried to devise ways to ameliorate its effects. Factions based on common values or interests are critical elements of our political system. To a substantial degree, democracy is a system of contending factions. "That people with common interests should be allowed freely to attempt to sway government policy is, in fact, democracy's whole point," according to John Mueller.[8] The legislature is the principal arena in which such interests contend with one another and vie for advantage.

There are at least two sides to issues with which the legislature deals, with each side represented by one or several groups or a coalition including multiple members. Gun control is an issue that is fought over just about everywhere in the country. Concealed weapons held center stage in the 2001 session of the Ohio and Minnesota legislatures. Ohio's House Bill 274 would have permitted qualified Ohioans to carry concealed weapons on a restricted basis. Proponents included the National Rifle Association (NRA) and the Ohio Gun Rights Coalition. Opponents included the Ohio Association of Chiefs of Police, the Ohio Coalition Against Gun Violence, and chapters of Ohio's Five Million Mom March. NRA and local gun-rights supporters endorsed a bill to provide citizens greater access to concealed weapons, while Citizens for a Safer Minnesota lobbied against it.

Drunken driving is another national issue that divides interest groups. By the start of the 2001 session a number of states had passed legislation lowering the blood-alcohol threshold for drunken driving from 0.10 percent to 0.08 percent. Maryland passed such a bill in its legislative session that year, with Mothers Against Drunk Driving (MADD) on one side and liquor interests on the other. In Minnesota the bill had failed to pass for four years, despite support from MADD and the national liquor distillers. It was opposed by the Wine, Beer and Spirits Federation of Minnesota.

If one group tries to lessen a burden on itself, another will resist taking on a heavier load, as can be seen in a number of bills faced by the Maryland legislature during the 2001 session. For instance, manufacturers backed legislation to shift some of the state's corporate income tax to out-of-state companies. Predictably, large nonresident companies, such as Kraft Foods, opposed. If one group wants to use legislation to expand its domain, another will regard such an action as incursion into its own territory. Another bill allowed HMOs to assign patients to nurse practitioners as primary care providers, instead of requiring assignment only to physicians. Nurses maintained that they were well qualified to do the job, while doctors argued that patient care might suffer as a result. Teachers tried to expand their control by sponsoring a bill that allowed teachers to bargain curriculum and classroom assignments, as well as salaries and working conditions, but school boards opposed the bill. Often the battle between groups is over public resources. For example, $8 million of Maryland's proposed budget was allocated for textbook aid to private and parochial schools. Groups such as the Catholic Conference on the one hand and Orthodox Jews on the other supported the appropriation because their schools would benefit. PTAs, teachers, school boards, and the American Civil Liberties Union opposed it.

Hundreds of lobbyists can be found in the capitol when the legislature is in session. Singly, or more likely in coalitions, they promote bills that will advance their organizations' or clients' interests, as they oppose bills that will threaten their organizations' or clients' interests. Lobbyists and group members testify before committees, buttonhole legislators in their offices and wherever else they can find them, and work together with lawmakers when their objectives coincide. Interest groups and their lobbyists are a key part of the process, which means that their support or opposition may be instrumental in ensuring a bill's passage on the one hand or its defeat on the other.

Intraparty Division

The legislative party provides much of the cohesion that exists in state senates and houses. This is because on a number of principles and issues Democrats tend to agree with one another ideologically, while Republicans also tend to agree with one another ideologically, with partisan agreement running in opposite directions. Not only do partisans see eye to eye on some important issues, they also have stakes in their own party's performance. They are rewarded, or punished, at the polls in substantial part because they run as Democrats or as Republicans. Their agendas normally benefit if their party wins control of, and consequently organizes, the chamber in which they serve. In competitive, two-party legislative bodies majority members do better than minority members when it comes to getting bills passed or projects included in the appropriation act.

Nevertheless, party loyalty is not sufficient to engender support on each and every such issue. As one legislative leader in Vermont explained: "We don't control our caucus. They [the members] are independent contractors." Leaders can use information to persuade their colleagues, argue the importance of party unity, and even lean on members a little bit. But such tactics do not necessarily overcome party divisions based on the districts legislators represent and the beliefs legislators hold. Most lawmakers behave independently of party on the key issues of constituency and/or conscience. On Vermont's Act 60, for example, legislators differed according to whether their constituencies received more or less school aid compared to what they had to pay in taxes. Neither Republicans nor Democrats as a party were unified on the issue.

Legislative parties can achieve unity at times, but not always. Some issues pit the interests of one type of district or area of the state against others, as did Vermont's Act 60. In Washington, for example, the Democratic speaker and his Transportation Committee chair disagreed over a regional transportation plan. The former favored a plan for South Sound commuters, many of whom lived in his district; the latter preferred one that would aid the state ferry system, since many ferry commuters lived in her district. Another case in point is New York, where majority Republicans in the senate have a number of incumbents from Long Island who want more money for school aid in order to keep down increases in property taxes. The upstate delegation wanted to cut taxes. Senate President Ralph Marino found it difficult during the early 1990s to get Long Island Republican members to accept tax cuts if doing so would mean less school aid.[9] His successor, Joe Bruno, found it virtually impossible to do the same ten years later.

Whether the caucus is Democratic or Republican, several members will be to the left or right of the center of gravity. Sometimes, as is the case of New York assembly Democrats, the caucus is split almost down the middle. Liberals represent New York City and less liberal Democrats represent upstate. In Washington majority Democrats in the senate showed remarkable discipline in the 2002 session, with some members sticking with their party at the expense of their districts. But even with such discipline, one member—Tim Sheldon—often voted with the Republicans, thus requiring the Democrats to get at least one Republican vote in order to prevail on the floor.

Intraparty division that results from the combination of conscience and constituency, rather than just one or the other, is not unusual. Both majority parties in Minnesota are divided. House Republicans have a caucus that, in the words of the majority leader, "runs the gamut from almost Democratic to almost Libertarian." [10] The Democratic-Farmer-Labor Party (DFL) has maintained a substantial majority in the Minnesota senate for years and therefore could afford to allow members to stray from party positions. But that caucus is severely split between liberals, generally from urban areas, and conservatives, generally from "out state." [11]

For example, a concealed weapons bill in the 2001 session split senate Democrats in Minnesota, with rural members supporting it and urban and suburban members in opposition. Momentum shifted back and forth, with Democrats seeking to find grounds for a compromise on which most of them could agree. "How should we frame it, so guys understand that we have to stick together?" one senator asked. The majority leader, Roger Moe, faced with a split, needed to know how many members he could depend on to beat back the bill legalizing concealed weapons. He also had to know how to amend the bill to keep enough members of his caucus satisfied.

Partisans and Partisanship

In every state, with the sole exception of Nebraska, whose legislature is nonpartisan, the two political parties vie for control. Each party wants to win a majority in the senate and house, so that its members may occupy dominant positions and control issue agendas. On the overwhelming majority of bills that legislatures consider, partisanship plays no role—that is, no role independent of constituency and interest group affiliations. But on some of the most important issues—notably the budget—party matters, as Democrats generally line up against Republicans. Partisanship, of course, makes lawmaking more contentious than it would otherwise be.

The Legislative Party in Five States

Party is a factor in each of the legislatures under special study here, although in Maryland Democrats have a substantial margin and in Ohio Republicans have a comfortable margin. As of the 2001 legislative sessions, Democrats had the barest of majorities in the Washington senate and house, while in both Minnesota and Vermont the senate was Democratic and the house Republican. Only in the Minnesota senate did the majority party have firm control; in the three other chambers, the division was close. The Democratic legislature in Maryland had the benefit of working with a Democratic governor, while the Republican legislature in Ohio had a Republican in the governor's office. Washington's Democrats, with narrow margin, had a Democratic governor, as did Vermont's divided legislature. In Minnesota the Democratic senate and Republican house were obliged to deal with a governor from a newly established Independence Party. In each state the majority party has principal responsibility for determining the chamber's agenda. Majority control is reflected on standing committees, where majority party members outnumber minority members and where a majority party member is normally appointed as chair. The majority, through its leadership and caucus, also determines which bills proceed to the floor and when. However, out of all of the bills that are introduced, that receive serious consideration, and that are reported favorably by standing committees, only a small proportion find most members of one party opposing most members of the other.

The Minority

Given control by the majority party, the minority has certain options. It can go along with a proposal pretty much as formulated by the majority, try to modify the majority proposal in committee or on the floor, or oppose it in the hope of defeating it. The precise role of the minority varies according to the party's strength. But it has to choose how it will generally relate to the majority. Maryland house Republicans, for example, saw their choices as straightforward: either cooperate with the speaker, maintain generally good relations with the speaker, or pursue an adversarial relationship with the speaker. The first choice would mean no separate Republican identity but a better chance for Republican-sponsored bills; Republican members would be treated about the same as Democrats. The second would allow minor, but not major, Republican bills to pass, with party affiliation becoming salient. The third option would entail Republicans challenging the speaker at every opportunity but seeing few or none of their bills pass, thus increasing rancor and engendering extreme partisanship.[12]

In Maryland the minority had traditionally pursued a good relationship with the majority, but as Republican members increased, the minority moved to greater independence. In more competitive two-party legislatures—such as Minnesota, Ohio, Vermont, and Washington—the minority strategy ranges between good relations and constant challenge. The more competitive the situation, the more likely the minority will stand in opposition whenever it can.

The minority can also succeed in modifying the majority's proposals. This normally happens in committee, where legislation is crafted. Here is where expertise counts most and relationships are more likely to extend across party lines. Thus, the minority may influence the shape of legislation before party lines harden. In Washington, for example, while the house Republican minority in 2002 chose not to work with the majority, the senate Republican minority worked with the Democrats on the shaping of critical bills. The closer the margins, the stronger the bargaining power of the minority. And where an extraordinary majority is required, as it is to override a gubernatorial veto or end a filibuster, the minority's bargaining position is enhanced. If the majority is large and can afford to lose the votes of some of its members, it may choose not to invite minority party participation in shaping a measure. Moreover, what the minority insists on in return for the votes of some of its members may be more than the majority is willing to give.

What the minority can and hopes to do is raise issues of its own. It has little chance of garnering the votes to enact them, but it suggests alternatives and develops its own agenda. The minority, in the words of an Ohio legislator, can "kick up sand" about broader issues that ought to be considered. Some of these issues inevitably enter into the next campaign for seats in the legislature. Often the minority party is in a campaign mode, offering alternatives and making cases that will underpin the next election campaign. By offering amendments, the minority frequently wants to force majority members to go on record and risk losing voter support on controversial issues. Or, alternatively, it wants to build support of its own with voters and interest groups.

In the process the minority usually succeeds in slowing things down. Guerilla warfare takes its toll. As a Republican member in Vermont characterized Democrats: "The minority on the House side has learned to be troubling faster than the majority has learned to be skillful." Some of the trouble is caused by the minority's careful scrutiny of legislation and some by the fact that the minority has chosen, or been forced into choosing, "bomb throwing" as its *modus operandi.*

The fact is that the two parties usually oppose one another on some of the most important issues of the session. The budget always ranks at the top in importance, and it is likely to be the measure most likely to divide the senate and the house along party lines. Here one can observe partisanship in standing committees, in caucuses, and in the roll call votes cast by members on the floor. Ohio is an interesting case of partisanship. The tradition in past years has been a pragmatic one. Whichever party controlled the legislature and whichever controlled the office of governor, it was possible for Republicans and Democrats to work together. But the era of cooperation gave way in the mid 1990s to an era of conflict, with budgets dividing Republicans and Democrats.[13] In 2001, when the budget passed the house by 53–45, six Republicans voted no, largely because of a lottery provision and additional taxes. The majority caucus did not need their votes, even though not one Democrat voted for the budget. Jack Ford, the Democratic leader, boasted, "We stood together." But, he had to add, "the [speaker's] caucus stood together, too." [14] When the budget bill reached the Ohio senate, three Republicans voted against it, while every Democrat did the same. Still, the budget passed, 18–14. Similar divisions on the budget could be seen in Minnesota. In Washington, with the house tied 26–26 during the 2001 session, the two parties managed to pass a budget 52–46, but only after several special sessions. The choice was to stalemate and shut the state down or to break the tie somehow. In 2002, however, with Democrats narrowly controlling each chamber, the 26–23 senate and 50–47 house votes were nearly a straight party division. On the senate side, only one Democrat voted against the budget, while only two Republicans voted for it. Parties also oppose one another in Maryland and Vermont, but partisanship is less of a factor in these two states.

Why Democrats and Republicans Disagree

That legislative parties oppose one another should cause little surprise. First, their members tend to represent different constituencies. Their principal supporters consist of people who differ from one party grouping to the other. In Minnesota, for instance, house Republicans come mainly from rural, conservative districts, while senate Democrats hail chiefly from urban and suburban districts. According to the house speaker, Steve Sviggum: "The division has been deeper and more pronounced in recent years, and it can make things difficult."[15] Second, their members tend to be affiliated with different interest groups. John A. Straayer provides confirming evidence for this obvious point in his study of the Colorado legislature. He reports the support scores for senators and representatives on items of importance to each of four interest groups. Two—the Colorado Union of Taxpayers (CUT) and the Colorado Conservative Union (CCU)— are conservative; two—the senior lobby and six groups comprising the environmental lobby—are liberal. Ranging from 0 to 100, the scores are shown in Table 5-1. The differences in the support scores accorded Republicans and Democrats are enormous.

As fundamental as district and group differences, and overlapping them, are the ideologies and policy preferences shared by most Democrats on one side and most Republicans on the other. Generally speaking, both geographical and interest constituencies and conscience reinforce one another. The beliefs and ideas of legislators cannot be discounted; they have independent strength of their own.

Minnesota exemplifies this tendency and is worth examining in some detail. Even though neither the house Republicans nor the senate Democrats are ideologically homogeneous—and on such issues as abortion and gun control are split—there can be no doubt where the preponderance of ideological weight lies in the two political parties. The differences between them pertain to core values and, in particular, the use of state funds. According to the senate majority leader, Roger Moe: "We basically have some real, solid philosophical differences." [16] In 2001 Minnesota projected a surplus of revenues over expenditures and the major battle between the Republican house and the DFL senate was over how to use the monies. Senate DFLers insisted on splitting the budget surpluses between tax cuts on the one hand and increased spending on education, health care, and transportation on the other. House Republicans, in contrast, wanted to devote the entire surplus to reducing property taxes. The former's budget proposal called for a 7.9 percent increase in state spending, the latter's a 5.4 percent

Table 5-1 Interest Group Support Scores for Colorado Legislators, by Party

Interest group	House Democrats	Republicans	Differences	Senate Democrats	Republicans	Differences
Environmental lobby	91.6	18.8	*72.8*	83.7	17.0	*66.7*
Senior lobby	88.8	39.4	*49.4*	91.0	57.4	*33.6*
Colorado Union of Taxpayers	20.0	80.1	*60.1*	19.8	80.6	*60.8*
Colorado Conservative Union	15.6	56.2	*40.6*	12.6	54.0	*41.4*

Source: Adapted from John A. Straayer, *The Colorado General Assembly,* 2nd ed. (Boulder: University Press of Colorado, 2000), 153–155.

increase. Consequently, the DFL's proposed tax cut was less than half of that backed by the Republicans.

Philosophical differences played out over the specifics of the tax bill, which involved not only how much would be given back to Minnesotans but also who would benefit and to what extent. The DFL argued that under the Republican plan too much of the tax relief would go to businesses, to people with expensive homes and second houses on lakefront properties, while those with lower to mid-valued houses and farms would have to assume more of the tax burden. "It's like modern art," said House Majority Leader Tim Pawlenty, "people look at the picture and see very different things." [17] That made agreement difficult, to say the least. Not surprisingly, the political base of each party strongly supported its legislative contingent's position.

Philosophical differences between the Minnesota parties extended beyond property tax relief. DFLers and Republicans also disagreed on matters of education policy such as graduation standards. In addition, the DFL would have spent more on health and human services and welfare, while the Republicans would have spent more on mental health. In the view of a DFL member of the State Human Services Committee: "It's been hard to find middle ground." The lead negotiators for the senate and house were committed to very different philosophies. Linda Berglin, the senate chair, was an outspoken advocate for the poor and the government's responsibility to help them. Fran Bradley, the house chair, believed that government should play a limited role in families' lives and was concerned about welfare dependency.[18] Other issues—prescription drug prices among them—also divided Minnesota's legislative parties.

What makes agreement even more difficult to achieve are the political stakes involved for each of the political parties. Unlike urban-rural and other cleavages, partisan division in the legislature is carried into the next election, which enhances and prolongs its saliency. Competition between the parties for seats in and control of the senate and house is intense, even in states like Maryland, where one party dominates, and Ohio, where one party has the upper hand. Individual members keep a watchful eye on their constituencies, never losing sight of how their legislative behavior may affect the next election. Party leaders are even more aware of the next election, since they and their caucuses are responsible for winning seats and maintaining or gaining control. Partisan competition at the polls makes joint problem solving and consensus building Herculean tasks.

Despite partisan contention, in some states, such as Vermont, legislators continue to bond across party lines as well as within. But in most places the bonds among members are becoming frayed. The approaching election—and an election is always approaching—permeates the legislature process. One's colleagues in the house or senate are being targeted for defeat by colleagues on the other side. In terms of who wins and who loses, much is at stake. It is little wonder that civility suffers. The rhetoric becomes more extreme, as illustrated by Democratic senator Michael Shoemaker's scornful remarks—those of the minority party not running the show—on the legislature's response to the Ohio Supreme Court's decision on educational finance:

> I have absolutely no confidence in the legislature to fix school funding. I wouldn't trust them with my pickup truck, let along school funding for the children of Ohio. No one's going to watch the store. You might as well put Jeffrey Dahmer in charge of the school cafeteria.[19]

Or as an editor of one of Minnesota's dailies opined, the legislature is "becoming increasingly polarized and politicized." In his view, members of the two parties tend to approach issues on an all-or-nothing basis and have even lost respect for one another's views.[20]

Most of the pressures that legislators feel work against interparty conciliation on major issues. Democratic and Republican caucuses are ideologically at odds, if not absolutely polarized on some major issues. Legislative leaders have to be especially solicitous of their party's extreme wing. Related to the dynamics of the caucus is what John Hottinger, a Minnesota senator, refers to as "caucus ego." DFL senators and Republican house members are so intent on winning—for reasons in addition to ideology, constituency, and election—that they are unwilling to make concessions. "You don't want to lose," said Hottinger. "Even if you lose, you don't want to be perceived as losing."[21] In Minnesota, senate Democrat Roger Moe acquired a reputation for getting the better of the Republican house in negotiations that took place every year, and the pressure was on him to live up to that reputation. Across the capitol building, the house speaker, Steve Sviggum, was seen as a loser in negotiations, prompting members of his caucus, who thought he was too willing to give in to senate demands for higher spending, to put pressure on him to stand firm.[22]

Committee Disputes

A legislative body is organized into standing committees to which members are appointed. Depending on the state and chamber, each legislator may sit on one, two, three, or more committees. This division of labor, expertise, and responsibility enables a legislature to craft legislation through study, public hearings, deliberation, bargaining, and consensus building among members. In most legislative bodies committees are key agencies of the lawmaking process.

But the very division of a senate or a house into standing committees, each with its own jurisdictional area, creates problems. A natural rivalry exists among committees and their chairs, one that is exacerbated by jurisdictional division and conflict. Most referred bills go to one committee or another. But sometimes two different committees have legitimate jurisdiction according to the rules, and occasionally the presiding officers decide, for strategic or other reasons, that committees ought to share jurisdiction. In Minnesota, for example, two committee chairs developed different bills on workforce development, requiring leadership intervention to work out differences. In Maryland health issues were of highest priority, and both the Economic Matters and Environmental Matters Committees had health within their domain. On pharmaceutical legislation two subcommittees of the two full committees claimed jurisdictional authority. Normally, there is tension when two or more committees share a subject, with each chair or subcommittee chair defending the prerogatives and product of his or her own group. Often the house speaker or senate president is called upon to mediate the dispute.

Much intercommittee contention occurs when money is involved. In most legislatures bills with fiscal implications are referred both to a standing committee concerned with policy (for example health, education, or transportation) and then to the standing committee concerned with money (appropriations, ways and means, or finance). In a few legislatures the policy and appropriations committees are one and the same. Minnesota is a case in point. In this state the policy committees spend the first three months of the session on their subject matter responsibilities. Five weeks before the adjournment deadline these committees cease their business on policy matters and address the state's budget. The Finance Committee by resolution sets budget targets for each budget division, which then takes its allotted amount and allocates funds to agencies and programs within its jurisdiction. Intercommittee conflict is avoided because members carry over from the policy committees, where they deal mainly with matters of substance, to divisions, where they deal mainly with funds for these and other substantive matters. Minnesota is the exception, since in most legislative bodies membership on policy and appropriations committees are different. How much a program can spend and how much an agency will be allocated is up to appropriations, ways and means, or finance.

It is unusual not to have a clash between a policy committee and an appropriations committee during the course of a legislative session. Therefore, legislative leaders can be expected to spend some of their time mediating between the chairs of respective committees. Policy committees normally take pains to craft a bill, and often that bill requires state expenditures. When appropriations fails to provide for it in the budget, funds it below the level requested, or simply lets it die, the chair and members of the policy committee object. They claim that they are the experts in the policy area, while appropriations responds that it has to consider the budget as a whole and set priorities. Ordinarily appropriations has the last word; it is rare that a policy committee prevails. The Senate Institutions Committee in Vermont, for instance, drafted sixty amendments to the budget; all were ignored by the Appropriations Committee and none won the day on the floor.

The tension that exists everywhere is illustrated by the budget process in the Maryland house. In the 2001 session much of the money that the chairs of the five policy committees wanted did not get in the budget. For example, Sheila Hixon, chair of Ways and Means, wanted to pass a mass transit initiative that cost a lot more than Appropriations budgeted. Howard "Pete" Rawlings, chair of Appropriations, blamed the shortfall largely on what the governor requested in the budget he proposed. It would have been fiscally irresponsible to think in terms of new money, given the revenue projections, Rawlings explained. The base budget was about all that could be funded. At a meeting of senior leaders, Rawlings justified reductions in the budget made by his committee, and each of the policy committee chairs objected to the cuts made in his or her particular area.

Overcoming the animosity toward the Appropriations Committee in the Maryland house requires strenuous efforts by legislative leaders. Rawlings had to appeal for support. Addressing his colleagues on the floor as the budget came up on second reader (where amendments are permitted), he urged them to support his committee's budget recommendations. "We make hard decisions," he said, "but we respect various interests"—that is, the interests of the policy committees. At meetings of his leadership team, the speaker stressed time after time that members had to defer to committees in order for the committee system to function well. He expected that ordinarily members would uphold committee recommendations, and he insisted on deference to committees from members of his leadership team, mainly the six committee chairs.

Senate-House Differences

Only in Nebraska, with its unicameral legislature, can one house of a legislature enact law without the assent of the other. In forty-nine states the senate and house must agree on an identical bill before it goes to the governor. That means that the bill must ultimately pass both chambers in precisely the same form.

Resolving Disagreement

Agreement between the houses can be reached in several ways. One chamber may consent to the other's bill after negotiations. Or a conference committee comprised of members from the senate and house may be appointed to resolve disagreements and report a single bill to both chambers. Whether the issue is major or minor, the senate and house have to come together if anything is to pass. As Republicans in the Vermont house explained succinctly: "We're going through a process in the house. The senate will have the bill. And we'll have to compromise. And then we'll have to fix it later on."

Sometimes agreement is achieved informally before a measure has passed both houses, but otherwise it goes through a more formal process. In his examination of the 1995 and 1996 legislative sessions in Colorado, in which 620 bills passed, Straayer found that in about 40 percent of the cases the bills passed the two chambers in identical form the first time. Either they were noncontroversial or the disagreements that existed could be worked out in advance. Of the 381 bills on which senate and house versions differed, differences were settled in almost three-quarters of the cases by the house of origin accepting the changes made in the second chamber. Conferences were required on the remaining bills, a total of 104. Straayer concludes: "So while conference committees are very critical parts of the committee system and the legislative process, and while they are more frequently employed on high-stakes contentious legislation, most bills, by far, pass without them." [23] Either way, agreement has to be reached.

Not all states use conference committees. Delaware, New Jersey, and New York, for example, negotiate differently. But some states rely on conferences for reconciling intercameral differences. Minnesota exemplifies the extensive use of conferences on complex, controversial legislation. If differences exist between senate and house versions, the house that acted first, on being notified that the other body had passed its bill, formally "refuses to concur." A conference committee is then formed. In the 1990s Minnesota's conference committees handled about 130 bills per session. More important, in this state, one study reported, "almost all major legislation is produced through the conference-committee process; thus, oftentimes what happens in conference is more important than what happens in either body." [24]

Reasons for Differences

One important reason for senate-house differences on legislation is divided partisan control, with one party having a majority in the house and the other in the senate. In 2001 control was split in fourteen states, including in Minnesota and Vermont. The differences on major issues in senate and house versions in most of these places is attributable more to partisan contention than to disagreement between the chambers. But even when either the Democrats or the Republicans control both houses, as in Maryland, Ohio, and Washington, intercameral differences are common. Such differences occur naturally and for a number of reasons.

First, the senate and the house are very different bodies, with dissimilar cultures and contrasting perspectives on their roles in the legislative process. In every match-up, houses exceed senates in size. As a consequence, house members have fewer committee assignments and can specialize to a greater degree than their senate colleagues. Thus, the house may initiate more legislation and the senate may look over broadly what the house sends over, as in Vermont. Here the house does the crafting of the major legislation in committee and the senate often acts as an appeals board, dealing with the issue after it is refined.

Because the senate is smaller, it is normally less formal than the house. Again, consider Vermont, with its 150-member house and 30-member senate. Each senator is more independent and more autonomous than his or her colleagues in the house. Power is dispersed. The body is more like a "club," with greater collegiality among members. Social events are more likely to include both Democrats and Republicans. Or take Minnesota, where the senate, with sixty-seven members, is the largest such body in the states but still is only half the size of the Minnesota house. According to one recent study, partisanship in the senate has been less important than in the house, with senators acting more as individuals and the minority party having greater influence. As in other senates, Minnesota's senate leader (in this case the majority leader rather than the president or president pro tem) has less formal power than the speaker and shares power with others on the leadership team.[25]

Senates are more stable in their membership than are houses, since in most states their members have four-year rather than two-year terms, and generally are more experienced. The fact that house members run every two years, while senators run every four, affects the way members deal with issues. The political temperature of the house rises higher. In Washington, for instance, during the 2002 session the house insisted on putting a gas tax package on the ballot in a statewide referendum, while the senate wanted simply to enact it into law. House members were under greater political pressure; they did not want to be accused in their election races of raising taxes without obtaining the consent of the people.

Second, not only are cultures and processes in senates and houses dissimilar, but so are the standing committees that shape legislation. Often the jurisdictional committees correspond from one chamber to the other. Transportation, health, human services, and criminal justice matters tend to be handled by roughly parallel committees. To some extent these committees are competing with one another. Each wants to be the major focus of influence within the policy domain under its jurisdiction. Occasionally, parallel committees will come into conflict, regardless of the substance of particular issues. In Vermont, for instance, the president pro tem had to intervene in a dispute between the transportation committees. The house chair wanted to monitor proceedings of the senate committee, the meetings of which were open anyway. He explained that his purpose in monitoring was to see whether and how the testimony of executive agency witnesses varied. But the senate chair objected, indicating that while such behavior might be appropriate in one's own body, it would not be suitable in the other. "It's uncomfortable for us to discuss your bill when you're here," he explained.

Third, individuals may differ in their views on either broad or specific aspects of proposed legislation. And they are almost certain to differ on details. The individual members of a house committee may see the same issue differently than the individual members of a senate committee. Even more important, the chairs of the respective committees may not have the same ideas for dealing with issues, nearly all of which have some degree of complexity built in.

Fourth, the house and senate are rivals for influence. Each wants to prevail. Each has its own institutional pride. Criticism freely flows back and forth. A Maryland house leader's complaint, addressed to colleagues on an issue in contention, that "The Senate's been making fools out of us, and they've been doing it for five years" illustrates the mutual suspicion. To add fuel to the fire, there is often a lingering fear on both sides that the other body may team up with the governor to create a two-to-one situation in negotiations.

Budget Disputes

As a consequence of these and other differences, it is understandable that the house and senate will disagree on many items that eventually require concurrence. The budget is probably the most important bill to pass each year or each biennium, and it is the one on which the largest number of disagreements exists.

Many pertain to amounts of money to be appropriated, while others are matters of public policy. In Maryland, for example, the senate approved spending $5 million for textbook aid for students in private and parochial schools, while the house removed the item from the budget entirely. Although disputes over dollar figures can be settled, policy matters, such as on textbooks for private and parochial schools, are tougher to resolve. Budgetary differences reflect the priorities for spending of the two chambers. In Washington the budget had to be cut in 2002. The senate opted for deeper cuts in higher education and state employee salaries, while the house preferred to make the cuts in human service programs.

Ohio illustrates how the two chambers—and the governor as well—fashion budgets that are not easy to reconcile, even though one party has control of both the legislature and the executive. After passage in each house in May 2001, there were 268 pages of differences between the senate and house bills. They had started out with very different amounts to be cut from the budget. Gov. Bob Taft proposed $610 million in reduced funding, the house upped the cuts to $660 million, and the senate raised them to $833 million. As they went to conference, the house and senate disagreed over tuition caps at the four-year universities, money for economic emergencies, assistance to needy families, the state's rainy-day fund, and a Board of Regents program to lower tuition. They also disagreed on minor business taxes, additional cuts in agency operating budgets, a multistate lottery, the use tax on leased vehicles, and a two-day sales-tax holiday.[26] All of these differences were manageable; but time, effort, deliberation, attention to detail and precise language, and willingness to compromise were required for agreement.

Frequently, the devil is in the details of legislation. Should the gas tax increase in Washington be .08, as provided in the house bill, or .09, as provided in the senate bill? Both houses in Maryland adopted measures to license recreational crabbers and reduce their harvests. But the senate version exempted crabbers who caught two dozen or fewer hard crabs a day, while the house exempted those who caught up to four dozen.

The Scarcity of Resources

In the states, unlike in Washington, expenditures and revenues have to be about the same. The budget of every state except Vermont must be balanced when the annual or biennial appropriation act is passed. In Vermont, as well as in the other states, budgets do get balanced year after year. It is easier to achieve this end in a good economy than in a poor one.

Whether economic times are good or bad, one of the major obstacles that has to be overcome in the legislature is the disparity between the state's resources and the demands for them. Not only does the budget process itself have to deal with the dilemma of almost unlimited demands and limited resources, but also any bills that have fiscal implications are subject to similar constraints. Money, even more than policy *per se,* is at the heart of the legislative process. According to Richard Westman, chair of Vermont's House Appropriations Committee,

"Much of what goes on here is a search for money." Whatever the state, the question arises: "Do we have enough in the budget?" Howard Rawlings, who chaired Maryland's House Appropriations Committee, also understood the problems of limited resources. Under fire in 2001 for cutting the governor's budget for nursing home care by $1 million, he responded: "We can't do everything in every area." If the cut were to be restored, a proposed prescription drug program for the elderly might have to be cut by the same amount. Legislators, especially those dealing with the budget, have to decide among competing "goods," not between the "good" and the "bad."

Even in healthy economic times, there is seldom enough. Nonetheless, when tax revenues are flowing into the treasury and surpluses are accruing, it is possible to try to solve problems by spending. Indeed, spending may help, and at least it will satisfy advocacy groups and their publics. In periods when the economy and/or the stock market are performing less well, revenues slow down; but demands do not. There are always many competing needs for the funds that can be made available in any state. Even a small state like Vermont needs money for its public services. During the 2001 session, for instance, the House Ways and Means Committee had bills listed on its meeting board to benefit all sorts of groups. But members realized that there was no money to accomplish even a little of what they would have liked. In another part of the capitol, the disabled community sent six of its members to testify before the Senate Appropriations Committee. Although they asked for additional funding, there was little chance that the legislature would give it to them. That same year in Minnesota, the Environment and Agriculture Budget Division set aside twenty-one bills to review for possible inclusion in the omnibus funding bill. Among the requests were $500,000 for the purchase of wetlands; $7 million for a loan to an ethanol processing facility; $1.4 million for trial development; and $270,000 to the University of Minnesota to determine why so many bald eagles had suffered lead poisoning. However, the total dollars required for all these bills greatly exceeded the division's spending target. Also that year advocates for every conceivable cause were trying to get members of the Maryland General Assembly to support their programs, even though the legislature constitutionally could not increase but only reduce the budget formulated by the governor.

Budgeting in 2001 was especially dicey for state legislatures. Revenues were down and would get even lower in subsequent years. Maryland's fiscal staff projected a $200 million deficit by 2003. Projections in Minnesota indicated a $60 million drop in revenues, which meant smaller tax rebates and less spending. In Ohio, after Governor Taft proposed a budget in January, an additional $800 million shortfall emerged. By April revenue estimates for the next two years were reduced by a further $562 million and expenditure projections increased by $175 million. Just as the house and senate were about to convene in conference to resolve differences between the two bills, another $145 million shortfall appeared because of Medicaid costs due to increased numbers of cases projected for the next two years.[27]

Anything can go wrong, and something frequently does. An example is the heavier than normal snowfall that hit Vermont during the winter of 2001. "It just kept snowing and snowing," wrote Sen. Susan Bartlett in her report of the Budget Adjustment Act. The snow required more plowing, sanding, and salting of roads than state transportation officials had expected. The result was a $5 million deficit in the Agency of Transportation budget. The first bill passed at every legislative session in Vermont is the budget adjustment act, which makes changes in the prior year's budget. The house passed the bill without knowing of the emerging maintenance shortfall. The issue the Vermont legislature faced was where to get the money to meet the unanticipated costs. The House Transportation Committee wanted to get $5 million from the $24 million the governor set aside for debt reduction, but others wanted that reserve left intact. It took strenuous efforts to work through the disagreements.

The challenge that both legislators and advocates often face is that the funding to pay for what they collectively want is not available without raising taxes. Legislative leaders and appropriations committee members are used to saying no—at least that is the case in Colorado. Straayer describes the situation in the Centennial State, focusing on Sen. Elsie Lacy, who in alternate years chaired the Joint Budget Committee. Lacy and her committee colleagues were targets of every group and agency seeking more money. Midway through one session, she reached her limit and exhorted the supplicants to "get out of the faces" of Budget Committee members. Indicating the lobby corps gathered outside the chambers, Lacy exclaimed, "everybody's like a bunch of vultures out there," adding "there is no money." [28] Lisa Brown, chair of Washington's Senate Ways and Means Committee, expressed the frustration that all legislators feel: "I've said no to so many of my friends, I don't know that I've got any left." [29] When a member of his caucus approached Ohio's senate president, Richard Finan, with a budget request, the leader responded bluntly: "You can talk all you want, but we don't have any money."

Legislators share an interest in enriching one program or another, or undertaking a new one, or getting a project for their district. "We all have an interest in raising the block grant," said Cheryl Rivers, chair of Vermont's Senate Finance Committee, "but where do you get the money?" This question is raised more than any other in the legislative process. Everyone has an idea of how to spend money, but few know where it can be gotten without grave political risk. "Put the five million in," says Finan, "and we can see in conference committee." That is, see how to come up with the amount necessary.

"There are any number of ways you can go to find the money," Maryland's house speaker, Cas Taylor, told his leadership team; but few if any of these ways are easy. And there are a large number of needs competing for very limited funds. One source of funds is taxes. Income, corporate income, and sales taxes are raised from time to time, but few lawmakers want to risk voting in favor of higher taxes. The possibility is usually on the table, however. Minnesota's Democratic senate leader, Roger Moe, needed more money with which to negotiate the 2002–2003 budget with the Republican house. He would have liked to have seen the Senate Tax Committee expand the sales tax so that more money would be available for property tax reform. Such an action would have been akin to taking money from one pocket and putting it in the other, but it would have been money nonetheless. House Republicans in Vermont were considering a similar strategy. They wanted to revise Act 60, which provided state aid for schools. In order to increase state aid, and thus permit local property taxes to be reduced, it would be necessary to find other funds. Where would the money come from? House Ways and Means considered raising the sales tax to 6 percent in all but the five Connecticut River counties that bordered tax-free New Hampshire. The committee also had to consider an increase in the statewide property tax in order to raise the statewide block grant to schools for each student. House Republicans were very reluctant to raise taxes, however. They themselves did not believe in it and their constituents did not want it.

One way to generate money on a one-time basis to plug budget gaps is by enacting a tax amnesty. By forgiving penalty payments, the state tries to encourage delinquent taxpayers to pay up. And some do, resulting in a one-time windfall. Maryland passed a tax amnesty in 2001, with the idea that the proceeds would pay for mental health and prescription drug programs. "If we don't use that tax amnesty money," argued one legislator, "our institutions will go belly up." That small pot of new money was important to the legislature, but, according to the chair of Ways and Means, "Everybody is trying to load up on the tax amnesty." Just so much money could be raised.

Money can be generated by user fees rather than taxes. The amounts may not be large, but they are critical. Vermont's Department of Environmental Conservation derives about half of its budget from fees for discharge, which go into its special fund. Its proposal to increase fees, which is tantamount to a tax hike, went to House Ways and Means for approval. The committee's inclination, however, was to hold the fees down. Maryland resorted to a fee increase of $3 on auto registration in order to raise funds for the state's emergency medical system. The year before, the bill had been killed in a senate committee because members did not want to raise taxes when there was a budget surplus overall.[30]

Reserve funds can also be exploited when deficits have to be eliminated. The state's rainy-day fund is the largest pot of money available. And in hard times governors and legislatures tap into that reserve in an effort to balance their budgets. For fiscal conservatives, using the rainy-day fund is a last resort. Ohio's Finan had no more loopholes to close, tax credits to be delayed, or cuts to be made in order to balance the budget. "I didn't have many options left," he explained. Funds from the tobacco settlement are also up for grabs when budgets are tight. The $6.1 billion expected from tobacco companies by Minnesota had previously been allocated, with $250 million dedicated to a youth tobacco prevention fund. House Republicans wanted to take the money out of that fund and put it into medical education and research or for tax relief.[31] DFLers objected. Other pots of money were also up for grabs. Sen. Dean Johnson, who had been developing major legislation on workforce development, was relying on certain funding sources but discovered that one of his colleagues was relying on the same sources for a workers' training program. The colleague intended to raid funds outside his own committee's jurisdiction, which was considered inappropriate committee behavior.

Gambling offers states the possibility of additional revenues. That is why most states have lotteries, with a share of the profits earmarked for public education. Slot machines were proposed as an answer to revenue problems in Maryland. For Del. Howard Rawlings a bill to legalize slot machines offered "the surest and least painful way" to increase funding for public education. For Maryland's race-tracks slot machines would have enabled them to compete with tracks in other states such as Delaware, where slots are permitted. When the bill appeared to have no chance of passage, horseracing interests placed their bets on another horse, backing legislation to take $10 million from lottery revenues to subsidize purses at Maryland tracks.[32] Powerball, a multistate lottery, appealed to many legislators in Ohio, although the governor was opposed to the game. It surfaced in Vermont, as well, as the House Ways and Means Committee searched for revenues to pay for a revision of its school finance formula. Not only was Powerball a possibility, but the chair, Richard Marron, remarked (albeit in jest): "Maybe we'll have to create a casino."

If established or new revenue sources cannot be exploited, a last resort is to cut expenditures. Many legislatures during the 2001 sessions had to trim budgets proposed by the executive. In Ohio, for example, after drawing heavily on its rainy-day fund, the legislature still was short of the monies required to finance elementary and secondary education, as ordered by the state supreme court. Senate and house leaders went through the budget line by line, item by item, making selected cuts. They were still short, so they had to cut an additional 1.5 percent across the board. Higher education suffered reductions, as did other budget areas. Ohio's universities and colleges, however, could look forward to better years ahead, if the economy took an upswing. "If there's more money, higher ed will be first in line," said Senate President Finan. Universities and colleges would just have to wait. But Ohio had managed to piece together the money required to fix a budget that started out with what might have been a $1.5 billion deficit. The fix included cuts in programs, drawing on the tobacco settlement, tapping into the state's rainy-day fund, a tax on financial institutions, and a multistate lottery.[33] It wasn't pretty by any conventional standards, but the obstacles to settling on a biennial budget had been overcome.

An Uphill Process

Disagreement is a normal part of the legislative process. In large part the differences legislators have reflect the different values, interests, and priorities in state and district populations. In large part, too, conflict is built into the structure and processes of the legislature itself. As pointed out, many bills are noncontroversial and engender no conflict whatsoever. On other bills, conflict is easily worked out. But on a substantial number of measures differences arise. That is because in any legislature the sources of opposition to a proposal are multiple. Opposition is always possible because individual members have agendas that are contrary, committees within the same house come into dispute, the two parties take different positions, or the senate and house may have contradictory views. All of these obstacles are part and parcel of the lawmaking process.

Another major obstacle involves the limited resources available to pay for policy and programs, and the constitutional prohibition on the legislature's spending more on services than it takes in by way of taxes and fees. There never seems to be enough money to pay for the many worthwhile programs and projects legislators and their constituents want. And rarely nowadays does the electorate appear willing to pay higher, or additional, taxes for the goods that it wants. That is why the state budget, reflecting expenditures and revenues, has nearly always been among the most contentious issues the legislature deals with. There are nothing but obstacles to overcome here.

NOTES

1. *Olympian,* March 18, 2002.

2. Ember Reichgott Junge, unpublished manuscript, 2001.

3. John E. McDonough, *Experiencing Politics* (Berkeley: University of California Press, 2000), 268–269.

4. Harriet Keyserling, *Against the Tide* (Columbia: University of South Carolina Press, 1998), 144–145.

5. Bruce Feustel, "Building Consensus One by One," *State Legislatures* (March 2001), 32.

6. See Alan Rosenthal, *The Third House,* 2nd ed. (Washington, D.C.: CQ Press, 2001).

7. John A. Straayer, *The Colorado General Assembly,* 2nd ed. (Boulder: University Press of Colorado, 2000), 2.

8. John Mueller, *Capitalism, Democracy, and Ralph's Pretty Good Grocery* (Princeton: Princeton University Press, 1999), 142–153.

9. Jeffrey M. Stonecash, "The Rise of the Legislature," in Sarah F. Liebschutz et al., *New York Politics and Government* (Lincoln: University of Nebraska Press, 1998), 88.

10. *St. Paul Pioneer Press,* May 27, 2001.

11. Daniel J. Elazar, Virginia Gray, and Wyman Spano, *Minnesota Politics and Government* (Lincoln: University of Nebraska Press, 1999), 100.

12. The analysis was provided by Del. Robert Kittleman, minority leader of the Maryland house.

13. Lee Leonard, *Columbus Dispatch,* May 7, 2001.

14. *Cincinnati Enquirer,* May 4, 2001.

15. *New York Times,* May 20, 2001.

16. *St. Paul Pioneer Press,* May 20, 2001.

17. *Minneapolis Star Tribune,* May 21, 2001.

18. Ibid., June 27, 2001.

19. *Columbus Dispatch,* September 7, 2001.

20. Steven Dornfield, *St. Paul Pioneer Press,* June 24, 2001.

21. *St. Paul Pioneer Press,* June 14, 2001.

22. Steven Dornfield, *St. Paul Pioneer Press,* June 18, 2001.

23. Straayer, *The Colorado General Assembly,* 138–139.

24. Elazar et al., *Minnesota Politics and Government,* 107–108.

25. Ibid., 102–103.

26. *Columbus Dispatch,* November 25, 2001.

27. *Cleveland Plain Dealer,* May 26, 2001.

28. Straayer, *The Colorado General Assembly,* 2001.

29. *Seattle Times,* March 11, 2002.

30. *Baltimore Sun,* March 29, 2001.

31. *Minneapolis Star-Tribune,* April 7, 2001.

32. *Baltimore Sun,* March 30, 2001.

33. *Cincinnati Enquirer,* December 6, 2001.

6 LAWMAKING:
PUTTING IT TOGETHER

From reading about lawmaking in the press, one would conclude that the fate of proposed legislation depends on campaign contributions, the finagling of lobbyists, partisan maneuvering, and the career ambitions of everyone involved. That is normally the story line. The media give little prominence to how the merits and demerits of competing positions affect legislation. Substantive disagreement stemming from different political philosophies, constituency interests, views on detail, and interpretations of consequences rarely loom as major factors in the media's coverage of lawmaking.

From watching lawmaking up close, it is clear that substantive, as well as strategic, considerations are essential to what goes on. Indeed, the language—certainly the public language—of lawmaking deals mainly with substantive matters. Discussions in committee and caucus and in debate on the floor are on the substance of legislation, not on the politics. This language is not simply for show, and thus it has to be taken into account.

Take, for example, a bill sponsored by Del. Sandy Rosenberg in the Economic Matters Committee of the Maryland house. The bill would provide compensation for business owners who suffered a loss of good will because the government's condemnation of their building forced them to move. The major stumbling block, as evidenced in the discussion of committee members, was that there was no objective way to quantify "good will." In short, opponents argued, the legislation would not work—not an unreasonable position. In Vermont the House Ways and Means Committee in a section-by-section review of the draft of a school finance bill considered, among other matters, how school districts would know how much money they were getting from the state before they prepared their budgets, the role of the price index, and the timing and setting of block grants. Members inquired into the most specific details in what was a very complicated issue.

At a senate Democratic-Farmer-Labor Party (DFL) caucus in Minnesota, LeRoy Stumpf, chair of the Education Appropriations Division, familiarized his party colleagues with the E–12 education finance bill in terms of underlying objectives: strengthening early childhood programs and helping troubled districts. He explained just where all the money would go and how his division's recommendations compared with those of the governor. Some of Stumpf's colleagues from the western suburbs of the Twin Cities fired questions at him regarding the impact of the budget allocations on their districts. On the floor of the Ohio senate the budget debate saw the minority Democrats challenging the proposals of the majority Republicans. The legislature had been ordered by the Ohio Supreme Court to remedy school finance inequities. The Republican proposal did not adequately do so, according to Democratic senators. In addition, it not only raised state taxes, it also cut funding for local school districts, which would have to raise their own taxes. Republicans responded and both sides engaged in an informed and spirited debate that may not have changed members' minds but that did present the arguments for both sides.

Especially in the formal and open-to-the-public spaces of the legislative process, such as standing committees and the chamber floor, the substance of legislation is paramount. Strategic or political considerations are by no means absent, but they play a secondary role. Even "behind the scenes," as it were, substantive considerations count heavily. Joseph Bessette, in his study of deliberation in the U.S. Congress, makes a distinction akin to the one made here. He contrasts deliberation on the one hand with nondeliberative activities or influences on the other. For him, the former includes "problem solving," "persuasion," and "analytical policy making," while the latter include "bargaining" and "politics." [1] The purposes of deliberative (substantive) and nondeliberative (strategic and political) activity in the lawmaking process are first, to *fashion* legislation that is meritorious, i.e., that solves a problem or meets a need; and second, to *enact* such legislation into law. Fashioning legislation places greater emphasis on matters of merit, particularly at the initial stages, while enacting legislation brings to the fore matters of politics and strategy, as opposition has to be overcome and majorities built. The merits are still the basis for a legislative position, but when people see the merits differently, merits are not always sufficient to forge a settlement.

Hearing the Arguments

The legislature spends much of its time listening to the arguments of proponents and opponents of measures that it is considering. The measures themselves may be initiated by citizens from a constituency or by representatives of one interest group or another. In any case, different points of view in support and in opposition are heard on matters of even minor import. The lobbying is continuous and constant, and it takes place everywhere—at a committee hearing, in a member's office, on the steps of the capitol, or at a downtown restaurant. It is conducted by contract lobbyists employed by a client, by in-house lobbyists working for associations and corporations, by lobbyists for advocacy groups, by individual citizens, and by legislators themselves. No one is denied access, and just about everyone appears to have a bill they want passed or killed.

Bessette estimates, at least for Congress, that more than 99 percent of the lobbying effort is spent "trying to persuade minds through facts and reasons." [2] This assessment might appear to be on the high side, but still there is little doubt that the preponderance of lobbying entails making a case on the merits. This is done by lobbyists, reports a study of lobbyists and interest groups in California, South Carolina, and Wisconsin, in a variety of ways: testifying at legislative hearings, contacting legislators directly, helping to draft legislation, alerting legislators to the effects of a bill on their districts, and engaging in informal contact with legislators.[3]

Today's lobbyists, far more than some of those of earlier years, cannot rely on their relationships, the standing of their clients, or campaign contributions and the like. They have to make a strong argument for the merits of their case. A reasonable position, supported by facts and communicated to members, is what a Minnesota lobbyist said counted as far as his job was concerned. According to legislators, the principal benefit of lobbyists is the provision of information. Lobbyists will make reasoned arguments, trying to persuade legislators on the basis of principle, the public interest, constituency interests, and political benefits. For example, the Minnesota Twins baseball team, represented by four or five contract lobbyists, supported a bill for a new stadium that would involve a large state subsidy. No one doubts that they were trying to advance a special business interest, but their argument was based on the economic benefits to the state, the promise of the team, and state pride. Their case is a persuasive one, even more so when the Twins are winning. An analogous argument was made by a group of investment counselors and brokers who, in a meeting with the senate majority leader in Minnesota, objected to the governor's proposal to add a sales tax to investments. It would obviously hurt their businesses, but their stated arguments were that plain people would be hurt by the tax, economic development would suffer, implementation would be difficult, and the administrative costs would be high.

Sometimes a case can be very persuasive, as when the Boeing Company in Washington State asked for an overhaul of the state unemployment taxation system. Retail stores and manufacturers, such as Boeing, complained that they paid more in taxes than their laid-off workers took out in benefits. The construction industry, by contrast, paid less in taxes than its laid-off workers took out in benefits. Boeing, which had recently relocated its headquarters from Seattle to Chicago and could move other facilities as well, maintained that Washington had the worst business climate of any state in which the airplane manufacturer operated. Organized labor also supported the bill, believing that addressing the tax fairness issue would reduce pressure for business to cut benefits to their workers.[4] Self-interested or not, these arguments were substantive in nature.

Often justification and information in support of interest group claims is pretty well balanced between both sides—those favoring a particular bill and those opposing it. A prescription drug bill in Washington saw AARP, doctors, pharmacists, labor, and patient advocates on one side and pharmaceutical companies, biotechnology firms, and the Association of Washington Business on the other. In Vermont developers, home builders, and the construction industry favored legislation to speed up the environmental permitting process under Act 250, while environmentalists opposed anything that would impede citizen participation at the initial stages. Minnesota's small gasoline retailers favored a bill that would prohibit gas stations from selling gasoline below cost. Their competitors, large corporate interests, were opposed on free-market grounds. In these disputes each side justified its position on the basis of economy, efficiency, public participation, and the well-being of an industry.

One of the big issues in the 2001 session of the Maryland General Assembly was an $8 million item in the budget for textbook aid to private and parochial schools. This hot-button issue promoted more lobbying than any other bill during that session. In favor of such aid was mainly the Catholic Church, along with Orthodox Jews. Opposed were PTAs, teacher unions, school boards, and the American Civil Liberties Union. One side favored limited and highly specific assistance for children; the other side focused on the constitutional requirement for the separation of church and state. Another heavily lobbied bill in Maryland would have allowed teachers to bargain curriculum and classroom assignments, as well as salaries and working conditions. Teachers cited the need to have a say on educational issues, while school boards claimed education policy was properly their domain. A turf battle between nurses and doctors also evoked public policy justification. Nurse practitioners pushed a bill to allow patients in HMOs to select them as their primary care providers, maintaining that they were specially trained and already treated patients and wrote prescriptions. Moreover, they added, in some states they functioned as primary care providers under Medicaid. The doctors opposed, questioning the qualifications in training and experience of the nurses and suggesting that such legislation would be harmful to patient care.

The legislature is awash in argument and analysis, which are staples of the lawmaking process. The contestant who omits policy justification is unlikely to get far. Especially when a bill is heard in committee, the merits and demerits are the focus. What is the problem, what is needed, how will it work, what good will it do, who is in favor and who opposed, how much will it cost? All are central questions in committee deliberations. Some members may know where they stand, because they are familiar with the issue or allied with the sponsors, but the record still has to be made. And ordinarily, no matter what the issue, some members have not yet made up their minds, and with them testimony and lobbying can make a difference.

Lobbying, of course, is more than simply making a reasoned case in written or spoken word. It is not only testimony delivered by a representative of an interest group at a committee meeting or a pitch made in a legislator's office. It can be a more dramatic production in which a human face (or faces) is put on a more analytic presentation. Grassroots lobbying is premised on the importance of political persuasion, not on substantive information, *per se*. It is intended to convey a powerful message—that people care enough to turn out. For example, in an effort to get the Environmental Matters Committee of the Maryland house to vote for a bill affirming the right of mothers to nurse in public, a dozen women nursed their babies right in the hearing room—allegedly in the first "nurse-in" ever held in Annapolis. Several hundred senior citizens gathered in the Minnesota Capitol Rotunda to support the Fair Drug Pricing Act, which would mandate drug companies to offer Minnesotans the same bulk discounts negotiated by the federal Medicaid program. During the same session more than two dozen mothers spoke out at a rally in front of the Minnesota Capitol against a concealed handguns bill. A similar rally, by Ohio's Five Million Mom March chapters and the Ohio Coalition Against Gun Violence, was held at the capitol in Columbus. Not every manifestation of grassroots capacity requires large numbers of people, however. For instance, a small-group appeal was made in St. Paul, where about thirty student constituents traveled to the capitol to lobby the senate majority leader on an antismoking program that was being funded out of the state's tobacco settlement money. The youngsters wanted to ensure that money for what they believed to be an effective program would continue to be budgeted.

Nevertheless, turning out people is important. Legislators are impressed by numbers, such as a three-thousand-person rally on the steps of the Minnesota Capitol to increase E–12 school spending, or the six thousand people who called lawmakers in response to television ads sponsored by the local teachers' organization. At the University of Minnesota students, staff, and alumni made hundreds of telephone calls from alumni association offices urging people to get in touch with their legislators and press them to support the university's budget request.[5] Lobbying can also be conducted through a public relations campaign making use of the mass media. The Minnesota Twins, in their quest for a new baseball stadium, campaigned from the broadcast booth during home games. Twins' announcers interviewed legislative sponsors and other supporters on Channel 9 and urged viewers to call legislative leaders and the governor.

One way or another, just about every proposal that the legislature considers gets some kind of hearing. Both substantive and political information are communicated, sometimes in rather aggressive form. Not every legislator listens, however; a number already have positions of their own. But some can always be swayed, and they can influence others. On the more important issues, both proponents and opponents of a measure try to rally support and win over the undecideds. On the most important questions, the debate is intense and lengthy, with the undecideds fewer in number. But the merits of the case still count in reinforcing support or opposition. And whether they are persuaded by substantive arguments or by other factors, the merits of the case are what legislators use to justify their positions with the folks back home.

Studying the Problem

Part of the study process for legislators is hearing from proponents and opponents—the various interest groups that have a stake in the issue. But part also is soliciting information from sources that have something to add. Study is most intense at the committee level, but it goes on throughout the entire process.

One source of information is the executive branch, which provides legislators with information in major governmental policy areas and data accompanying administration policy and budget proposals. At a hearing of Vermont's Senate Transportation Committee, for example, members listened to the secretary of transportation testify on a departmental bill. The administration official went through the bill section by section, in extraordinary detail, and answered members' questions about specifics. Nothing controversial was discussed, but the details were important to all involved. Administration officials are constantly providing legislators information. The appropriations process, with executives' testimony on their agencies' budget proposals, is probably most informative of all. Executive briefings and testimony before standing committees other than appropriations also provide much grist for the legislative deliberation mill. Typical was the scene at a 2001 session meeting of Vermont's Senate Judiciary Committee, where the secretary of the Agency of Human Services and her entire senior staff briefed senators on the state's care of its youth. The secretary described Vermont's substance abuse initiatives, while other executive officials detailed the nature of the problem. Senators could not help but learn from all that they heard in these sessions.

Not all of the information that is conveyed is done in an objective, lifeless manner. Much of it supports one position or another. Many of those who testify are lobbyists or representatives of groups whose interests ride on the proposed legislation. Their testimony naturally conveys information that confirms their group's position. Some of those who take on an advocacy role at committee hearings are not professionals, but rather citizens with interests that coincide with one position or another. For example, during hearings by Ohio's Senate Finance Committee the issue was whether to increase the cigarette tax from twenty-four cents to seventy-four cents a pack. The president of a company that operated eleven convenience stores testified in opposition, on the grounds that cigarette sales would decline, business generally would suffer, stores would close, and some of his two hundred employees would lose their jobs. On the other side of the issue was a woman who informed members of the committee that her father, his brother, and a cousin—all smokers—died from pulmonary emphysema. Now she had lung cancer.[6] The legislators had to weigh the two sides presented to them.

At a committee hearing the Senate Ways and Means Committee in Ohio was considering a resolution calling for the legislature to put a proposed constitutional amendment on the ballot requesting slot machines at seven horse-racing tracks. Several representatives of horse racing in the state testified that the machines were needed for the economic survival of the tracks. On the other side of the issue was the mother of a former star quarterback at Ohio State University who had later played for the Indianapolis Colts of the National Football League. Her son had been addicted to gambling, she told legislators, which led to his committing credit card fraud and money laundering and his eventual prison sentence. She believed horse racing was the root cause of her son's gambling addiction.[7]

Another source of information for legislators is the commission or task force that pays special attention to a problem and offers recommendations. The study agency may be appointed by the executive or the legislature. Its members may or may not include legislators, but the results feed into the legislative process, mainly through the committee that has jurisdiction over the subject matter. In many states, where legislative sessions are limited rather than essentially year-round, interim committees of legislators take on the job of intensive study. The work done by these groups can furnish an important part of the agenda of the next legislative session. Tom Loftus, former speaker of the Wisconsin assembly, describes the interim study process in his state. In Wisconsin the best forum for studying an issue was the Legislative Council, which had study committees composed of both legislator and citizen members and supporting research staff. From June to January of election years, when the legislature was out of session, "these study committees would take a vexing problem, study it, find a consensus, and then prepare a bill," writes Loftus. The Wisconsin legislature would usually pass a bill embodying the committee's recommendations.[8]

Another important means of acquiring information in the legislature is the professional staff, many of which vary greatly in size and organization. The larger states—California, Florida, New York, Pennsylvania, and Texas—have over two thousand persons on their staffs. Maryland, Minnesota, Ohio, and Washington have five hundred to six hundred. The smaller states—Delaware, Idaho, New Mexico, North Dakota, South Dakota, and Wyoming—have fewer than sixty persons on their legislative staff. Vermont has thirty-five. In the larger states staff tend to be allocated broadly—to legislative party leaders; party caucuses; standing committees; and individual members; and to the senate, house, or legislature as a whole for bill drafting, research, and analysis. In the smaller states staff tend to be centralized, primarily nonpartisan, and serving the legislature, its committees, and its members.

Staff can be both partisan and nonpartisan, as in Minnesota, Ohio, and Washington, or they are predominantly nonpartisan, as in Maryland and Vermont. Either way, they will provide at least cursory analysis of just about every bill brought up in committee and on the floor. On anything important, however, staff input is likely to be substantial. Nonpartisan staff will confine themselves to substance—the nature of the problem, how other states are handling it, what the effects of a measure are likely to be, how much it will cost, what groups favor and oppose it, and where the relevant state department or agency stands. Partisan staff will attend to the above factors but also take into account political considerations. Staff are especially critical on budgets, taxes, and state aid formulas. It is their study and analysis that serve as a foundation for legislative deliberation. In these areas in particular it is common to see a staff professional explaining a complex formula for school aid, state property taxes, or other formulas to members of a standing committee. It is difficult for legislators to grasp all of the implications of many provisions of proposed law. But committee members have an incentive to understand, because they have to explain a bill and defend the committee's actions to their colleagues, who have less special knowledge than they do. Lobbyists provide legislators with important information, but when it comes to closing in on a solution to a problem there is no substitute for professional staff.

Among other things, standing committees function as study groups for the legislature. Here is where most substantive learning takes place, where members develop some familiarity with a subject matter. Even if they have served on a committee for only a session or two, they are specialists—at least compared with members who have never served on such a committee. Study is a big part of the job of standing committees. It overlaps or merges with the hearing processes on the one hand and deliberation on the other.

Years ago in an insightful book William Muir Jr. likened the California legislature to a school where learning is constantly taking place, emphasizing that study is a good piece of what legislatures and members do.[9] Sometimes informal educational sessions help committee members prepare for an issue they know will be coming up; other times committee leaders bring in state and national experts to educate them and their colleagues on an issue. More frequently, study is tied to a bill, such as Act 60 on school finance in Vermont. In this case, study was nonstop, as committees and fiscal staff went back and forth trying to figure out a way to modify the funding formula, making it more agreeable to both the high- and low-wealth communities across the state. Committee study normally is practically oriented, responding to an issue or shaping a piece of legislation. It does not involve learning merely for learning's sake.

A good example is related by John E. McDonough, the former Massachusetts legislator, who describes how the Health Care Committee under its chair, Rep. Carmen Buell, approached an issue involving hospital regulation. At the outset Buell spent those months meeting with consumer groups, labor unions, and academics who warned against competition, as well as with hospital leaders, Blue-Cross members, and the state's HMOs and business groups who urged a market mechanism. In working through the opposing arguments, she also relied on a group of Brandeis University academics who were trying to devise a solution to the problem.[10]

Legislatures have been accused of calling for an issue to be studied as a substitute for action. Certainly, task forces and commissions are established so that a legislature can postpone addressing a problem. It would seem, however, that these instances are the exception, not the rule. Legislators often want more information, especially on complex or technical problems. That is why study is an important part of the legislative process.

Deliberating

Hearings and study are part and parcel of the overall deliberative process, which can be defined generally as "reasoning on the merits of public policy." This is what the framers of the Constitution had in mind for representatives of the new nation. They were to be above private interests, acting on what they thought best for the public good.[11] Deliberation in a legislature would require that representatives have ideas on what the public good is, but that they would also be willing to modify their ideas in response to reasons offered by those with different ideas. Representatives, then, can be expected to engage in intelligent, civic-minded deliberation, using their skills, experience, and the information available to them. For deliberation to take place, according to Bessette, participants must be willing to learn and be open to persuasion on the basis of the merits of an issue. They must be willing to change their positions as a response not to pressure, bargains, or blandishments, but rather to reasoned argument.[12]

In Committee

Not all legislators participate in deliberative activities at the same time. But an enormous amount of give-and-take does go on, as lawmakers search for solutions to what they perceive to be public policy problems. Much of the discussion at the committee stage is essentially deliberative. Take, for example, a hearing of the Vermont House Ways and Means Committee on a petroleum cleanup fund bill. Participating in the discussion was an administrator from the Department of Natural Resources and a representative of the Vermont Petroleum Association. The bill before the committee dealt with releases from above-ground storage tanks. Several years ago the department had set aside funds to deal with the problem, but the demand for money exceeded the amount available. The department, therefore, wanted to use money generated by fees on underground storage tanks for above-ground leakage. The proposed bill would have taken money from a weatherization fund for the purpose, but the administration was opposed to the idea. Moreover, the Vermont Petroleum Association representative argued that the money already collected should all be spent on the purpose that had been specified. Committee members supported the bill's objective but wondered where they could find a source of funding. A home-heating-oil tax was a possibility, as was a fuel tax, but there were disadvantages either way. Despite much discussion, deliberation did not produce a solution at that session. Yet it exemplified how a standing committee engaged with a tough problem, albeit one that was below most people's radar.

Deliberation is a central element of lawmaking. It is at the heart of the legislature's review of the budget. In Ohio, for example, the House Finance Committee met for 263 hours and heard testimony from 868 witnesses, according to the chair, John Carey. In his words: "This budget has received more debate, more ideas and more scrutiny than any budget in modern history." [13] Throughout both house and senate consideration of the budget, emphasis was on trying to work out problems and get the support of as many members (or at least majority party members) as possible—on the merits, as well as on the politics. In Minnesota, twenty-five members of the Senate Tax Committee worked at session after session on an omnibus educational finance bill, examining one formula after another for the distribution of state funds to local districts. Their staff produced a succession of computer runs for the committee, with one particularly imaginative run designated: "The run to end all runs" (or the "end-run" formula). As one DFL senator observed: "Every year it seems the formula gets more complicated."

In Maryland the drafting of a measure to provide pharmaceutical benefits to senior citizens aptly illustrates the nature of legislative deliberation. With about $11 million to spend as a result of cuts by the House Appropriations Committee in the governor's proposed budget, the speaker directed staff to draft a bill. The draft included four different approaches, agreed to by the chairs of two standing committees that were sharing jurisdiction. One approach was a waiver provision similar to that granted by the federal government to Vermont. Another was an allocation of $9 million for seniors at the 175 percent of poverty level to get a discount on pharmaceuticals. Still another was an expansion of Med banks—groups that receive free pharmaceuticals from manufacturers—to five areas to service senior citizens with no resources. A last approach was the use of funds for a prescription drug program for seniors with some measure of need. At a meeting of two subcommittees working jointly, twenty-five legislators discussed these different approaches: How would the program be marketed and promoted? How would a means test work? What would it cost pharmacists? The committee discussed, among other things, the possibility of the federal government taking over the program, whether benefits and premiums could be raised slightly, if a risk existed that a contractor might drop out, and how the program would work in rural areas. The questions and discussions ranged broadly. One committee chair concluded: "On balance, we've addressed many concerns." Intertwined in the discussions were political considerations, particularly the opposition of the pharmaceutical industry to the type of waiver obtained by Vermont and the possible opposition of pharmacists to a bill that squeezed their profits. But, deliberatively, the committee considered how to meet the opposition's objections.

Consideration of substance is central to the committee stage of the legislative process that, along with floor debate, are what Bessette refers to as the "formal channels" of the deliberative process.[14] This is where members receive further education in a subject area with which they already have some familiarity and where they can exchange views and ideas. The Vermont House Ways and Means Committee's effort to revise Act 60 went on day after day for a few months. Rep. Richard Marron, the Republican chair, began working on revisions just after the 2000 elections and, right after the legislature convened, the committee began to deal with legislation to modify a most complex and controversial educational finance system. Marron steered the committee's discussion, which was tantamount to a continuing education program for the members, including the chair himself. Lengthy and detailed consideration of an index to be used for expansion of the block grant—whether it be the price index, the grand list (a formula used in Vermont), or some other device—and what kind of equality mechanism to use—were typical of the committee's agenda during the period during which it was trying to produce a school finance revision. At the committee level partisanship was not a factor. Even members who favored Act 60 as it operated, and were not in favor of revision, participated in the committee's effort to fashion a bill that made sense and could ultimately work. Rep. Gaye Symington, who would have voted against revision if it came up on the floor, contributed substantially to the work that went on.

On the Floor

Substantive discussion not only dominates committee work, it is also the principal feature of debate on the floor of the senate and house. Frequently debate on the floor—on a bill or an amendment—influences how some members vote, and at times it may even determine the outcome. A few members are generally so respected that they command the attention of their colleagues, no matter what the issue. Other members command their colleagues' attention because they are regarded as experts on particular issues. Most members know how they intend to vote on issues taken up on the floor. But some members still have not decided. So issues can remain open until practically the last minute. One such example was a Maryland bill to provide immunity from prosecution for abandonment as a means of discouraging mothers from leaving their babies in dumpsters and other places where they might not be found or cared for. The question was whether to allow babies to be dropped off at firehouses, as well as at police stations and hospitals. A number of legislators—who were also volunteer firefighters—objected during debate on the floor because fire stations were not always manned. They wanted to amend firehouses from the bill, while the reporting committee wanted firehouses to remain. The floor debate mattered to the outcome. Another Maryland bill decided on the floor concerned car safety for children. The bill reported from committee, by a vote of 16–2, would have required Maryland drivers to put passengers eight years old and younger and weighing less than eighty pounds in car safety seats. The measure was supported by health and automobile safety groups and by the state police. But one house member thought the law would discourage drivers from other states who lacked booster seats from coming to Maryland. As part of debate on the floor, he displayed a map that showed Maryland was the only state with such a law and traffic arrows indicating how cars would drive around it to avoid fines. His argument raised doubts among his colleagues, and the bill was sent back to committee.[15]

By the time most important bills get to the floor, their course—at least in that chamber—is pretty well set. A majority or more of the members can be counted on to support a bill and to resist amendments. At this point, deliberation is unlikely to change a decision that has already taken shape, but it still takes place. For example, a measure related to abortion passed the Minnesota senate in 2001, by a vote of 37–30. The outcome had pretty well been settled earlier. Still, the debate went on for three hours, with more than half the members speaking in what one member referred to as one of the senate's finest debates, one "that will likely shape this issue for years into the future." [16] No one's mind or vote changed, but the discussion was significant nonetheless.

The Maryland senate and house also debated the budgetary provision for private school textbooks, as though the issue were in doubt—which it was not. By the time the issue got to the floor, nearly all the members had taken a position.

As one senator put it: "This is an issue on which you cannot not have made your mind up." But his colleague thought there still might be "leaners" to sway. The debate was vigorous, sharp, and informative. Opponents argued for the separation of church and state and noted that not even public school students were getting the benefits being proposed. The proponents maintained that the aid did not go to parochial school, but rather to children. Moreover, it was being provided for only one year. Few if any votes changed. The outcome was as expected, but the case for each side had been articulated.

Although one purpose of floor debate is to change votes, and also outcomes, it is by no means the only one. Floor debate also provides a valuable record of the substantive arguments on each side. Furthermore, it gives individual members opportunities to score points, play the gadfly, show off for their constituencies, posture for relevant groups, or simply spout off. Debate tends to fill the time available for it. When thirty, forty, one hundred, or more members with different ideas, agendas, and constituencies assemble, different styles and perspectives will be on display in any debate. One Maryland legislator referred to the budget debate in the house as "a mass of energy looking for an outlet." [17] Proponents of an amendment, even if it is headed for defeat, get a hearing and make a record. But they can also send a message to others, as during house debate on a moratorium for the death penalty. As one of the supporters said: "the governor is now aware that there's a fairly large community concerned with the fairness of the death penalty." [18]

Members use the floor to express their philosophies, whether they persuade anyone or not. It is not at all unusual for legislators to be motivated primarily by their beliefs about the issue in question rather than by political or strategic factors. Typical is the discussion on third-reader in the Maryland house on a bill to allow youngsters to seek medical advice on their own. The proposal would have eliminated the legal obstacle to children seeking care for drug or alcohol problems, but who were being turned away by psychologists. A strong argument was made, but another member opposed the bill on the ground that it eroded the rights of parents who should have the power to seek such advice for their children.

Behind the Scenes

Deliberation also takes place in informal locations such as the caucus, private meetings among legislators, and even among lawmakers and representatives of interest groups. The problem, of course, is to identify these deliberations, since they are closely intertwined with essentially nondeliberative activities that go on "behind the scenes." In informal settings deliberation, strategy, and politics tend to comingle. As Bessette writes: "It is almost second nature for journalists and political scientists to assume that whatever occurs behind closed doors in Congress must be something other than genuine deliberation about legislative issues. Yet there is nothing about the nature of reasoning on the merits of public policy that restricts it to public forums." [19]

On critical issues deliberation sometimes occurs behind closed doors rather than onstage, under the spotlight. Take, for example, the passage of a billion-dollar health care bill in New York. The bill raised payments to hospitals and nursing homes, allowed Empire BlueCross BlueShield to become a for-profit company, simplified Medicaid enrollment, and increased cigarette taxes. Yet, as reported in the January 17, 2002, *New York Times,* the bill had no expert testimony, no public hearings, and no general discussion. There was little public involvement, and even discussion in the legislature's public arenas was limited. One member, who voted against the package, remarked: "When nobody sees a gigantic bill until 20 minutes before they're supposed to vote on it, that's irresponsible." Deliberation among legislative leaders and their staff, interest group representatives, and executive branch officials did take place, however; perhaps it was not as extensive nor as inclusive as many observers felt such a major issue was due. And it certainly was not center stage, spotlighted for the press and public.

What Goes into Deliberation

What, then, are the components of deliberation, as it goes on in the legislature? First, information is conveyed. Second, arguments are made that connect facts to desirable goals. Third, persuasion is attempted.[20] Fourth, participants can be swayed.

The element by which arguments are made with regard to goals is of special interest. Such arguments mediate between facts on the one hand and desired achievements on the other. In the deliberative process, one side may use one standard in making an argument, while the other side employs another to rebut it. The issue of carrying concealed weapons is a good example. Proponents use *rights* as a standard for their case. People need to be able to carry concealed weapons to protect themselves from criminals. Opponents use workability as their standard. This will allow people with poor judgment or sharp tempers to carry guns in public places, thus increasing the incidence of violent behavior. Or consider a debate in the Minnesota house on the use of tobacco settlement funds. Democrats generally wanted the monies to be devoted to antismoking programs. Republicans, on the other hand, wanted the monies allocated to health education and research. Another standard often used is *balance,* and whether taxes, spending, and some policy "lack balance" or are in "proper balance." Still another standard is that of *precedent.* Frequently, what other states have done will be an important part of the argument for a measure. On drunken driving legislation under consideration by the Minnesota senate, the sponsor of an amendment strengthening a measure to discourage such behavior pointed out, "We are joining the other 39 states to say, people who have a fourth DWI will be sentenced to a three-year prison term." [21]

The standard that most frequently is made explicit in the deliberative process is *fairness.* Legislators do not want to favor one group over another, and measures that appear to do so invite opposition. A senator representing the community of International Falls, Minnesota, appealed to the Tax Committee on an

omnibus education bill to allow school districts to levy for a swimming pool. His question to the committee raised the fairness standard: "Why can you levy for a hockey arena and not a swimming pool?" The chair's reply invoked the same standard: "You can't do it just for International Falls."

One measure in Minnesota would have given the St. Paul school district special authority to borrow money for construction projects without having to go to the voters for approval. The opposition maintained, "From a policy standpoint, we should treat all school districts the same." Why should some districts have an unfair advantage over other districts that had to win support from the voters for such bonding authority? "Everyone else has to go to their voters," a Republican senator argued. "St. Paul should have to also." Discussion on a transportation bill, being reviewed by the Senate Rules Committee in Minnesota, ranged widely. It even questioned the membership of a transportation board provided for in the measure. Why is there one member from each county, even though the populations of the counties vary substantially? asked one senator of the bill's author. In senate debate over a provision to provide state funding to help solve odor problems at an ethanol plant in St. Paul, opponents argued that if the Minnesota legislature went along every community with an ethanol facility would look for similar help.

Whenever benefits are at issue, chances are that the question of fairness will enter into debate. A bill before the Maryland legislature required that a portion of the fees collected by the sale of tobacco tax stamps be returned to the wholesalers who administered the system. Supporters maintained that retail merchants and others who collected taxes in Maryland get some compensation for their work. Since tobacco wholesalers were acting as agents for the state by collecting tax, why shouldn't they also be compensated for their services? It was not a question of supporting tobacco, but one of fairness.

The Limits of Deliberation

Deliberation goes on throughout the legislative process. Probably, the more significant the legislation, the more deliberation is involved. A measure is drafted and redrafted on its way to final decision. In committee members receive one draft after another and additional amendments, all of which are argued back and forth. Further discussions take place in caucus and among groups of legislators and lobbyists, or legislators and executive branch officials. Measures are changed and changed again, in order to respond to suggestions of participants and to gain the support necessary for their enactment. One compromise after another may be necessary in the fashioning of legislation. Compromises that occur because merits are in dispute, with neither side able to persuade the other, are in part a product of deliberative activity.

The effort to revise Act 60 in the Vermont legislature exemplifies how the process works over time. It began with the Ways and Means Committee chair, Richard Marron, crafting a plan after the November 2000 elections. And it continued in his committee, as well as in the corresponding senate committee, most

of the session. Almost on a daily basis proposed provisions were revised and revised again—to accommodate different points of view and preferences of legislators. One version contained financing from the Powerball lottery; a succeeding version did not. One version did not include an increase in the sales tax; another did. And still another exempted the counties on the border of New Hampshire from paying the higher rate.

While deliberation accounts for much of the conversation throughout the lawmaking process, it is seldom viewed as critical in changing the decisive votes—that is, the votes that result in 50 percent plus one being reached. Deals, bargains, payoffs, pressure, and less substance-based techniques are deemed to be the factors that finally put one side or the other over the top. That may indeed be true; but without all the votes influenced by substantive considerations, there would be no "decisive votes" to be won over by intriguing political techniques. In his exploration of lawmaking in Congress, Bessette asks: "[H]ow many votes in Congress are the result of bargaining at each decision stage and how many must be explained on other grounds, such as judgments on the merits[?]" In his view, even if bargaining is the capstone in putting together a majority, it may only explain relatively few of all the votes cast. Often, however, reasoned appeals are what prevail at the committee level and subsequently are the basis for assembling comfortable majorities at various stages of the process. In such instances, other techniques are unnecessary. But sometimes reasoned appeals fall short in majority-building efforts. Then, as Bessette notes, additional support is sought through essentially nondeliberative means. Suppose, for instance, that the legislative body divided about evenly on the actual merits of a proposal, whereupon bargaining moved one member to create a majority. Would we conclude that bargaining made the difference to the bill's enactment? Or would we determine that deliberation, which largely affected all but the deciding vote, made the difference? The answer is that bargaining is certainly important, but deliberating on the merits ordinarily dominates the process.[22]

Building Support

Part and parcel of the deliberative process is that of building support for—or against—a measure at step after step along the way. Making a case, of course, is one method of gaining support. But the way in which the case is made—and a variety of accompanying appeals—also matters. The merits still count, but strategy comes to the fore, sharing center stage with deliberation.

The Job of Committees

As with the back and forth of deliberation, the building of support is the special business of standing committees. The principal role here is that of the chair. Probably the chair's most important job is that of setting the committee agenda, and mainly determining which referred bills will not be on it. In some legislative bodies a committee is required to take action on every bill referred to it, and some committees are required to report out every bill, with a "do pass" or "do not pass" recommendation. In a large majority, however, committees have considerable discretion and, for the most part, the chair is the screening authority who separates the wheat from the chaff.

Those who chair committees have authority as gatekeepers. They can bury bills, not bringing them up for consideration. Or they give them a hearing without calling for a vote. The sheer volume of bills introduced and referred makes it virtually impossible for committees to deal with them all. The chair then can choose which ones will be dealt with, postponing the others indefinitely or reporting them out too late for floor action. The chair will not bring up bills unless the sponsors want them to do so. Many bills legislators introduce are intended to placate groups and individuals in their districts. The sponsors themselves do not believe them very meritorious. In the Maryland senate, for example, of the bills not voted on by the session's end a number are ones the sponsors did not really want enacted. Controversial legislation that might lead to legislator casualties also is likely to be filed in a bottom desk drawer by a committee chair. "We do it mostly to protect the senators from themselves," said Maryland senator Walter M. Baker. "So many of them don't know how to say no." [23]

The committee is the burial place for "bad" bills—"bad," of course, being in the eye of the beholder. These include proposals that arouse intense interest group opposition. Many groups take a defensive posture, and their objective is mainly to stop measures from passing. "That's basically our agenda," said a Maryland lobbyist, "as long as everything dies in committee." A "bad" bill also is one that a chair simply does not like or one that a majority of members opposes; or one that has gotten nowhere session after session. Bills that the leadership wants killed are also disposed of by chairs acting in their capacity as members of the leadership team. "What do you want us to do in Appropriations?" asked a Vermont legislator of a Republican leader. "I want you to hold it," was the answer. "No problem," the legislator replied. Not much needed to be said, for the two understood one another; they were on the same team.

Generally, chamber rules provide for circumvention of a committee, through discharge petitions and other mechanisms. But chairs usually have their way, unless they have virtually no support from members on their committee. Beyond that, they do the scheduling of just when a bill will be taken up and how much time will be devoted to it. If they do not agree, it does not get done. In Maryland, Del. Sandy Rosenberg wanted action from a subcommittee chair of the Environmental Matters Committee. "I'll have to check with our chairman," the subcommittee leader said. "He runs the trains in our committee." Rosenberg understood: "The railroad operates similarly in my committee." [24] Even legislative leaders defer to committee chairs on scheduling matters. Vermont's senate president wanted his chamber to send a major environmental bill over to the house for action. But the senate committee chair wanted to go slowly; it required more time, he insisted. The president had little choice but to wait.

Chairs not only set the agenda and determine the timing, they also are responsible for building support for certain measures in the committee. On major issues the chair may champion particular legislation. Cheryl Rivers, who chaired the Senate Finance Committee in Vermont, knew just what kind of bill she wanted as a modification of Act 60. She thought she could get her committee members to go along—or planned at least to work at it. Larry Pogemiller, who chaired Senate Taxation in Minnesota, also had definite preferences when it came to an omnibus education finance bill. "I have a dog in this fight," he told his colleagues. The chair may have his or her own ideas; the chair may be carrying out the wishes of legislative leaders or the governor; or, alternatively, the chair may be carrying out the will of his or her committee colleagues. Either way, members have to get on board if a bill is to receive favorable action.

Building Consensus in Committee

The first place to build support is in the committee itself. Different chairs have different styles, but ordinarily it requires time and effort—talking to members issue by issue, so that one's colleagues feel consulted about and included in the decisions that are made. An effective committee leader will be constantly engaged in bringing colleagues along. Mike Busch ran his Maryland house committee this way, giving all the members a chance to develop their own areas of expertise, and delegating them some power. In return, he could count on their support when he really needed it.[25] Howard Rawlings built consensus in House Appropriations by delegating authority to his subcommittees and inculcating pride in the committee and its process. In the senate, Barbara Hoffman, who chaired Budget and Taxation, made it her business to help members whenever she could and even abandoned some of her own bills in order to develop membership loyalty. If a consensus already exists, building support is not a problem. That seemed to be the case when the head of the Maryland State Police testified before the Senate Judicial Proceedings Committee on a bill to ban racial profiling. No one had signed up to testify against the bill, and it was apparent, as the chair stated, that "we are all singing from the same hymnbook." More often than not, if the issue is of any significance, support is not automatically at hand. It is up to the chair to develop it.

Ralph Wright, the former speaker of the Vermont house, describes Edgar May, who chaired a committee on which Wright served before attaining top leadership: "The give and take in the committee could get heavy, but May would see to it that it always rolled to a consensus. His greatest attribute was bringing people together." This was not a negligible accomplishment, especially in a committee "filled with committed people and not, incidentally, as devoted to the Chair as I was," Wright said.[26] Vermont committees, like those in other states, try hard to fashion consensual positions—the greater the degree of agreement among members, the better a measure's chances. A chair, like Marron of House Ways and Means, may have an almost insurmountable job. On Act 60 some committee members wanted to keep the school finance plan essentially intact, others wanted to repeal it entirely, and still others wanted to modify it in one way or another. The chair's challenge was to get the two sides, as well as the middle, to agree on something. He reasoned that if he could get the committee to agree, his chances in the Republican house would be good. That was only the beginning. The Democratic senate would still be another matter, as would the Democratic governor. So Marron worked at bringing the committee along—slowly, tediously, probing continuously to see what aspects of a revision would garner support. Piece by piece, he would try to forge consensus.

Richard Westman, who chaired Vermont's House Appropriations Committee, had an advantage over Marron in building support. On the budget everyone knows what the bottom line will be. That is, the budget will come out in balance. The committee will not appropriate more monies than projected revenues will permit. Beyond that, however, Westman has to work with a diverse membership, some on the left and some on the right, and some who are advocates for one governmental program or another. His approach, as he describes it, is to leave his own preferences outside the committee room and take a middle course. "You can't be so far out of the mainstream that you lose people," he says. Moreover, he gives each member of his committee the opportunity to lead by assigning each a section of the budget to handle and on which to make recommendations. When it is time to vote, section by section, members are very much in a consensus-building frame of mind. Because of Westman's approach, as well as the delegation of authority, the committee manages to report out bills, not unanimously, but by large majorities. The 2001 budget effort surprised even Westman: "I had people vote for the budget who in my nineteen years never voted for it."

Many committees elsewhere operate in a similar bipartisan fashion. Indeed, it is at the committee stage in the legislative process that the minority party usually plays its most constructive role. A chair looking to maximize support, as most of them do, will accept minority-sponsored amendments, if they do not go completely counter to the majority position. In a partisan legislature, especially, minority party members have far more opportunity to affect the shape of a proposal in committee than anywhere else. In a more deliberative setting expertise and preparation count heavily, so both majority and minority members have input. Anyone can get changes made, if he or she—and of course the changes—are considered reasonable. For example, in the E–12 Education Finance Division of the Minnesota senate, LeRoy Stumpf, the chair, was willing to accept minority amendments as long as they did not do what he considered to be damage.

Even when the majority dominates, minority members can make some headway at the committee stage. In the Ohio house, budget negotiations during the 2001 session were controlled by the Republicans. But some minority party members still managed to get a few items into the budget. One Democrat, Rep. Dixie Allen, expressed disappointment with the lack of her party's input on the Finance Committee. Nevertheless, she succeeded in restoring funding for a radio reading program for the blind.[27] Sometimes a committee chair will intentionally seek bipartisan support, which requires more accommodation by the majority to minority requests. This may occur because of the nonpartisan content of the subject matter, the political need for both parties to share responsibility for unpopular action, or because divided control of government or of the legislature necessitates bipartisan cooperation. Therefore, it is not unusual to find chairs working to fashion a bill that is acceptable to members of both parties as well as a wide range of interest groups. This results in nobody getting everything he or she wants, but in most members getting something.

Building consensus can be slow and arduous business. As in all phases of the legislative process, timing is extremely important. The subcommittee chair in the Maryland house, Sandy Rosenberg, could sense whether or not a consensus was forming. If there was none, or if a majority was moving in a contrary direction, he would postpone the vote. For instance, at one subcommittee meeting the votes for one of the governor's priorities were not there, at least not yet: "I quietly advised the department's lobbyist he needed to lobby my colleagues so that the votes would be there the next time." [28] In the process of building support, chairs receive help from a measure's proponents. The governor's administration officials, interest group lobbyists, and legislative leaders are used to helping a chair get the votes that are needed. They seldom have to work alone.

It does not always succeed, however. On occasion, a committee cannot establish the consensus necessary to prevail on the floor. On some issues committee leaders fail entirely; the votes are simply aligned against them. For example, despite their efforts, the chair of the House Appropriations Committee and the speaker could not convince Maryland legislators to support the governor's budget proposal to provide state aid for private school textbooks. They were beaten in subcommittee and by a 14–12 vote in the full committee. The leadership, moreover, was unable to retain the support of one member who reversed herself, having voted in favor of such a provision in the 2000 session.

Support in Caucus

Support building, or support mobilizing, also takes place in various legislative caucuses. County and city delegations, women's caucuses, black caucuses, and other groups in which members share interests are places where support is mobilized. For example, in Maryland the delegations of Montgomery and Prince George's Counties and Baltimore City—the major delegations in the house— meet from time to time to deal with state-aid formulas and local legislation. If the group is large and cohesive it has to be taken into account. The Black Caucus during the 2001 session had 38 out of the 188 members of the Maryland General Assembly. It has proven to be a formidable legislative force. It focused its efforts on bills involving minority businesses, a death penalty moratorium, racial profiling, and voting rights for ex-felons. A ban on racial profiling had died in the 2000 session, primarily because of infighting among Black Caucus members, but the following year members put aside their differences and pushed passage of the bill through the legislature.[29] In its drive for a death penalty moratorium, the

Black Caucus managed to win in the house but not in the senate. The caucus also organized support for a bill extending voting rights to convicted felons, lobbying their white colleagues effectively and winning 2–1 on the house floor.

On a minority business enterprise bill, an initiative of the governor, the Black Caucus joined forces with the Women's Caucus, a group with sixty-five legislators as members. Together the two groups had a majority of Maryland legislators. A similar bill had failed in 1995, partly because the two caucuses could not agree. But in 2001 the bill passed both houses without any significant compromise having to be made. At one point the bill was stuck in committee, but the black/women's coalition forced the leadership to persuade the committee to move on it. As the speaker described how legislators—and even contractors who opposed the bill—regarded the issue: "Here comes a train that isn't going to stop, so get out of the way."

The natural tendencies toward party cohesion are reinforced by the legislative party caucus. The party caucus is a key mechanism in three out of four legislative chambers in the country. Caucuses do not function in bodies dominated by a single party, but they tend to be organized in bodies in which the two parties compete for control or where a one-party system is in the process of evolving into a more competitive one. In many legislatures—Minnesota, Ohio, and Washington among them—the caucus meets each day that there is a floor session. In other places, such as Vermont, the caucus will meet perhaps once a week. Elsewhere caucuses meet less frequently or, as in Maryland, only at the outset to plan for the chamber's organization. (In the house, the speaker's leadership team meets on a regular basis, partially substituting for a majority party caucus.)

Whatever the exact frequency of their meetings, caucuses not only select party leadership but serve a number of other purposes as well. They convey information to members on the bills that are slated for consideration that day (or that week), or bills that are under consideration by the legislature. They provide an opportunity for members to pose questions to party and committee leaders and at the same time enable leaders to get an idea of how members and the people in their districts feel about issues. Caucuses also afford members an opportunity to learn about where their colleagues stand. They give members a chance to air their complaints. They serve as vehicles for building intraparty consensus on legislation and enable leaders to count votes available for a measure and decide whether or not to call up a bill on the floor. Few caucuses require members to vote with the majority, but most exercise at least subtle pressure on them to do so. And, finally, caucuses are places in which strategy can be discussed and agreed.

Caucuses held by the majority Republicans in the Vermont house during the 2001 session illustrate the functions of such sessions. The major issue facing the Republican Party was Act 60, which specified a complicated formula for state financial aid to local school districts. The House Ways and Means Committee, chaired by Marron, had the task of reporting out a school aid bill for consideration by the caucus and the house. Marron would brief the caucus on a weekly basis, presenting the plan as it had thus far been agreed on, informally if not offi-cially, in his committee. Local property taxes would be reduced, but a statewide property tax and the sales tax would be increased. The burden on wealthier dis-tricts would decline. Caucus members were concerned about any increase in taxes. One member asked: "Why not let the governor (who had also campaigned for revision of Act 60) do what had to be done?" to which the Republican major-ity leader responded: "As the majority, we have the responsibility to stand up and lead." Perhaps, someone suggested, why not get more revenue from sales taxes on out-of-staters? Another asked: "Why not broaden the tax on junk food?" In response, Marron pointed out that "It doesn't produce enough money and you have everyone ticked off at you."

It would take seventy-six votes to pass a school finance revision in the Ver-mont house. Republican leaders calculated that in order to bring the bill to the floor for a vote they would need the support for a revision from about sixty-five of the eighty-three Republicans. They anticipated a dozen or more Democratic votes. The majority leadership did not intend to push ahead unless they were sure of winning. So they took repeated head counts. As it turned out, the lead-ership was unable to get enough support for a Ways and Means Committee bill in caucus. Consequently, no Republican bill made it to the house floor in that session of the legislature.

But there was still dissatisfaction with Act 60 in Vermont. The legislative effort to modify it continued, with Marron taking the lead. Two sessions later, in 2003, revision was achieved in the new Act 68, which took away the much-criticized "sharing pool" and replaced it by raising the statewide property tax.

Building consensus is probably the most important business of the majority party caucus. Consensus is built, in the first place, by keeping members informed of what is going on. This is a basic function of a caucus session, particularly when the legislative party is trying to build support on major issues. It is also accom-plished by getting members to buy into strategy. Sen. Steve Kelley of Minnesota, in trying to discourage amendments to the energy bill, warned his DFL col-leagues that "We ought to be careful about last-minute inspiration." One of his colleagues thereupon announced: "I'm not going to introduce an amendment—I'm a team player." Others also pledged their party loyalty. Caucuses also try to build consensus by responding to members' questions and/or complaints about a bill or provision. At a Republican caucus in the Ohio senate, one member ques-tioned why some of his colleagues seemed to have something in the budget for their districts when he and other members did not. In defending the allocation, the chair of the budget committee pointed out that so-called pork could benefit the entire state, not only individual districts. The questioning senator was not entirely satisfied, however.

Giving members a voice in the shaping of a measure is still another caucus function. The following is how the revision of Act 60 was handled by house Republicans in Vermont. The Ways and Means chair, Richard Marron, would run his committee's deliberations by his Republican caucus. "This is a long-term

effort," one Ways and Means committee member said to his Republican colleagues in caucus. "We'd like you to stick with us, and we welcome your ideas."
The Ways and Means chair constantly checked with his leadership and caucus,
so that his committee could formulate a measure that would have enough support to pass the house. He was willing to give on important matters, as well as
minor ones. Most of his committee's members were against instituting Powerball, a multistate lottery, in Vermont in order to raise revenue. But Marron was
flexible: "If there is consensus in this caucus to put Powerball back in, we'll do
that." Marron was not willing to put pressure on his committee—not until some
package appeared to have sufficient support in the Republican caucus.

On occasion a caucus can participate rather directly in the shaping of a bill.
That is certainly a good way for leadership to build support for a measure. In the
2001 session House Republicans in Ohio took the budget on en masse. Speaker
Larry Householder decided to let the fifty-nine-member caucus write the house
version. One of his intentions was to give his Republican colleagues, many of
whom were new to the legislature, a view of the entire state and its various constituencies; another was to get his Republican colleagues to buy into the budget
that the caucus developed. After more than twenty hours of closed-door meetings in which Republicans went over the budget line by line, the product that
emerged got six days of public hearings, an eight-hour committee amending session, and then a floor debate and vote. Democrats were not happy, but Speaker
Householder got every Republican vote.[30]

Persuading Members on the Floor

Building support is an ongoing activity; it continues as a measure progresses
from committee to caucus and beyond. Even though most of the hard work is
done before then, majorities continue to be constructed as a measure gets taken
up on the floor.

Often the sponsor of the majority party has the votes committed before bringing up a measure on the floor. Sometimes, however, support has to be won on
the floor. Probably the main argument made at this stage, as well as in caucus, is
the need to defer to the standing committee. (A similar argument is made at the
committee stage with regard to a subcommittee's recommendation.) In some
legislatures, such as Maryland's, committees are relatively large and representative of the entire body. This is one reason why deference to a committee can be
the norm. Committee members, moreover, are deemed to be experts in their
domains. However, in term-limited states it would appear that committee
expertise is accorded less deference than formerly—mainly because with rotat-
ing memberships committees have less expertise. The importance of the legislative division of labor and expertise, as reflected by the standing committee system, is explained by Tom Loftus:

> Like students with a declared major, members of a legislature begin to specialize
> in the issues addressed by the committee or committees on which they serve.

Some legislators, usually committee chairs and ranking members, reach a sort of faculty status; other members defer to them and follow their vote on bills in their area. There is an important partisan element to this. When members follow the lead of the expert on their side of the aisle, they must trust that the political problems have been filtered through and that the chosen way to proceed is as politically safe as possible.[31]

Committee members obviously are more familiar with the bills they hear and craft in their committee than are other legislators. On important matters, they have worked through amendments and made compromises. They therefore cannot help but influence colleagues who defer to their judgment. As a former speaker of the Vermont house put it: "Committees reporting a bill on the floor of the House to the body, of whom 90 percent haven't any idea what the bill does, have to be trusted much as a child trusts the comfort of his mother's arms after having a bad dream."[32] A bit florid, but the point is well taken.

Deference to committees is most apparent when it comes to bills that the committee deep-sixes. In some legislative bodies standing committees are required to report out all bills referred to them. In most, however, committees have discretion and only those that a committee supports are reported for floor action. Those that a committee, or sometimes only the chair, opposes get no further, except when they reemerge in another committee, appear as an amendment on the floor, make their way in the other house, or get inserted into a conference committee report. But this does not happen often. Any of these actions would be a slap in the face to the committee, and particularly its chair. A committee rejection is extremely difficult to overcome.

Members prefer to be on the good side of the committee chair, so they are reluctant to do end runs. Maryland's Rosenberg recounts an appealing possibility of getting his way on a measure he favored. He could have quietly pressed for an amendment to be adopted in a conference committee on the budget, but colleagues would have found out what had happened. "I'm not concerned," Rosenberg wrote, "about those who opposed HB 437." Instead, his concern was over his ongoing relationship with the chair of the committee that had heard the bill. In any case, the chair agreed to work with Rosenberg on drafting legislation for the next session. The moral of the story, he concludes, is that "even though it may be legal to do something, it may not be wise to do so."[33]

In most legislative bodies, bills opposed by a committee get no further. The unwritten rule is that no one pulls a bill out of committee unless the chair assents. Loftus explains that pulling a bill out of a committee is "an act of mutiny" against the committee's chair. If one chair's authority is undermined, all chairs can be similarly undermined. Thus, he writes:

> If you were a Democrat, a member of the party in the majority, you dared not vote to pull a bill, any bill. It was the clearest of the unwritten rules and there were consequences if you broke this rule. There was the real possibility the Speaker would remove you from a choice committee, and the memory among all the members of

your treason would stay for your whole legislative career, like a scarlet letter only they could see.[34]

When the infrequent attempt is made to pry a bill from a hostile committee, it usually is repelled. Maryland's Judicial Proceedings Committee was sharply divided on a bill for a death penalty moratorium and would not report it out. One Maryland senator tried to bring it to the floor nevertheless, but he was beaten by a 35–9 vote. The committee was upheld. In the Maryland house an effort was made to pull a medical marijuana bill out of the Judiciary Committee. It fell far short of the seventy-two votes required. Of the thirty votes cast for overriding the committee, twenty-two were cast by minority party Republicans.

Deference toward committees was defended by two DFL senators in Minnesota. The Crime Prevention Committee failed to pass out a "right-to-carry bill," favored by sportsmen's clubs and by rural areas. In a joint letter to the editor of a local newspaper Sens. Doug Johnson and David Tomassoni explained why they voted against the motion to bring the bill to the floor over the committee's objections, even though they themselves favored the bill. First, the integrity of the committee process was necessary if citizens were to be able to offer opinions about legislative proposals. Second, as rural senators from an area of declining political strength, they desired a process that could in the future protect their interests from the powerful metropolitan area. For them, the vote on the floor concerned the merits of the committee process, not those of the bill itself. Johnson and Tomassoni, no doubt, were trying to justify their behavior to their constituents, but the argument was a sound one on procedural grounds as well.

For the most part, committees work to build support for measures they report with "do pass" recommendations. It is up to the committee chair to put legislation together so that it has substantial backing within the committee and can therefore be expected to garner similar support in caucus or on the floor. As an illustration of the committee leader's role Loftus describes Joe Czerwinski, whom he regarded as a very effective committee chair. He made competing interest groups compromise; he got both Democratic and Republican committee members to back the measure; and he made sure that it was in proper legislative form.[35] In other words, he got the job done. "No chairman," writes Del. Rosenberg of Maryland, "likes to see his committee lose a vote on the floor." [36] So chairs will try their hardest to get more than a simple majority to back a favored measure. "Generally," said Maryland delegate Salima Marriott, "when a bill passes 2–1 in committee, you don't have to work too hard to move it forward."

Usually legislative leadership will help committees fashion majorities and pass their bills on the floor. Leaders have their own investment in the integrity of the committee system. In the Maryland house, for instance, committee chairs are part of the speaker's leadership team. Speaker Cas Taylor believed strongly in the committee system, and when he was informed of a motion to bring a bill out over the objection of committee, he would urge his team to work for its defeat. Loftus was also a leader who insisted that members follow their committees. He would advise newer members: "Look, if you don't have the guts to vote with the committee on this one, it's damned unlikely that you have the guts to be a chair of any committee next session." [37]

In a few states, such as Oregon, committee recommendations do not mean much. But in those states, where committees generally represent the chamber's membership, where chairs hesitate to report a bill without a consensus, and where leaders support the committees, committees usually prevail. "Follow-the-committee" is the watchword. The Maryland General Assembly illustrates how influential standing committees can be in the lawmaking process. Seldom are committees overridden in either the senate or house. Bills reported by the committee pass, and their provisions have privileged status as the product of the committee of reference. The Appropriations Committee in the house and the Budget and Taxation Committee in the senate dominate the budget process. In the 2001 budget process, for instance, only one amendment to the house committee's budget bill passed. It restored $2 million that was cut in a $20 million increase in nursing-home reimbursements.[38] The stature of committees in Maryland does not mean that the process is uncontested. Members do try to amend the committee bill, in order to benefit their district or promote another policy end. Minority Republicans are likely to disagree with certain provisions and offer other ways to achieve a balanced budget. There are always opportunities to overcome a committee's action, but only rarely can the opposition achieve a majority necessary to amend what the committee has done.

Despite the fact that in Maryland and elsewhere committees have a good record of building support, on some hot-button issues the odds of their winning decreases. Abortion, the death penalty, and gay rights are the kinds of issues that can divide a committee sharply. Even if a majority can be cobbled together, a divided committee receives much less deference on the floor. For example, the Judicial Proceedings Committee of the Maryland senate would report out legislation with bare majorities. During one session it lost a bill and had another referred back to it. These bills, in leadership's judgment, should not have been reported out in the first place. Since the chair and the members were not sufficiently representative of the entire senate, leadership decided to change the composition of the committee.

Deference to the committee is a powerful support mechanism, but by no means is it the only one at work. Other appeals are also made along the way, usually by members of the committee. There is further appeal to the *process*, such as mention of all the work devoted to a bill reported by the committee: "The committee spent days on this issue"; "We spent a lot of time discussing those questions"; or "The committee really studied this issue and studied it hard." Translated, this means that the committee version is as good as any alternative; it should be kept intact; and legislators should vote against the amendment. There is also the appeal to *numbers,* which argues that "the committee overwhelmingly felt that . . ." or that the bill has already passed the other house by an "overwhelming margin." There is an appeal to *authority,* in terms of who is for the bill. "This bill is supported by everyone who testified on it" is how a sub-committee chair defended a bill on the house floor in Maryland. Authority is invoked not only by indicating all the groups that support a measure, but also by noting other states that have similar law. "This brings Maryland in line with what other states do" is one reason cited to vote for a bill allowing former felons to vote and run for office. There is, of course, an appeal to *politics*. "A vote against this bill is a vote against nurses" was part of the case for a bill in Maryland's house that permitted patients to select nurse-practitioners as primary care providers.

If a committee can satisfy a member's objections on the floor without changing significant parts of a measure, it will try to do so. Motions to special order or lay a bill over (or whatever the precise procedure) are frequently made. By mutual consent, the bill is put aside so that an objection can be met, a problem worked out, or clarification provided. Often a minor change agreed to by the committee manages to satisfy the objector. Bit by bit and person by person, the process builds support.

Deliberation and Support

Much of what transpires in lawmaking is relatively simple in concept. Proponents and opponents deliberate a measure's merits and try to win support for their side. The merits of a case are broadly construed, consisting of what appears to be good public policy, what is good for the constituency, and what is most acceptable to one's partisan, committee, and other legislative colleagues. Throughout the lawmaking process, the merits get studied, discussed, and argued back and forth. On that basis—and with the understanding that this encompasses both substantive and political considerations—the respective merits essentially account for most of the votes of most of the members most of the time.

NOTES

1. Joseph M. Bessette, *The Mild Voice of Reason* (Chicago: University of Chicago Press, 1994), 150.

2. Ibid., 50–51.

3. Anthony J. Nownes and Patricia Freeman, "Interest Group Activity in the States" (paper presented at the annual meeting of the American Political Science Association, San Francisco, September 1996). See also Alan Rosenthal, *The Third House*, 2nd ed. (Washington, D.C.: CQ Press, 2001).

4. *Olympian*, March 12, 2002.

5. *Minneapolis Star Tribune*, April 16 and May 6, 2001.

6. *Toledo Blade*, May 2, 2002.

7. *Dayton Daily News*, June 13, 2001.

8. Tom Loftus, *The Art of Legislative Politics* (Washington, D.C.: CQ Press, 1994), 117.

9. William K. Muir Jr., *Legislature: California's School of Politics* (Chicago: University of Chicago Press, 1982).

10. John E. McDonough, *Experiencing Politics* (Berkeley: University of California Press, 2000), 225.

11. See Cass R. Sunstein, "Interest Groups in American Public Law," *Stanford Law Review* 38 (1985): 45–49.

12. Bessette, *The Mild Voice of Reason*, 46.

13. *Cincinnati Enquirer,* May 4, 2001.

14. Bessette, *The Mild Voice of Reason,* 176.

15. *Baltimore Sun*, March 17, 2001.

16. Ember Reichgott Junge, unpublished manuscript, 2001.

17. Diary of Del. Sandy Rosenberg, March 14, 2001.

18. Del. William Cole, in *Baltimore Sun,* April 8, 2001.

19. Bessette, *The Mild Voice of Reason,* 176, 177, 179.

20. Ibid., 46–55.

21. *St. Paul Pioneer Press,* May 16, 2001.

22. Bessette, *The Mild Voice of Reason,* 71, 99.

23. *Washington Post,* April 2, 2001.

24. Diary of Del. Sandy Rosenberg, April 9, 2001.

25. *Baltimore Sun,* March 25, 2001.

26. Ralph Wright, *All Politics Is Personal* (Manchester Center, Vt.: Marshall Jones Company, 1996).

27. *Columbus Dispatch,* May 7, 2001.

28. Diary of Del. Sandy Rosenberg, March 2, 2001.

29. *Baltimore Sun,* March 29, 2001.

30. *Columbus Dispatch,* May 7, 2001.

31. Loftus, *The Art of Legislative Politics,* 111.

32. Wright, *All Politics Is Personal,* 163.

33. Diary of Del. Sandy Rosenberg, March 23, 2001.

34. Loftus, *The Art of Legislative Politics,* 79–80.

35. Ibid., 107.

36. Diary of Del. Sandy Rosenberg, March 9, 2001.

37. Loftus, *The Art of Legislative Politics,* 81.

38. Diary of Del. Sandy Rosenberg, March 14, 2001.

7 LAWMAKING:
MANAGING MAJORITIES

With the 2001 legislative session in full swing, Richard Finan, the Ohio senate president, told a statehouse reporter: "A lot of people think you can drop a bill in the hopper and something magic happens. You have to push and push and push—I don't care what kind of bill it is." [1] Some bills take more of a push, others less, but it is the responsibility of their sponsors and backers to do what it takes to get them enacted.

The "push" Finan was talking about, especially on less significant, less costly, and less contentious matters, involves making the case, arguing the merits, and building support on matters of substance, fealty to committee, or loyalty to party. But even in these relatively straightforward instances bills have to be managed, if on the way to enactment they are to navigate standing committees, caucuses, two chambers, and the governor's office. More significant, more costly, and more contentious bills require much more in terms of skillful management in order to achieve majorities through the course of enactment.

Those who sponsor and those who back legislation want to succeed. They not only believe in what they are doing by way of principle, constituency, interests, and politics, they also want to succeed legislatively. One measure of success is the enactment of legislation. By pushing their agendas, legislators try to establish as much control over the process as possible and leave as little as they can to chance. If the process were left to chance, rather than to the management of legislative leaders, committee chairs, and members themselves, it would be very different and would have different outcomes.

Strategizing toward Enactment

Strategizing is a major element in lawmaking, although it is usually commingled with deliberating. Take, for instance, the issue Maryland legislators faced of whether and how to aid horse racing in the state. Members of the industry wanted a law established that would legalize slot machines at the tracks, but the industry, as such, was split between harness and thoroughbred racers and could not present a unified voice. Consider the following discussion among the speaker of the house, his aide, the majority leader, the chair of the Ways and Means Committee, a former chair of the Maryland Racing Commission, the governor's legislative aide, and a subcommittee chair:

134

Speaker: Do you have a sense of where the committee wants to go?

Chair: We don't think much of the industry or commission.

Speaker: How do we go forward?

Chair: We can stand back and watch.

Speaker: What would happen if we pass nothing?

Former racing commission chair: "They'd run less days. . . .We have a completely divisive industry.

Speaker: Would the act of doing nothing shake up the industry?

Governor's aide [referring to a succession of meetings with the racing industry]: All we ended up doing is being mad at each other at the end of the session.

Speaker: Either do nothing or put everything in one bill.

Subcommittee chair [stressing that leadership has to back up the committee and subcommittee]: You've got to shut your office doors to them.

Former commission chair: There's no hope.

Speaker: Let's ask Ways and Means to do nothing. Why waste time on it?

The racing industry would have to get its act together, everyone agreed, before the legislature would even consider coming to its rescue. One can see that the merits of the case are at the base of the discussion. Legislators would like to help the horse-racing industry; its potential contributions to the Maryland economy are obvious. But they have little faith in the industry's ability to reach internal agreement and figure out what it needs and what it can settle for. Until the industry takes steps in the right direction, it cannot count on the house to help it legislatively.

"What do we want to do and how do we do it so that we maximize our gains?" is the strategic question underlying much of the conversation that goes on privately, if not publicly, in the nation's state capitals. Strategizing by legislators, and especially by legislative leaders, often includes "what iffing": what if this happens; what if this goes wrong; what if these votes don't materialize? Question after question is asked in the course of enacting legislation. "Should the bill begin in the house or senate?" is a question frequently raised. "What if the Republicans do this, and then the governor does that?" That question was addressed by the house minority leader to the senate majority leader midway though the 2001 session of the Minnesota legislature. Another question was: "What about campaign finance?" Even though no bill was likely to be passed by the house, the senate Democratic-Farmer-Labor (DFL) Party wanted to be prepared—just in case.

Partisan or Bipartisan

The principal strategic objective is getting the votes to pass a measure. In a partisan body, which most senates and houses are, the choice for legislative leaders is either to look for votes solely within one's own party or to look for votes on the other side of the aisle as well. Trying to develop a consensus within a party is a very different process than trying to win votes from the other party. What is the strategy to be, asked Roger Moe of his DFL colleagues, when it comes to a pro-life amendment on a budget bill? "I negotiate with people in this room or I negotiate with them [that is, Republicans]," Moe told the DFL senators. "I will do it either way."

On matters such as revenues and appropriations, especially, the majority party prefers to have some minority votes for its proposals. A show of bipartisan support makes it more difficult for the minority to criticize the majority. But the minority is not always willing to share responsibility, instead preferring to play the role of opposition that will use its criticisms in an effort to win seats at the next legislative election. The 2001 budget process in Ohio illustrates the difficulty of recruiting minority party members to the majority party's side. Both the house and senate Republicans had hoped to bring the Democrats into the process on school finance and the general budget. Despite the delay and cost it would entail, the majority believed it worthwhile to have the minority involved. On a few occasions at the outset the minority leaders were included in meetings with the majority leaders and the Republican governor. After one meeting, however, Democrats held a press conference criticizing the Republican proposals. At this point the Republicans concluded that the Democrats would not provide any votes for the budget and decided to exclude them from participation. They would get all the votes they needed from the majority party caucuses. After the budget emerged from committee, Speaker Larry Householder tried specifically to get some Democratic votes for passage. When he failed, he presented the case to the Republican caucus, whose members agreed to prepare the budget themselves, without Democratic votes. Why not? The Republicans would be blamed for unpopular cuts, so why give away items just to achieve bipartisanship? On the senate side, Finan stated the strategy: "We have no Democratic votes for the bill, and that makes it easier."

Two years later, in 2003, the Republican majorities in the Ohio legislature took another approach to the budget, a bipartisan one. A transportation funding bill received some Democratic votes in the senate because the minority had been invited in to help shape the bill. "We learned something here," said Greg DiDonato, the minority leader. "By simply putting us in communication, by simply allowing us to come to the table and being inclusive . . . the end result is you get support." [2] On the budget itself, antitax Republicans refused to vote for a proposed temporary one-cent sales-tax increase, insisting instead on more spending cuts. Speaker Householder, however, cut a deal with five African American Democrats, who along with forty-eight Republicans passed the budget, 53–46. The African American Democrats, in return for their support, had some funding restored for local governments, dental and vision services, Medicaid, and other items.[3]

Timing

Sometimes rounding up votes takes a while, delaying a bill's progress. Timing is a vital part of strategizing in the legislative process. Usually a bill will be held up until there are enough votes to pass it. In Maryland, for instance, the "safe haven" bill protecting abandoned newborns had a number of problems in committee, suggesting that there was still work to be done gaining support. Therefore, the committee had the bill laid over on special order, giving proponents time to round up votes.

The importance of timing as a strategic consideration is illustrated by the budget struggle during the 2001 session of the Minnesota legislature. Leaders calculated that it would be better to send the budget bills to conference committees later than they had done previously. In past years, when conferences began earlier, negotiators wasted weeks and did not come up with compromises until the last minute. However sound the strategy appeared in light of the legislative tendency to defer until the deadline, time ran out as conferees failed to resolve differences between house and senate bills before the end of the 2001 session. The legislature had to finish up in a special session called by the governor.

Majority Leader Moe's strategy might have been to delay until the last minute, because he felt at an advantage when negotiating in the final days when everyone's back was up against the wall and legislators were making compromises they really did not wish to make.[4] It did not matter that the legislature failed to finish on time. Perhaps this strategy worked after all, even though Minnesota did not resolve the budget until the special session. Although the Republicans won overall, it was Moe's belief that they did not win as much as they would have had the negotiations concluded earlier. The DFL made advances, which could not have been made at the outset of the impasse between the senate and house.

Few legislators have the incentive to negotiate and compromise on the big issues until the deadline is upon them. As Alexander B. "Pete" Grannis, a member of the New York senate, observed, "on the big issues, usually the last week of the session is when people make deals and get things done." [5] In the case of New York's budget, the deadline of April 1 has not been met for twenty years. Yet there have been no serious political consequences, and at some point—later rather than earlier—the deals do get made.

The Other Chamber, Other Party

Rarely absent from strategy is an assessment of what the other chamber might do. House-senate jockeying for position is a given, occurring whether party control is divided or not. When one party controls the senate and the other the house, each has to act with the other in mind if it hopes to settle difficult issues. The senate in Vermont was not anxious to revisit the subject of school finance, but the house was. What are the house Republicans likely to do in their revision of Act 60? Democrats had to ask. "My fear," said Senate President Peter Shumlin, "is if they send us a bill, we have to work it out." Both the Minnesota senate and house were crafting tax bills, and each had to take into account what the other was likely to do. The Senate Tax Committee, chaired by Larry Pogemiller, had to make sure that its bill was competitive with the house bill being crafted by the Tax Committee under Ron Abrams. "I want to tell you where we are going to get without telling you how we are going to get there," Pogemiller advised Moe. Thereupon, Moe thought ahead to what the speaker would probably do. While "we're out there fighting for welfare extensions and public employees," he pointed out, the house Republicans have $600 million in play that the senate Democrats did not. Pogemiller suggested supporting the governor's position on the sales tax on services, but he doubted that he could get the votes in committee. "I think it's a smart political vote and I think it's the right thing to do policy-wise," he said, adding, "this can work—we might get lucky." But the bothersome question remained: Why take a tough vote if the conference committee will eliminate the item? The tax chair wanted to stay with the governor, but the majority leader urged that the committee have a bill by May 2, because the house Republicans planned to have a tax bill on the floor on May 4.

Part of strategizing toward enactment is an assessment of the strengths and weaknesses of one's position vis-à-vis the opposition. This includes an accounting of allies and opponents. If the legislature is divided, with the Republicans controlling one chamber and the Democrats the other, the party of the governor normally has an advantage, at least on issues that arise to that level of importance. Thus, in the 2001 session of the Vermont legislature, senate Democrats had an edge on house Republicans because they could expect to have Democratic governor Howard Dean on their side. On the revision of Act 60, therefore, while house Republicans were trying to develop their own legislation, senate Democrats were working with the governor's office on more modest changes in the school finance system.

In Minnesota both the house Republican majority and the senate DFL majority tried to win over the Independence Party governor, Jesse Ventura. Each wanted Ventura on its side. In 1999 house Republicans had proposed cuts in income taxes and, when Ventura moved in their direction, the senate DFLers had no real recourse; they were outnumbered. Two years later the senate again seemed to be negotiating from a position of weakness, with the governor more aligned with the house on taxes and budget. The Republicans wanted to cut taxes by $1.6 billion over two years, the governor by $1.2 billion, but the DFL by only $609 million. Republicans originally had proposed cutting income tax rates, but they switched to favoring a reduction in property taxes in order to put themselves on the same side as the governor. Ventura wanted the state to pay a greater share of public school costs, thus reducing local property taxes. "If we're going to be bludgeoned into doing it by the governor," said Ron Abrams, the House Tax Committee chair, "why don't we take the ball and run with it?" [6] The DFL did not have the same flexibility given its constituencies of welfare recipients and state employees. "That's the dilemma I face," acknowledged the senate majority leader.

Each chamber was wooing the governor in order to ensure that the tax and budget situation would be two against one in its favor. House Republicans and Governor Ventura generally agreed on most major items: they were in accord on the overall level of state spending, and both supported tax cuts, although the house did not want to expand the sales tax, which the governor did, to include most services as a way to pay for property tax relief. Lining up with the governor would lessen the DFL senate leverage when it came to final negotiations between the houses. "In a tripartite system, it's all about two against one," Speaker Steve Sviggum said. "We want to be one of the two." [7] DFLers might have thrown in their hand, but they continued to pursue a strategy of winning over the governor, even if doing so meant adopting his position. Senate committees treated Ventura's education proposals well in an effort to soften him up. The senate also supported the governor's campaign finance package, which the house opposed. DFL leaders hoped to keep the governor in play, as it positioned itself to deal with the house at the end of the session. Despite its overall disadvantage, the senate's strategy was to negotiate from as much strength as possible. It knew the house's positions, but it also needed to know where the governor was or would be, and what it would take to lure him to the senate position. So, as bills were being put together in committee, a major consideration was the governor's position. The senate leader advised his staff to compile a list of items "that your instincts tell you the governor is likely to side with us on."

The Endgame

The "endgame" requires strategies to look ahead to where they have to be when issues are finally settled. It is an important part of strategizing. It is almost a certainty that the budget programs preferred by each chamber will differ, whether control is divided or not. Therefore, the strategy on major measures is to have a position from which to negotiate, either in a conference committee or informally between house and senate leaders. While the revision of Act 60 in Vermont had first to get support in committee and then in the Republican caucus and in the house, strategist Richard Marron always kept in mind the compromises that could be made with the senate in conference. The budget bill requires that leaders keep the endgame in mind. The Vermont house will usually cut the budget more than it might desire, anticipating that the senate would cut it less and the conference committee would split the difference. In Minnesota the half-dozen or so omnibus budget bills ordinarily are the most significant measures of a biennium. It is hardly surprising that each chamber's hopes, plans, and strategies are directed toward the conference committee. These strategies change constantly, as events unfold on a daily, even an hourly basis. "You can't plant your feet in cement," but you have to be flexible approaching final negotiations, indicated one participant. Among other things, therefore, the appointment of conferees is critical. "Who will be the house conferees for each budget bill?" is a question not far from the mind of the senate majority leader as the session draws toward its end. And who will be the senate conferees? Who can stand up to the house? Moe asked the chair of the E–12 budget, LeRoy Stumpf: "Let's just look down the road. Who do you want as your conferees?" "I need a hatchet man," Stumpf indicated. "You need a strong, very smart suburbanite," replied Moe.

In planning for the endgame, participants try to put themselves in the strongest position for negotiating. If one side is firmly committed to a proposal, it has little leeway to bargain. But what it can do is include in a measure material that it can give up in a negotiating process. In the words of Maryland's house speaker: "Let's load [a bill] down, let it sit, and then they'll make a deal." Any deal clearly would involve some unloading of the bill. So the senate will put "stuff" in to give up as part of bargaining with the house; and the house will do likewise. Minnesota's senate DFLers, for instance, in crafting a transportation package, not only included diverse elements to attract enough support in their own caucus and chamber; they also looked toward the conference with the house. "We can't leave Dean [Johnson] hanging out there with nothing to negotiate," said the majority leader. "What else does he need?" There is always a danger, however, that an item thrown into a bill as bargaining bait will not be taken out in negotiations. "Whatever we do, we have to be prepared to live with it," the majority leader's chief of staff cautioned. There are constraints on how much and what can be included for strategic purposes.

Strategy also dictates loading up the budget with policy. In a number of legislatures policy items, as well as appropriations, are inserted into omnibus budget bills. Doing so helps to facilitate passage of an item that is part of a large package, and it may also protect it from the governor's veto since the governor can only line-item veto appropriations, not policy. Minnesota leaders claim that they try to keep policy out of the budget bills so that it can be examined separately, on its merits. But they have not been entirely successful in this effort. Noncontroversial policy does get considered separately, but controversial policies often are included in omnibus budget bills. Take a provision—known as "informed consent"—pushed by abortion opponents in Minnesota during the 2001 session. This provision requires that a woman be given certain information about the abortion procedure, and alternatives, then wait twenty-four hours before undergoing the procedure. The previous year a similar measure was passed by the legislature, but it was not part of a budget bill and was vetoed by Ventura. By making "informed consent" part of a $6.7 billion health and human services funding bill, the strategy of proponents was to shield it from the governor's veto. They had enough votes in the senate to amend the provision to the funding bill on a 36–31 vote, after which abortion rights supporters tabled the bill, hoping that they could change some votes. After an unsuccessful attempt to move the abortion language to a less crucial bill and failed efforts to change votes, the omnibus budget bill passed the senate. A similar bill passed the house. The house bill was accepted by the senate, in anticipation of a gubernatorial veto, which Ventura had threatened from the outset—even if the entire health and human services budget suffered along with the anti-abortion provision. The senate strategy, in approving the house bill that most DFLers opposed, was designed to bypass having to negotiate the provision with the house at the end of the session. As expected, the governor vetoed the bill.[8]

Amendments

Critical to strategic thinking is the use of amendments. No bill is ever safe from being amended at various stages of the process. There are various ways to enact a measure. The most obvious is to pass it as a bill. Alternatively it may be buried in the budget act. Or it can also become law by being added as an amendment to another measure. In legislative strategizing, leaders and members alike think in terms of having "vehicles" available to carry amendments. If it appears advantageous to attach one measure to another rather than let it stand alone, that strategy will be pursued. Usually, all that prevents the use of vehicles is a germaneness rule, which requires that the amendment have some relationship to its host. Therefore, it is good strategy to have multiple vehicles available as the session draws to an end.

Amendments offer opportunities to one side, but threats to the other. Proponents of a measure have to be constantly on the alert and develop strategies to fight off unfriendly amendments. Meanwhile, a bill's opponents strategize about amendments that will weaken or kill provisions they oppose. Amendments are in order during both the committee and floor stages of the process. On minor matters, a bill's sponsors and backers figure out what amendments are likely to be headed their bill's way, and how to ensure that they do minimal damage, if adopted. On major matters, committee chairs along with party leaders take responsibility for defensive or offensive strategies. It is impossible for majority party leaders to know which amendments will be offered by the minority, and occasionally they are not even informed about those coming from members of their own party. They expect that their partisan colleagues will notify them of their intentions, while the opposition party will attempt to surprise them to gain advantage.

The majority party tries to keep its members united in the face of amendment threats. A Republican Party caucus in the Ohio senate anticipated the likely Democratic amendments that would be offered on the floor that afternoon. Two Republican senators indicated to the leadership that politically they could not afford to vote against one of the amendments. The discussion of strategy turned, therefore, to whether the majority should move to table all the amendments. "Is everyone comfortable with tabling?" asked the Republican leader. His members could vote in favor of the tabling motion and then not have to vote against the amendments, *per se*. Either way, the amendments would not pass. The minority party, however, could put the majority on record if it could force votes on the amendments themselves. In Ohio Democrats offered more than fifty amendments to the budget in the House Finance Committee and forty-one amendments in the senate. The Republicans were forced to vote against a number of politically popular expenditures.

When a conference is pending the majority party may simply allow amendments on the floor, expecting that if they do pass they can be discarded in conference. But if conferees for the other house favor the provision in the amendment, it will be difficult to jettison it. Therefore, each side plays it close to the vest and tries to keep amendments it opposes off the bill in question. In discussing the E–12 education finance bill in the Minnesota senate, Stumpf briefed his colleagues in the DFL caucus on a dozen or so amendments he thought would be proposed by Republicans on the floor. Referring to one, he said: "I would rather go into conference without it." In an executive board meeting across the capitol building, the house Republican majority also was strategizing for an end-of-the-session conference committee. "If you're going to negotiate with the Senate, you want it out," said the majority leader in reference to a possible amendment on a change to a 0.08 alcohol level as evidence of drunken driving. "Here's the script, then," Tim Pawlenty concluded, "on 0.08 we'd prefer to keep it out, but members can vote as free agents."

Amendments relating to guns and abortion are always possibilities because of the special passions these issues generate. In Minnesota the majority party could look forward to such amendments on the health and human services and state government omnibus bills. DFLers who opposed concealed weapons legislation were outnumbered in the senate, so they had to fight every step of the way. A number went so far as to boycott a meeting of the Senate Finance Committee, which prevented the committee from having a quorum necessary to transact business that included a concealed-weapon amendment to a shooting-range bill. "We were so desperate, we had no other choice," explained the boycotting DFLers. This, of course, was a dangerous strategy, since the other side could prevent quorums as well.

Amendments are offered to weaken, or even kill, bills more often than to strengthen, or perfect, them. Amendments may be a better means of opposition than a frontal assault on the bill itself. The senate DFL leadership strategy over concealed weapons in Minnesota is a good example. The bill would have required that permits be issued to citizens who pass a criminal background check, have no serious mental illnesses, and have been trained in the use of the weapon being purchased. It had been lobbied heavily by the National Rifle Association (NRA), had been supported by Governor Ventura, and had passed the house. Sen. Pat Pariseau, a Republican, offered the house bill as an amendment to another bill on the senate floor. DFLers, however, in opposing concealed weapons, offered an amendment to Pariseau's amendment. It would keep the current permit system intact but would grant an administrative appeal to applicants denied permits. In short, it weakened the intent of the house bill and the Pariseau amendment by not allowing more people to carry arms. The senate adopted the amendment, leaving the law unchanged in any major respect. The weakening amendment strategy had succeeded.[9]

The so-called "poison pill" amendment is intended to kill a bill—either by adding a provision that drives away enough votes or that makes the measure inoperable if enacted. A bill to require booster seats in automobiles was challenged on the floor of the Maryland house by members who questioned whether it could and should be implemented with respect to out-of-state vehicles. The poison pill amendment here provided that the provision would not go into effect until neighboring states had the same requirement—which was not likely to occur in the near future. The amendment would have crippled the bill, so the speaker requested that the chair of the committee reporting the bill move to recommit it.

An amendment can kill a bill even when that is not the intended consequence, as was the case with regard to a house bill that would have created the Office of Women's Health in the State Health Department of Maryland. Pro-life advocates intended to introduce an amendment to that bill that would ban the use of state funds for abortion clinics. The majority party caucus was split on the issue. Thus, although the governor and the speaker both backed the bill, the Women's Caucus decided not to risk opening the session to such a divisive issue. Instead of pursuing legislation, the Women's Caucus decided discretion was the better part of valor. It asked the governor to establish the office administratively, rather than through legislation, which he agreed to do.

Political Ramifications

Strategy is an important part of getting a bill passed; it is also an important part of preparing for the next election. Legislators not only plan ways in which to persuade their colleagues to vote one way or another, they also conduct their lawmaking with the next election seldom far from their minds. How they gain or lose votes as a result of positions they take and votes they cast may not be a conscious calculation, but it is a consideration nonetheless.

Electoral Positioning

Individual members consider what they support and what they oppose in light of the constituencies and constituents they represent. Implicitly for the most part, but explicitly on occasion, they ask whether a bill will help, hurt, or not really affect their district. And they also ask whether their positions on a bill will help, hurt, or not really affect them with their constituents. Most matters that come before the legislature do not resonate at all in their constituency. Legislators have a free ride there, at least as far as the constituency is concerned. Some matters arouse one or several organized interest groups that have a presence in the district they represent. On these matters legislators take into account whether the group is part of their base support or is generally opposed to them, as well as the group's feelings about the issue, its strength, and so forth.

Legislators try to explain their choices to their constituents and justify their votes. Sometimes this means disassociating themselves from the legislature, from their chamber, from their party, or even from their own vote (the latter being the most difficult to do). They will explain and justify in the district, in the state house, and on the floor of the chamber. "If my constituents are not to be well served by a bill," said a Michigan legislator, "the floor is the place for me to remind them it wasn't my fault." [10] Legislators would rather take credit and escape blame, which ought not to come as a surprise to anyone.

The overwhelming majority of issues do not involve partisanship and have little bearing on the constituency or the election. There is no political relevance one way or the other, and no way that the legislator could imagine a hit piece during his or her next campaign. The only question regarding these bills is: "What does it make sense to do?" Some issues, however, can have a great impact on people in the district. In Vermont, civil unions was one such issue. Every member of the legislature thought about where constituents stood on the measure that would afford gay couples rights similar to those of heterosexual couples. School finance was another. In crafting legislation to revise Act 60, the Ways and Means chair, Marron, kept checking with his colleagues in the house Republican caucus to see how they reacted on the basis of visiting with their constituents in the district. They doubted what Marron was proposing and several expressed critical views of their constituents on raising taxes. "I think we're going down the wrong path," one objected. Deciding on a tax increase would be a tough sell, mainly because of the opposition of constituents.

In Washington, Speaker Frank Chopp explained the Democratic legislative party's objectives: "Our first and foremost concern was doing the right thing for the people of the state. But we want to keep doing that, and that means we have to have a sustainable majority." [11] During the 2002 session the Democrats, who had narrow majorities in each chamber, had to deal with a budget shortfall without raising taxes. Otherwise, they feared they would lose their majorities. They could not help but recall that when they controlled the legislature in 1993 they approved a large tax increase. In the following year's election, they lost control. On their part, Washington Republicans were hoping that the Democrats would have to raise taxes so they would have a powerful issue in the November election. As one legislator described the session, "the battle is not won on the floor; the battle is won in November." The legislature ended its session with the Democrats claiming that "We did it, without a tax increase," and the Republicans rebuttal: "It's just pasted together, and you can bet the Democrats will raise taxes later on." To protect themselves, members of the Washington house insisted on putting the transportation package they were about to pass on the ballot. Otherwise, an initiative to roll back the transportation tax was sure to be circulated. The voters might repeal the law in a referendum and also punish legislators at the polls.

While individual legislators are concerned about their own electoral prospects, party leaders also care about their members' electoral prospects. According to Speaker Walter Freed of Vermont: "Politics is staying on the right side of the electorate." That means *responding* to what voters want, or, just as likely, *anticipating* what they want.

Take the issue of civil unions, for example. When the state's highest court put gay marriage on the legislative agenda, the Vermont house passed a civil unions bill after a stormy struggle. The senate president, Peter Shumlin, had second thoughts about the bill when his chamber had to act. Although he favored the legislation as a "moral imperative," he was afraid that it might cost

Democrats control of the legislature. He talked with Governor Dean about waiting to study the issue after the 2000 election, but Dean turned down any thought of delay.[12]

Just as Shumlin feared, the civil unions issue helped give Republicans control of the house in the 2000 election. Newly elected Republicans ran on a platform of repealing civil unions. Some wanted to modify it by enacting legislation that prohibited marriage between two members of the same sex, and others wanted absolute repeal. Something had to be done to help these Republicans get reelected. The strategy for the house speaker was to protect his new majority of eighty-three members in the house. The election would be fought out locality by locality, but still what went on at the capitol in Montpelier would be relevant to the election.

Each party tries to put the other in a bad position vis-à-vis the state's voters. If an issue can be exploited politically, the majority party will advance it. But more often the minority party, by means of amendment in committee and on the floor, will try to put the majority in a position that creates difficulties for its more vulnerable members. Maryland Republicans, according to Speaker Cas Taylor, "have the luxury of not governing." They had little prospect of seeing their amendments adopted, but they offered ones to provide benefits for citizens, such as an earned income tax credit for seniors. Democrats had to work within budgetary constraints and opposed such amendments. All along the line Republicans in the Maryland house and senate would criticize administration and legislative priorities—all of which were grist for the election campaign.

Protecting Members Electorally

Leaders have to take responsibility for protecting members from unnecessary political risk. In doing so, it is not that they try to respond to what people want, as might be indicated in public opinion polls. They have a pretty good idea of where various constituencies stand on major issues and what rank-and-file citizens would generally like. Their strategic stance is more to try to anticipate the public's response to legislative action, or inaction, by their party. More specifically, their concern is whether their legislative party would lose votes at the next election if it supported or opposed a measure or failed to get something done. Leaders and members alike operate in a manner that political scientist Jane Mansbridge refers to as "anticipatory representation," whereby legislators try to please voters in the next election rather than respond to constituents' preferences issue by issue.[13]

A senior leaders' meeting in the Maryland house provides an illustration of how public influence operates in the issue domain of health care. Democratic leaders expressed the fear that, because of the governor's inaction on the issue, their party would suffer with the public. "When we end this session, where are we?" one leader asked. "We have to be able to say we helped senior citizens with prescription drugs," responded another. "I want protection when I go home," added yet another. That means, added the majority leader, that "We have to tell the governor through a joint resolution or something else that he ought to put it in next year's budget." [14] The leadership group decided that three committees, with jurisdiction over health, would prepare a resolution to that effect—a choice they were satisfied would help their members politically.

Membership protection does not drive the process, but it is often a potent consideration. Members think of themselves in electoral terms and leaders think of their parties the same way. One device they use is justification to the public of the policies they had advocated and gotten enacted. During a DFL caucus, held after the senate, the house, and the governor had arrived at a compromise in 2000, one senator asked Roger Moe: "How do we even explain the tax bill?" Moe's response: "I'm writing your campaign literature now: DFL'ers deliver permanent tax cuts in 1997, 98, 99, 2000—and deliver strategic investments to help our children and our Seniors. That's how you explain it." [15] The following year a similar discussion took place in the DFL senate caucus. Some members were worried about how the distribution of school funds by the state would play out. "It is a very sensitive political issue," said one. "You can't explain in a brochure the merits of a formula," said another. "This is going to be an issue in the next election in the 'burbs,' " volunteered another. "You don't want to abandon good policy," added Sen. Julie Sabo, "but how do you explain good policy?"

Legislators are always at risk for the positions they take and the votes they cast. Naturally, they try to reduce the risks. That means they try not to take on issues when nothing is likely to be gained as a result. Why go on record merely for the sake of doing so? The records of legislators already provide a multiplicity of targets for their opponents. In Minnesota DFLers did not want to vote for a sales-tax extension for two principal reasons. First, ideologically the DFL opposed the sales tax. Second, DFLers were not about to vote for a provision to raise taxes when it could be abandoned in conference anyway. Why have such a vote added to their record when it might have negative political consequences without any positive ones?

In Ohio the Republican senate president and Finance Committee chair, along with staff, met on the amendments that would be offered to the budget bill on the floor. The minority Democrats had filed about seventy amendments. The Republican leaders decided to take up four or five for debate, but not ones that would be exploited by the Democrats politically. "If they try to fry a member in a campaign," said Douglas White, the Finance chair, "all bets are off." Analogously, why vote against a popular measure if that measure is sure to pass? A credit-scoring bill in Washington, which was sponsored by the Democratic administration and Democrats in the legislature, was generally opposed among the Republicans. But despite problems with the bill, most Republicans supported it. If they voted against it, the Democrats could make use of their vote politically. The bill passed the house 94–4, which was not a true indication of the support and opposition it engendered.

One way to provide cover for members of one party is by getting votes from the other. Washington's senate Democrats got twenty-one of their members to vote for a gas tax, part of a transportation package, in the 2002 session. But they wanted ten or so Republicans as well. That way, the Democrats thought, they would be protected from partisan attack. Another way to provide cover is to enable members to vote both ways, by offering amendments that permit them to cast popular votes while they also cast controversial votes. Both-way voting is not that common, but it does occur on budget bills. John E. McDonough recounts how members of the Massachusetts house had added about $200 million to the bottom line of the budget bill. But many members who themselves added, or voted for, amendments increasing total expenditures also voted "no" on the final 84–72 roll call to indicate displeasure with the house's inability to keep spending down. "If they felt a contradiction in their actions," McDonough writes, "they kept silent about it." [16] "We need cover," declared a member in a DFL caucus discussion of a tough vote ahead. The majority leader counseled his members: "Vote against the amendment, then if we need cover, we'll bring up the other amendment."

Sometimes political protection involves going through the motions to cover one's flanks. The strategy of Vermont senate Democrats was essentially to have a bill to modify Act 60, even though they believed no bill had a chance of being enacted into law. But who could be sure? And since the Republican house was putting together amendatory legislation, the Democratic senate felt it also had to grapple with the issue of school finance. Senate President Pro Tem Shumlin personally favored Act 60, as it stood. But Republicans had made the act a focus of their 2000 legislative campaign. Shumlin did not really want change, but he realized that because of strong opposition to Act 60 by almost half of the towns in the state, senate Democrats had to be prepared. Strategizing on the bill, the senate president pro tem noted that everyone favored some modification and that Governor Dean wanted the Finance Committee to produce something and not merely wait for the house to act first. "It's time for you all to hatch a plan," he told his lieutenants. "This bill probably will not become law, but we have to pretend it will." Figure it out and write up something that the caucus will support, he instructed. His instructions required staff to explore ways of finding revenues to finance the bill. Car rental and leasing taxes; higher taxes on beer, wine, and liquor, on snack foods and soft drinks, and on video games were all raised as possibilities. "Let's remember," said the Finance chair, "all this has to do is pass the Senate. It doesn't have to become law."

Getting a Party Edge

An important strategic objective is to gain partisan advantage on the few significant measures in which the two parties are at odds. This involves making distinctions between bills passed by the two majority parties in a divided legislature. The tax bill passed in Minnesota by senate DFLers differed substantially from that passed by house Republicans. Partisans of each claimed that their bill was the better one. A senate Republican, Kenric Scheevel, put it this way: "It seems to me the tax bill in front of us is a nice ham, but the house bill has got the whole hog." [17] Playing for partisan advantage also involves the introduction of amendments by one party in an effort to put members of the other party on record in a way that can be used against them in the next election. Senate DFLers, for instance, were looking for some way to criticize the tax-cut bill that was about to be passed by the house. One possible strategy would be to introduce amendments in the senate to the house bill that might force senate Republicans to vote against an income tax cut. If Republicans could be put in a position of opposing such a provision, Democrats would have a good campaign issue.

Criticism and blame are heaped on the other party's proposals. In Minnesota, in response to the passage of a Republican tax bill in the house, the DFL minority leadership in that body argued that first, the size of the tax cut means that there would not be enough money for education; second, anyway, cutting property taxes and a state takeover of a bigger share of school costs have been Democratic priorities for years; and third, an economic downturn could threaten the surplus.[18] Ohio minority Democrats challenged the majority Republicans on the budget that was being voted on the senate floor, trying to make a case that would resonate with the electorate. First, the Republicans' budget does not respond to the supreme court decision with the required overhaul of the school finance system; second, it raises taxes and cuts local funds; third, it requires localities to levy more in taxes; and fourth, it cuts basic services overall.

In the New York battle of the budget, Democratic assembly speaker Sheldon Silver's stance vis-à-vis Republican governor George Pataki illustrates how the blame game can be played.[19] The speaker, a supporter of public education, engaged in a public campaign attacking the governor's proposals to reduce state education spending by $1.2 billion in 2003–2004 and portraying him as an enemy of education. In his assault, positioning himself for photo ops among four-year-olds in pre-kindergarten classes, the speaker made no mention of how he would pay for restoring education cuts. He also kept his distance from advocating tax increases. Let Pataki take the blame. As one observer pointed out, even if local school districts raised their property tax to pay for pre-kindergarten programs, people would blame their local elected officials and school boards and, perhaps, the governor. Silver's stance would also help his Democratic assembly members from suburban districts where education is the major issue. "He is providing real political capital for his marginal suburban members, particularly in the downstate suburbs," was one explanation of his strategy.

Occasionally the contest between partisan sides on major issues extends outside of the legislature as well as in it. With the legislature in special session negotiating a budget and tax settlement in 2001, the Minnesota Republican Party ran a statewide radio advertisement that blamed the senate DFL for obstructing tax relief and reform. The sixty-second spot featured a woman's voice accusing DFLers of "fooling around and playing games" and intending to "shut down government" because, in their view, "tax relief isn't as important as new spending." The DFL objected, but Republicans refused to pull the ad.[20]

Positioning vis-à-vis the electorate involves free media far more often than paid media. Individual legislators, legislative party leaders, the governor, and others engaged in the lawmaking process all attempt to use the print and electronic media in their efforts to enact legislation and not lose electorally. How do they defend their positions and minimize damage that may be done by press accounts? How do they attack the other side and win the press over to their side? Individual legislators write columns in local weeklies. Leaders visit with editorial boards, hold press conferences, and make themselves available for radio or, if at all possible, television interviews.

Ember Reichgott Junge, a former member of the Minnesota senate, describes the battle of press conferences between Republicans and Democrats during the 2000 budget negotiations. After a DFL press conference, house Republicans responded. "It's not phony money, it's taxpayer's money," Speaker Sviggum said, holding up fake money with the caption: "Give it all Back." Majority Leader Pawlenty raised up white paper with doctored pictures of the senate and house DFL leaders, each wearing a pirate hat. "They have a boatload of Minnesota's money and it is time the pirates be thrown overboard and we give the money back," he said. [21]

Media dueling in Minnesota went on the next year, as the house and senate fought their battle over the budget in public. House Republicans, especially, focused on communications aimed at persuading the public of the merits of their respective agendas. Each party used the unveiling of its tax bill as an opportunity to claim credit and attack the opposition. "This plan is bigger and better than Governor Ventura's," claimed Speaker Sviggum. It would return all of the state surplus back to the people and would go a long way toward property tax reform. The contest within the legislature had become a public engagement, the objectives of which were to affect the immediate battle over law and the longer-term battle over partisan control.

Working It Out

Key legislative strategies in lawmaking are designed to reach agreement, gain the majorities needed to vote measures to final passage, and minimize electoral risk. Throughout the process legislators try to resolve issues by negotiating or bargaining—with one another, with the executive, and with interest groups— until a settlement is reached or sufficient votes are secured.

Deliberation and negotiation intermingle in practice. The merits enter into many discussions that are intended to arrive at a deal. Certain "merits" are chosen, while others are dropped by contending participants. When differences have to be resolved, negotiation and deliberation may take place simultaneously. Efforts are made by contenders to persuade one another that a settlement is fair in terms of the merits accorded to each side. Joseph M. Bessette refers to bargaining, rather than negotiating, but for present purposes the two are essentially the same, and usually involve deliberative elements.[22] The point is that in the lawmaking process neither deliberation on the one hand nor negotiating on the other are pure forms of activity.

Payoffs and Payments

The discussion of pork and projects in the popular press would lead one to believe that lawmaking depends almost entirely on such currency. True, in their representational role legislators try to get as much money, material, and employment for their districts as possible. Not only do they believe "bringing home the bacon" is an important part of their job, but they also think that it helps them get reelected. For the most part what legislators can do for their districts depends on leaders of the majority party and the governor as well. Legislative leaders and/or the governor, therefore, can use resources at their disposal in their bargaining to build support for a bill. And they do use them when necessary to win one or several votes on a measure that they deem important. For the most part, however, what legislators obtain for their districts depends on considerations other than one-shot payments. Such considerations include overall loyalty to the legislative party, their service on the committee where allotments are made, their need for electoral help, and, especially, fairness in the treatment of members (albeit with majority members getting a fairer shake than minority members). As a member of the Minnesota senate said, "Every time we design an omnibus [budget] bill, we try to build in balance." In an education finance bill, for instance, the balance has to be among the metro, suburban, and rural districts of Minnesota. The balance may not be perfect, but it usually suffices so that enough senators are willing to vote for the finance bill. The power of legislative leaders may only be used to reward members infrequently, but it is there. Members expect that if they go along they will get along—and that if they do not toe the line on the few partisan issues where their votes are needed, they may lose out when benefits are distributed. In most instances their behavior is shaped by these expectations.

The fact is that the legislature has only a limited amount of money for pork and projects. In the 2001 budget the Vermont legislature had extremely little to spend locally, a $20,000 project here, a smaller project there. The Ohio legislature had a system of "earmarking," whereby projects could be designated by the legislature, but it was still up to an executive agency director to fund them if they were deemed worthwhile. In 2001 there was hardly any pork to hand out in Ohio. Some nominal monies went to majority party senators who were in trouble in their districts, and a few majority party members got earmarked funds in the house.

The capital construction budget in Maryland illustrates the limits on the use of projects in negotiating for support. The senate had only $17.5 million to play with, which amounted to only $360,000 per senate district if it was spread equally. The total did not have to be divided equally, but it did have to be meted out "fairly," so that every area of the state got something. The capital budget subcommittee required that projects be worthwhile—that is, community need and community support (including a local contribution) had to be demonstrated. The more people affected, the better. And, if they were to be funded, projects had to be ready for construction. On the house side committee chairs were provided for and the various delegations consulted in the distribution of projects for legislators' districts. For example, at one hearing before the subcommittee a community recreation center was proposed for West Baltimore at a cost of $750,000. Testimony made a case for need, community support, the mayor's consent, and past progress on other projects. "Will the local match be ready?" asked the chair. The answer was in the affirmative. In choosing projects, the subcommittee chair met with representatives from the major regions of the state to establish guidelines and negotiate among contenders. Later negotiations included senators and their house counterparts.

Exceptions are made. Some legislators are denied pork and projects entirely. Despite the emphasis on merit and fairness in Maryland, senators can be singled out for "bad" behavior. Those who vote against the budget are not, in the view of legislative leaders, entitled to benefit from items in it. Thus, the requests of a few minority party senators who opposed the budget bill were not honored in the capital budget. The year before one senator not only voted against the budget but also introduced an amendment on the floor and called for a roll call vote with the intention of using the issue politically. That was considered beyond the pale, so any projects for his district were denied in the capital bonding bill.

"If you're not going to vote for the bill," said Ohio's senate president Finan, "you are not part of the process." Among other things, that means dissenting members reap no rewards for their districts—customary discipline in many legislative bodies. Therefore, chances are that if the minority party coheres in opposition, its members will get nothing. But if the minority party provides some votes for a budget bill, even though most minority members vote against it, the situation will be different. For example, in return for the necessary votes to raise the sales tax in Ohio, Democrats received about $140 million in projects and programs that otherwise would not have been in the budget. After some Democrats voted for the Republican budget in the Minnesota house, the majority leader, Tim Pawlenty, sent a note to the assistant minority leader thanking him for the Democratic votes. The note was written on an amendment that Pawlenty would have introduced striking Democratic projects from the bill if the Democrats failed to provide votes for the budget bill. Republicans, moreover, had sweetened the budget bill in order to attract some minority members, and they were successful in doing so.

Normally, legislators may be won over by those benefits that can be conferred on their districts. On occasion, however, they agree to vote for the budget in return for extra-district accommodation. Such was the case with passage of the budget in 2002 in Washington. One of the bills approved by the House Ways and Means Committee would allow former public-hospital paramedics who are now employed by fire departments to join more lucrative pension funds. Unless this bill passed, one of its supporters refused to vote for the budget. With a two-vote margin in the house, and with no help expected from the Republicans, the Democrats felt they had little choice but to endorse the member's bill.[23] The year before, two senate Republicans agreed to vote for the Democrats' budget bill. One succeeded in getting $72 million in restoration of nursing home funds, and the other got an additional $10 million for aid to cities.

The members who barter their votes for district benefits are few, but these cases tend to be exaggerated in the folklore of legislatures. The ability for legislative leaders to provide pork and projects scarcely fuels the process, as some might believe. But it does help lubricate it so that the business of putting together a majority can proceed more expeditiously.

Trades and Hostages

Trading one bill for another is another important method employed in legislative negotiations. If the senate passes HB 159, the house agrees to pass SB 72. The two bills may be completely unrelated, but the fate of one could hinge on that of the other. Although trading does occur, it is not commonplace. Ordinarily, it takes place during the closing days of the session. If it is only implicit, and reflects the legislative norm of reciprocity, where members support one another whenever they can, a trade is not actually being made. Reciprocity or trade, both parties benefit from the transactions. "We passed her bill unanimously," said a house leader of a senate leader's bill. "Well, then, we can expect something from her," replied a staff aide to the speaker. Logrolling is one type of trade, usually between individuals but also between chambers. "I will vote for your bill, if you vote for mine," is the normal exchange. The major trading that goes on at the leadership level is when one bill's advancement depends on another's. Committee chairs manage the agendas within their domains, while party leaders arrange for trades in order to gain necessary support at the caucus or chamber stage or to reach an agreement with the other house. The discussion that took place in the Maryland speaker's office is illustrative. The question was who to deal with in the senate. "Bromwell is difficult to get to change, Hoffman will listen," went the conversation. "With Miller, let's hope there is something he wants over here so that we can get what we want over there."

Trading becomes especially critical as the legislative session draws to a close. In Maryland, for example, the passage of a DNA testing bill was thought to have little chance until it was given the green light by the senate president in exchange for the Legislative Black Caucus giving up on another bill. The caucus had supported a moratorium on executions, but it did not have the votes to pass the bill. Yet proponents continued their fight, and the threat of a filibuster loomed. By refusing to back down, African American legislators could have interfered with the heavy schedule on the final day of the session, and consequently other bills could not have been taken up and passed. The deal offered to the caucus included not only passage of the DNA bill, but also legislation to study whether two-time felons should be allowed to vote. According to the delegate who headed the caucus: "When they [his colleagues] realized they couldn't pass the moratorium . . . they saw this as something to walk away with, instead of walking away with nothing." The senate's president also got what he needed: a controversial issue was put aside so that the senate could complete its business.[24]

An important reason why so many bills are passed in the final days of the legislative session of a legislature is that they are being held "hostage" by one chamber that wants something from the other. If, for instance, the senate has passed a bill that has to be acted on by the house, one way for the senate to have leverage is to hold a bill that the house wants passed by the senate. Bills passed by one chamber often will be held in the committee of the other chamber. Anticipating end-of-the-session trades, Senate Majority Leader Moe suggested to his DFL colleagues in caucus on several occasions: "Let's keep as many House-filed [bills] in the bank as possible." And that is the practice just about everywhere. Maryland's party and committee leaders constantly look for leverage to use with the other body, focusing on individual members and what each of them wanted. The house, for instance, kept its eyes on the location of the senate president's bills; it wanted to have something to trade in order to get senate agreement on the construction of a new house office building.

The result is that many bills are kept for the negotiations that conclude the legislative session. The former speaker of the Vermont house recalls the "annual end-of-session ritual and the normal 'hostage' taking of bills" between the house and the senate. His role in this positioning was "threatening the Senate with a promise not to move their priorities unless they agreed to move those of the House." [25] During the tenure of Willie Brown as speaker and Patrick Nolan as minority leader of the California assembly, "Each searched for the levers to force the other into concessions, each linking passage of one unrelated issue with another unrelated issue. . . . It usually took until the last night of the legislative session to unravel the political knots as each side tried to bluff the other." [26] A number of bills are set aside to be used in negotiations over the principal bill of the session, ordinarily the budget. The session ends, but many of the set-asides do not become part of last-minute trades and die, having passed one house but not the other. In New York, for example, after the 2001 session ended the senate majority leader, Joseph Bruno, accused the assembly of "holding everything in the state, practically, hostage." As evidence, he noted that 900 bills had passed the senate but not the assembly. In rebuttal, Speaker Sheldon Silver pointed out that 823 bills had passed the assembly but not the senate.[27]

Negotiations

On most issues the objective of the legislature is to build consensus through mutual accommodation. While disagreement is endemic to lawmaking in the legislature, working toward agreement also characterizes much of what goes on. At every stage, legislators negotiate in one way or another to try to meet objections that are posed, often by making changes in the bill in contention. If there is a problem with a bill—in committee, in caucus, or on the floor—a legislator may request that it be set aside in order for the problem to be resolved. At any given floor session it is likely that members will object to one or several bills. Such objection is expressed differently in various states.

In Maryland, for example, a request is made for a "special order." "I have no problem if you special order it, so we can talk it over," said a senator to a colleague who wondered if a bill was specific enough in defining an educator who sexually abuses a child. In Minnesota, however, "progress" is requested, and normally granted, if a member is not ready when a bill is called up or would like more time. Or a bill can be "tabled" if there is a problem that legislators would like to work out. Sometimes objection is made, in which case the bill's chief author responds during the course of debate. In Vermont if there is objection on the floor, the normal procedure is to settle the matter before going on. The house may recess while members assemble and discuss an amendment. All of these devices allow pause and/or postponement, during which members try to resolve their differences.

Occasionally an amendment can be drafted quickly, and the bill's progress resumes. Sometimes the bill returns to the committee for the drafting of an amendment. For example, a bill to allow optional county license plates led to questions on the Maryland house floor as to residency of the owner and the vehicle. It was special-ordered until the following day so that a clarifying amendment could be prepared. A bill's manager normally will accept an amendment that builds support for the legislation without seriously weakening the bill's intent. Thus, much of legislative business is done through "friendly" or "perfecting" amendments—that is, by accommodation.

Negotiations are conducted not only by legislators themselves but also by interest group lobbyists, who are either proponents or opponents of a measure in contest. Sometimes lobbyists are delegated the job of forging agreement between opposing sides on a measure before the legislature will take it on. The legislature, then, is likely to enact the measure that the groups have agreed to, as long as no opposition remains. Sometimes, a committee or subcommittee chair or a legislative leader functioning as mediator steers the discussion among the groups, pressing for agreement. At the very least, committees take into account the cases made by groups in testimony and lobbying before they report a bill. Either way, interest groups are very much party to negotiations on legislation that affects them.

One method that legislatures—and governors—employ to get agreement is the formation of a commission or task force, which includes as members representatives of the major interest groups. Everyone wants to have a say in the resolution of the matter and to sit on the body charged with conducting a study and/or making recommendations. In his book on lawmaking in Massachusetts, McDonough discusses the inclination of the legislature to create special commissions to examine complex and/or controversial problems. "When outsiders can be brought together in a way that leads to consensus," he writes, "the route to legislative approval can be considered smoothed." In his effort to improve health care, McDonough convinced legislative leaders to establish a commission that would bring key parties together to figure out what should happen to the state's health care rate-setting system when the law mandating it expired. Appointed as commission members were all the usual suspects: the hospital association, life insurance association, HMOs, BlueCross BlueShield, AFL-CIO, Associated Industries of Massachusetts, a community health center, a health care advocacy group, and others. It should be noted, however, that commission members could not reach agreement because, according to McDonough:

> Health care providers and insurers simply had too much at stake to make their deals at the commission stage, which preceded normal legislative considerations. Final deals usually were cut much after in quieter rooms where the brokers were Ways and Means chairs, House Speakers, or Senate Presidents.[28]

A diverse and conflicting membership obviously makes it more difficult to reach a settlement. But should participants hammer out agreement, the legislature is inclined to ratify it. In Ohio, for instance, a 2001 task force on unemployment compensation, which had representation from the major interests, agreed on a bill that made major revisions in the process. It sailed through the insurance committee and passed the senate by a 33–0 vote.

If groups come to the legislature united behind a measure, their chances at getting some of what they want are excellent; it is hardly surprising, therefore, that legislators encourage them to work out their differences beforehand. Richard Finan orchestrated an arrangement with Ohio State University that allowed it to change its investment strategy and then had it adopted in the conference committee report on the budget. OSU, however, was not satisfied with the language of the amendment, and other universities also objected. Finan's rejoinder was to advise the universities to get together and reach agreement. "Then come to the legislature," he said, "and we'll see about a bill."

The legislature normally plays a substantial role in helping groups arrive at compromise. Perhaps the most dramatic example is the "napkin deal," as recounted by James Richardson in his book on Willie Brown's legislative career. As speaker of the California assembly, Brown, assisted by Sen. Bill Lockyer, tried to get representatives of the insurance companies, trial lawyers, doctors, and manufacturers to agree to sweeping changes in the civil liability laws of the state. He brought them together in a private dining room at Frank Fat's, the speaker's favorite Sacramento restaurant. As the night wore on, with the talks still not resolving issues, Brown went from participant to participant in order to help expedite the process. Finally, the groups closed a deal, the outline of which they scrawled in ink on a cloth napkin. It was the final step in negotiations that had been going on for days. Legislation implementing the agreement was quickly drafted, and it passed on the final night of the legislative session that year. Brown regarded this deal to be one of his most notable accomplishments, and Lockyer justified it as follows: "The public is better served when these groups are trying to mend rather than tear the fabric of society." [29]

A deal can be consummated anywhere the so-called "players" come to the table. Usually negotiations involving conflicting interest groups take place at the committee stage. A bill is introduced and referred to committee, then representatives of the groups, in the parlance of legislative negotiations, "come to the table" and are steered toward a resolution they can "all sign off on." Interest groups want a seat at the table and legislators want all of them to sign off on a measure. That makes things much easier, as was the case when, under the management of the Economic Matters Committee of the Maryland house, the Maryland Port Administration on one side of the issue and the environmental community on the other side managed to craft a delicate balance with regard to the prohibition of dumping dredge in the Chesapeake Bay except for one location. Each group backed the bill that emerged from the negotiations.

The way the Minnesota legislature handled a measure to deal with an impending electricity shortage illustrates how consensus can be built, even when the interest groups concerned have very different objectives. The electricity issue certainly had the potential to become polarized. On the one hand, the business community and major utilities were seeking deregulation of electricity pricing, which they maintained was necessary to stimulate investment in plants and facilities. On the other hand, consumer, environmental, and labor groups wanted greater investment in conversion, renewable energy, and cleanup activities. The Republican chair of the house committee and the DFL chair of the senate committee were determined to have a bill that would be supported by a wide range of stakeholders, and by members of both parties. Both chairs "made it clear from the beginning," said a lobbyist, "that everyone was going to see some forward steps in the bill, but that nobody was going to get everything they wanted." The bill passed the house 98–35 and the senate 64–0.[30]

Compromise

Although many Americans regard it as "selling out," compromise is a virtual requirement of democratic politics and of the legislative process. Richard Posner makes the case that representative democracy encourages compromise—that is, compromise of interests, not of ideas:

> The ethics of political responsibility require a willingness to compromise, to dirty one's hands, to flatter, cajole, pander, bluff, and lie, to make unprincipled package deals, and thus to forgo the prideful self-satisfaction that comes from self-conscious purity and devotion to principle.[31]

Legislators are disposed to compromise, although on occasion the parties in interest cannot quite come together.

Legislators individually have to compromise between what they believe in on the one hand, and what they are willing to settle for on the other. Most realize that if they stick to their principles they may lose an issue completely, having done nothing at all to promote their cause. A good example of the willingness to compromise is Rep. Bill Lippert, who chaired the House Judiciary Committee in Vermont when civil unions was first debated. Lippert would have preferred a gay marriage bill, but recognizing that it would be impossible to achieve, he settled for less.[32]

On most bills that a legislature enacts compromises occur not only within members but also among members. They are negotiated somewhere along the line—in the formulation of the measure; in committee consideration; or on the floor, with the other house, or with the governor. Compromises occur when one or more positions on a bill are in conflict. The options in enacting a measure are either to put it to a pass-or-fail vote on the merits or to effect a compromise that gains support from both sides. Compromise is usually the preferred option: first, because if the votes for passage are not there it is necessary to build support, and second, because even if the votes are there, legislatures try to build as much consensus as possible.

Bessette tries to distinguish compromises that are strictly bargains from those that are a result of deliberation. However, the distinction is difficult to make.[33] The substantive merits are at issue, and it is these that are negotiated by the participating parties. In one case negotiations may result in a modification that each side regards as an improvement. This, according to Bessette, would be a deliberative process. In the other case negotiations may result in a modification in which each side gives up some of what it considers to be the merits. This is clearly a less deliberative process, but it is by no means bereft of deliberation. The merits, as such, are less relevant when inducements and trades are the currency, but they still drive the process. Moreover, the norm is for some type of compromise to be engaged in, so that each side is better off in terms of winning what it deems meritorious than if it had lost a vote.

Although compromise would appear to be required in the legislative process, only the budget bill or bills have to be passed annually or biannually as the state constitution dictates. Passing a budget bill necessitates any number of compromises, culminating in the reconciling of differences among the senate, the house, and the governor. Even in a state where both houses of the legislature and the executive are controlled by the same party, differences in budget positions can be substantial. Take Ohio, a state in which the Republicans are in control. A senate-house conference committee had to resolve differences such as the following:

- More business taxes, favored by the governor and the house but opposed by the senate.
- Additional 2 percent cuts in most agency operating budgets and a 6 percent reduction in local government and library funds, adopted by the senate but not by the house or governor.
- A multistate lottery proposed by the governor and the senate but opposed by the house.
- Acceleration of the use tax on leased vehicles—a senate provision only.

- A two-day sales-tax holiday proposed by the house but restricted by the senate to shoe and clothing purchases of $200 or less.
- Differences over the amounts of money to be removed from the state's rainy-day fund and from tobacco-settlement accounts.
- Differences between the house and senate on taxes on trust income, passive investment companies, and business transactions between affiliates.[34]

There are other instances in which legislatures have to pass measures. When the state's highest court requires action, such as a revision of school funding formulas or a redistricting plan, the legislature is compelled to respond. In other cases, such as federal requirements or the possible loss of federal funding, the legislature is under great pressure to act. Such action, of course, is apt to require compromise. Most legislative introductions, however, do not have to be enacted. The legislature can let them expire, and thus there is less pressure to compromise. Obviously, die-hard opponents reject compromise. Many bills are disposed of right off the bat, usually in committee. These bills either have little support—and, in some instances, not even the support of the sponsor—or strong opposition from the majority leadership and/or a committee chair. The other bills, however, are pushed toward passage, which entails compromise of one sort or another along the route. Proponents almost always are willing to sacrifice something in order to gain passage; opponents can hang tougher. Sometimes, too, proponents are willing to tailor a bill simply to broaden their base of support.

Some issues, however, do not lend themselves to compromise. These are issues—like abortion, guns, and gay rights—where legislators have strong convictions, interest groups are insistent, and substantial numbers of constituents are in one camp or another. It may appear better, both morally and politically, to meet these issues head on rather than to cede the high ground. Tom Loftus, who served as speaker of the Wisconsin assembly, acknowledged that "although the legislature is designed to produce compromise, the process will not work if the issue is one where strong interest groups do not seek compromise, and the politicians can discern no point of consensus among their constituents." Such is the case with abortion, where the opposing interest groups—pro-choice and pro-life—believe that any compromise is a sign of weakness and a step toward defeat.[35] Many legislators do not want to have to deal with this issue, but if one side or the other can put together enough votes it will push forward with a pro-life or pro-choice measure. Compromise, however, is out of the question. Parental notification and partial-birth abortion, for example, might be viewed as middle positions by some. But they are seen as victories in the war by the pro-life side and as defeats by the other.

Civil unions legislation in Vermont also illustrates the kind of issue on which there appeared to be little room for compromise. Civil unions was enacted into law during the 2000 legislative session. The battle divided not only the legislature, but the entire state. Most people had a position and many held their positions firmly (as was discussed earlier). The November elections were fought out over the issue, and when Republicans won control of the house it was assumed that they would make a good-faith effort to repeal or modify the law. In the 2001 session the opposing sides dug in. The House Judiciary chair, Peg Flory, offered a bill to eliminate sexual orientation as a factor in deciding who receives the same rights as married couples. But members who sought to repeal civil unions did not think her bill went far enough, and those who favored civil unions wanted to leave the law alone.[36]

Even on issues such as these, compromise is always a possibility, although it may be a long shot. When it occurs, it is hard won and at the margins. Gun safety education in Maryland is illustrative of this point. The bill to require schools to offer gun education courses for children in kindergarten through the twelfth grade was prompted by a thirteen-year-old's death at the hands of a nine-year-old playing with a handgun. A dispute between gun and antigun lobbies over what should be taught, and to whom, threatened to derail the bill after it passed the senate 41–3. The differences, however, did not appear irreconcilable. Both sides favored teaching gun safety in schools through the twelfth grade. They could accept a variety of teaching programs as well. But they disagreed over who would control the curriculum and some other matters. Many lawmakers believed that the bill was dead. One, Maggie McIntosh of the house, a sponsor of the legislation, said that the hearing in committee on the bill was "one of the best policy discussion I've had since being here." She hoped that somehow the bill would survive.[37] It did, after the bill's proponents worked and reworked it until both sides were satisfied. The compromise would allow local school boards the option of using various courses. They could use the NRA's "Eddie Eagle" program, the "In the Flesh" or "Star" programs developed by gun-control groups, or they could develop their own.

The majority party caucus is one place where compromises are fashioned. Without compromise on a number of issues, the legislative party would be unable to play a leadership role in the lawmaking process. For example, a concealed weapons bill in the 2001 session split senate DFLers in Minnesota, with rural members supporting it and urban and suburban members opposing it. Momentum shifted back and forth, with the DFL seeking to find grounds for a compromise on which most members could agree. "How should we frame it, so guys understand that we have to stick together?" one senator asked. The majority leader, Roger Moe, faced with a split, needed to know how many members he could depend on to beat back the bill legalizing concealed weapons. He also had to know how to amend the bill to keep enough members of his caucus satisfied. DFLers finally agreed on an amendment by their colleague, Steve Murphy, a hunter and NRA member, which would keep the present permit system essentially intact; they made only minor changes.

Compromise comes in a variety of forms, the most familiar of which is "splitting the difference." Differences in dollar figures, as in house and senate appropriations, can be resolved by taking a figure halfway between the two bills. Or items of similar value may be traded, with the senate getting one of its preferences in return for the house receiving one of its own. On the expansion in the budget of mass transportation in Maryland, for instance, the governor asked for a 14.3 percent increase, the house agreed to 10.3 percent, and the senate to 8.9 percent. The conference committee decided on a 9.9 percent increase. Splitting the difference can be a compromise method on nonbudgetary matters as well. A recreational crabbing bill in Maryland was opposed by waterfront property owners who objected to a license fee that they felt was substantial. The compromise exempted from the fee those who caught fewer than two dozen crabs (but about four hundred watermen who crabbed for a living still turned out in opposition to the bill).

Related to the above technique is that of simply "dividing up the pie." One side gets half the funds in question to control; the other side gets the other half. Or in the case of the Minnesota budget, in 2000 the senate, house, and governor were unable to settle their many differences. They finally negotiated a three-way split of $525 million. As described by one of the participants: "What could be a more tripartisan solution than ending the session by using a meat cleaver and splitting the spoils in thirds?" Each party agreed to use $175 million in permanent surplus revenues the way it wanted. The house Republicans opted for income tax relief. The senate DFLers divided their share among K–12 education, health care for seniors, and the environment. The governor put his money into license fee reductions and a transit initiative.[38] Everybody left the table with less than they wanted but something for which they were willing to settle.

Another common compromise model is that of "getting something—giving something." In discussing DFL strategy vis-à-vis negotiations with the governor, Roger Moe mentioned that "He'll want something, I'll want something, we'll get there." Each side comes away with part of what it wants, while giving up part. Illustrative are two major compromises agreed to by the Washington house and senate in the 2002 session. The first involved collective bargaining for state workers, which was a priority of the Democratic senate. In order to get the Republican house to endorse it, proponents agreed to civil service reforms and contracting out by state agencies. The compromise succeeded in getting sufficient Republican support in each chamber to pass it. The second compromise was on a statewide transportation plan, which the senate would endorse only if the house agreed to a congestion relief package for Puget Sound highways. House Democrats were not pleased with the highway plan, but they had to go along in order to get the statewide transportation package they desired.

Alternatively, each side may surrender provisions that the other side opposes. In the 2001 Ohio budget struggle senate Republicans, house Republicans, and the governor all gave ground. House Republicans dropped a provision for a sales-tax holiday to lure shoppers to stores and thereby boost the economy. Senate Republicans dropped their opposition to using more of the state's rainy-day fund. And Gov. Bob Taft agreed to cut spending even more than he had already done. In Minnesota that same year each party gave up something it really wanted in the budget for health and human services. "It was," according to the agency head, "a classic tough compromise." The Republican house agreed to remove language prohibiting family planning grants to agencies that provide abortions or refer women for the procedure. The DFL senate agreed to take out a new teen-pregnancy prevention program.[39] The Republicans also had to yield on a twenty-four-hour waiting period for abortions, since the senate refused to include it in the omnibus spending bill.

"Watering down" is another common method by which compromise is reached. The price of support may be to reduce the scope, penalties, or impact of a proposal. A good case in point is when concealed weapons legislation was introduced in Ohio. The bill was similar to the law in Vermont, with no requirements for a permit, firearms training, or a background check (beyond that required by federal law). A less permissive measure, such as was the law in Kentucky, would have been a compromise that some antigun legislators could endorse. It would require a written permit, proof of at least eight hours of firearms training, and would not license anyone with a criminal record. In Minnesota a proposal to establish felony penalties for chronic drunken drivers was watered down in order to gain support. That would increase sentences, but compromise would have allowed judges to reduce sentences if they thought it appropriate. One legislator complained that the resultant bill was "almost a sham." The sponsor acknowledged that the bill was not as tough as the one he had drafted, but, "You've got to crawl before you can walk. We're not even rolling over on our tummies on felony DWI." [40] A proposed tightening of the seatbelt law in Minnesota also had to be watered down in order to convince the house to agree to a senate measure. The senate recommended allowing police officers to stop drivers solely for failing to buckle up. As a compromise the house proposed that only anyone under eighteen would be required to wear a seatbelt.

Reaching Agreement

Trying to forge agreement is probably the most difficult work legislators engage in. As tough as anything else are the negotiations that transpire toward the close of the legislative session, normally on the budget but on other items as well. Former senator Ember Reichgott Junge described budgetary negotiations at the end of Minnesota's 2000 session. Leadership had closed "the big picture deal" covering tax rebates and new monies for E–12 education, health care, transportation, and bonding. Next, it would be up to a number of conference committees to work out details before the close of the session. She wrote:

> Throughout the weekend, conferees walked around bleary eyed, with no sleep. Many stayed up between 24 and 48 hours straight; some even got to 62 hours. No wonder tempers flared, tears flowed, legislators walked out, and even-tempered legislators showed frustration. . . . Virtually nothing goes on in public. Conferees meet privately in offices where they can't be found. Conference committee meeting rooms look the way a transatlantic plane looks after the end of a long flight: food everywhere, papers strewn about, chairs tipped, legislators and audience with big

bags under their eyes. People doze in their chairs, spread out over two or three chairs if they can. Time doesn't exist. It's like Las Vegas where there are no clocks on the wall. There are clocks, but they don't mean anything. Conferees announce they'll reconvene at 8 P.M. and maybe they'll get there at 10:45 P.M. They announce another offer for maybe five minutes. No response from the other side. Recess until 2 A.M. That's how it goes.[41]

Negotiating is an iterative, and therefore frustrating, business. Deals are offered, rejected, reoffered, accepted, and then fall apart—and then negotiations continue once more. On Wednesday prospects for a settlement look bright, by Thursday they are dim, and on Friday other elements have been added. The leaders reach agreement, their lieutenants are on board, but then one or the other caucus turns it down. The experience of Colorado's Joint Budget Committee, as detailed by John A. Straayer, shows how difficult it is to find compromise positions on the provisions preferred by the two houses:

> The JBC will meet for hours, even for days, as its members seek a middle ground that will be saleable to members of their respective caucuses. They bring a list of compromises on the budget lines where the chambers differ; some are accepted and some are not. Thus, the JBC must go through several iterations, slowly but surely settling out the points of difference until it has a complete budget that is acceptable to the majority party caucuses in both houses.[42]

Often negotiations fail. It is simply not possible to put together a measure that can secure sufficient support, at the very least enough votes to be reported favorably out of committee or to pass in the house or senate. In working on Act 60 Vermont's House Ways and Means Committee spent weeks on one possible revision after another. One version contained financing from Powerball; the next did not. One version did not include an increase in the sales tax; another did. Still another exempted the counties bordering tax-free New Hampshire from sales tax. Each provision was designed to win support from some groups of legislators.[43] But whatever plan the committee floated, it could not get enough support in the majority party caucus. In the 2003 session, all this work paid off, however. Act 60 was revised.

Some bills are not expected to go far. They die in a committee of one chamber or the other. Others make it through one house, but not the other. Some pass in both bodies, but a settlement eludes negotiators or time simply runs out. And in practically every legislative body, some important pieces of legislation expire at the close of the session. Agreement between the houses and contending parties cannot be reached; compromise does not succeed.

The Minnesota legislature did its best. It fashioned one compromise after another to help the Twins construct a new stadium for their baseball team. The issue was what the amount of state subsidization would be to keep the Twins in Minnesota. One bill passed a senate committee by a sharply divided vote; another passed a house committee, also by a divided vote. All of this occurred after the stadium bill had appeared dead. Yet, even after many changes designed to satisfy members of the senate and house, the governor, and the Twins, it was not possible to reach agreement in the 2001 session.

Negotiated compromises move things forward but leave many of the principals unhappy. Roger Moe, who negotiated the tax bill, ended up actually voting against it, though it passed the house 117–16 and the senate 55–11. One of his colleagues admitted that the bill was a compromise that did not satisfy him. "But make no bones about it, schools got the short end of the compromise," he said.[44] "Am I happy about it?" the Ohio speaker of the house asked as the budget went to conference. "No, but we did our job." His counterpart, the senate president, agreed. "This is the best budget we could do under the mandate of the court," whereby funding primary and secondary education had to come first, with everything else residual.[45]

"The 2002 legislative session wasn't pretty, but lawmakers did tackle tough issues—resolving most," editorialized the March 17, 2002, *Olympian* about the Washington legislature. Not pretty, but probably the best that could be done *under the circumstances.* And those circumstances are always in flux. In defending the ongoing negotiations that characterize lawmaking in Minnesota, the majority leader of the house, Tim Pawlenty, quoted a Rolling Stones song: "You can't always get what you want, / But if you try sometimes, / You just might find, / You get what you need." [46] And, if nothing else, "try" is what legislatures do—they try to work it out, reach agreement, and then move on to a never-diminishing workload.

Legislative strategy is crucial in reaching agreement, forging majorities, and protecting members from electoral risk. Wherever legislators stand on the merits of a measure, enacting it into law depends on figuring out when to deal with the issue, what ought to be in the bill, and how it ought to be taken up. It also depends on the many negotiations and compromises that take place along the way.

NOTES

1. *Dayton Daily News,* April 17, 2001.
2. *Cincinnati Enquirer,* March 27, 2001.
3. *Akron Beacon Journal,* April 11, 2003.
4. Ember Reichgott Junge, unpublished manuscript, 2000.
5. *New York Times,* June 21, 2001.
6. *St. Paul Pioneer Press,* April 26, 2001.
7. Ibid.
8. Ibid., May 9 and 12, 2001.
9. *St. Paul Pioneer Press,* May 16, 2001.
10. William P. Browne and Kenneth Ver Burg, *Michigan Politics and Government* (Lincoln: University of Nebraska Press, 1995), 124.
11. *Seattle Times,* March 17, 2002.
12. David Moats, *Civil Wars: A Battle for Gay Marriage* (New York: Harcourt, 2004), 224–225.
13. "Rethinking Representation," *American Political Science Review* 97 (November 2003): 516–520.

14. The Maryland legislature cannot add to the governor's budget, nor can it switch around funds; it can only reduce items. Therefore, the legislature had to persuade the governor to put an item—such as funding for prescription drugs—in his next budget or in a supplemental budget.

15. Reichgott Junge, unpublished manuscript, 2000.

16. John E. McDonough, *Experiencing Politics* (Berkeley: University of California Press, 2000), 151.

17. *St. Paul Pioneer Press,* May 10, 2001.

18. Ibid., May 5, 2001.

19. *New York Times,* March 4, 2003.

20. *Minneapolis Star Tribune,* June 17, 2001.

21. Reichgott Junge, unpublished manuscript, 2000.

22. Joseph M. Bessette, *The Mild Voice of Reason* (Chicago: University of Chicago Press, 1994), 56–63.

23. *Seattle Times,* March 14, 2002.

24. *Baltimore Sun,* April 18, 2001.

25. Ralph Wright, *All Politics Is Personal* (Manchester Center, Vt.: Marshall Jones Company, 1996), 83.

26. James Richardson, *Willie Brown* (Berkeley: University of California Press, 1996), 309.

27. *New York Times,* June 21, 2001.

28. McDonough, *Experiencing Politics,* 254.

29. Richardson, *Willie Brown,* 347–350.

30. *St. Paul Pioneer Press,* June 24, 2001.

31. Richard A. Posner, *Law, Pragmatism, and Democracy* (Cambridge: Harvard University Press, 2003), 166–167.

32. Moats, *Civil Wars,* 210.

33. Bessette, *The Mild Voice of Reason,* 61.

34. Lee Leonard, "House, Senate to confer on budget bill," *Columbus Dispatch,* November 25, 2001.

35. Tom Loftus, *The Art of Legislative Politics* (Washington, D.C.: CQ Press, 1996), 76–77, 85–86.

36. *Burlington Free Press,* April 2, 2001.

37. *Baltimore Sun,* March 27, 2001.

38. Reichgott Junge, unpublished manuscript, 2000.

39. *Minneapolis Star Tribune,* June 29, 2001.

40. Ibid., May 8, 2001.

41. Reichgott Junge, unpublished manuscript, 2000.

42. John A. Straayer, *The Colorado General Assembly,* 2nd ed. (Boulder: University Press of Colorado, 2000), 233.

43. Chris Graff, "Be Careful with Act 60 Version," *Burlington Free Press,* April 8, 2001.

44. *St. Paul Pioneer Press,* June 30, 2001.

45. *Columbus Dispatch,* May 31, 2001.

46. *Minneapolis Star Tribune,* June 12, 2001.

8 BALANCE: THE EXECUTIVE'S UPPER HAND

"It is no trick to invent a government and devise a strong executive," wrote Tom Loftus. "The trick of democracy is to devise a strong legislature that can survive transfers of power and shifts of party control." [1] In the colonial period state constitutions served to weaken executive power and grant power to legislatures. But the framers of the U.S. Constitution retreated, concluding that in a republican form of government the legislative branch had a natural tendency to exert control over other departments. Therefore, they increased the executive role so that the governor could act as a check on legislative power.

By the early nineteenth century the role of governor had become stronger. While executive power was still limited, governors were clearly gaining on legislatures. By the mid-twentieth century the executive had succeeded in carving out a distinct advantage over the legislature. The executive advantage—some would say executive dominance—continues to this day. There are exceptions among the fifty states—places where governors tend to be constitutionally and/or politically weaker than elsewhere.[2] Indeed, there may be a few places where the office of governor is so limited that the legislature can lay claim to being the dominant branch of government. If one assesses their constitutional authority alone, governors are at the greatest disadvantage vis-à-vis their legislatures in Alabama, Georgia, Nevada, New Hampshire, North Carolina, Oklahoma, South Carolina, Texas, and Vermont.[3] But even these governors possess important powers when it comes to dealing with their legislatures.

Governors vary not only from state to state but also from individual to individual in the power they wield in relation to the legislature. The partisan composition of government is important. A governor with a legislature controlled by his or her own party has a better chance of dominating than one who faces a legislature in opposition hands. The way the governor approaches the legislature—which is a function of belief, agenda, personality, experience, and skill—counts as well. Individual governors have different ways of dealing with their legislatures. The nature of the legislature, including its identity as an institution and the way leaders see their roles, has a substantial impact on what the governor can or cannot do as "chief legislator." Finally, circumstances of all sorts often enable or disable governors who care to exercise power.

The simplest view of the separation of powers between the executive and legislative branches is that the legislature makes laws and the executive administers them. A more sophisticated view recognizes that both branches engage in law-making. Today governors are generally believed to have the principal role in the

165

lawmaking process, even though lawmaking is one of the legislature's three principal functions. "The governor proposes, the legislature disposes" is how the relationship is often characterized. This may be an exaggeration of executive dominance; nonetheless, governors generally have the upper hand because of a combination of constitutionally, statutorily, institutionally, and politically derived powers.

The Power of Unity

Perhaps the greatest advantage the governor possesses regarding the legislature stems from the constitutional fact that he or she is one while they are many—188 in Maryland, 201 in Minnesota, 132 in Ohio, 180 in Vermont, and 147 in Washington, for example. And they are organized in two houses and two major parties, just to complicate things further. Whether governors are the only state officials elected statewide, as in New Jersey, or whether they share governance with other independently elected officeholders, they still are very unitary creatures compared to legislatures. Consequently, although governors have to be sensitive to various constituencies and normally have to consult and even heed advice, they have a far easier time arriving at a consensus than do legislatures, where—as the previous three chapters demonstrate—it is far more difficult for members to come together. Try to imagine how the balance of power would shift if a multiheaded executive were dealing with a multimembered legislature.

Because the governor is a single person elected by all the people of the state and the legislature is a collection of individuals, each of whom is elected from a small part of the state, governors are the ones who command the attention of the public and of the media (that is, insofar as the public and media pay attention to state government). "The cacophony of legislator voices," writes George W. Scott, a former member of the Washington legislature, "can rarely compete with a governor who can capitalize on his singular visibility in the media." Or, as political scientist Thad Beyle writes, "Probably the most significant source of informal power available to governors is their relationship with the public through the media and through other modes of contact." [4]

Because the governor speaks with one voice, the governor, and not the legislature, has a "bully pulpit"—a prominent public position that provides an opportunity for expounding views—at his or her disposal. Governors can make use of it to contact the public directly or through the media. In a small state like Vermont, it was not difficult for a governor like Howard Dean to spend considerable time in the various communities, getting to know people, and helping them get to know him. "He knows what districts want," a member of his staff said, "sometimes better than the legislators from the districts." Usually, governors can travel around the state, talk directly to citizens, and—most important—get coverage for their trip in the media as well. No legislative leader or backbencher can match such coverage.

Jesse Ventura of Minnesota certainly knew how to go to the people—to promote himself, win support for his agenda, and blame the legislature for what was wrong. If a governor has an advantage, a celebrity governor has an even greater advantage. Ember Reichgott Junge, a member of the Minnesota senate at the time, describes one of Ventura's bus trips to rally support during the 2000 legislative session:

> The Governor's tour was a wild success by any measure. In Zumbrota, the high school band played "Born to be Wild" at a pep fest in his honor. Another school band played "Rocky." Whatever happened to "Hail to the Chief"? Elementary students and soon-to-be-voter teenagers were screaming as they would for a rock group. Ten middle school students painted on their t-shirts letter by letter—"We love [heart] Jesse." Jesse addressed the students in a turtleneck and sportjacket, holding up a packet of papers and reminding them to learn to read well, and ending with vintage Ventura, "I got you out of class, didn't I?" In Rochester, Ventura action figures served as the centerpiece at a Chamber of Commerce luncheon. People lined up along the streets to glimpse the governor, forcing unscheduled stops. Over 700 people packed the Whistle Stop Café in Frontenac, with a like number outside. The place only had six or seven tables. Some staked out their tables 3 hours ahead of the visit.[5]

Neither the legislature nor the capitol press corps were gentle in their treatment of the former professional-wrestler governor. But Ventura was able to go over the heads of the political insiders in appealing to the public. Reichgott Junge recounts how he addressed a town hall meeting in Wabasha on the subject of unicameralism, which was not moving in the legislature. His plea was passionate:

> "While the legislature has caucuses for Democrats and caucuses for Republicans, I don't have a caucus. I stand alone. But I have you. Don't let me down." Tears started down his cheeks. "Because you're all I got," he paused, as if to compose himself. "I got elected alone and I stand alone." His voice trembled ever so slightly. "I need you. If I don't have you I can't be successful. Thank you very much." The scene was played on the news many times.[6]

Ventura's appeals for a unicameral legislature were not successful, in part because the public could not be roused on the issue and most legislators were opposed.

As a celebrity governor, with a distinct approach to governance, Ventura may be peculiar in using the bully pulpit for self-promotion as well as for promoting his agenda. Arnold Schwarzenegger, who became governor of California in 2003 after Gov. Gray Davis was recalled in a referendum, is another chief executive who uses his celebrity in governing. But Schwarzenegger appears to use the bully pulpit more as a threat than as a weapon with which to subdue the legislature. He manages to play an inside game, negotiating with legislators, more than an outside game of going to the people over their heads.

Other governors make use of their position to build up public support for items in their legislative program. Gov. James McGreevey of New Jersey, for example, will approach legislative leaders first for their support. If they do not grant it, however, the executive will end run the legislature by appealing to the public through the media. Parris Glendening of Maryland traveled around the state to round up public support for his budget in 2001. He also focused on a gay rights bill, having included it in his State of the State address and having testified in its favor before a house committee. "This was a classical case of using the bully pulpit," Glendening said.[7]

A coordinated operation by the office of governor in pursuing a public strategy can be very effective, as it was when Gov. Carroll Campbell traveled around South Carolina speaking directly to people, held news conferences, and focused his office's press operation in order to mold public opinion. As a policy advisor to the governor explained, first, "We had the best messenger in the state"; and second, "We understood how to use the tools we had to communicate what we were about to the public, and that's how you build political capital."[8] Such a strategy, if effectively implemented, will likely generate support within the legislature. That is, in part, because legislators wish to please their constituents and, in part, because they wish to please a popular governor. In addition, they may be intimidated by the governor's ability to make a case to the public, with no real opportunity for them to rebut it.

The governor of Rhode Island, whose constitutional powers may be weaker than those of other governors, recently was given a powerful amplifier for his bully pulpit. Statutorily, the governor is permitted to place a question on the ballot for an advisory referendum from the electorate. The governor chooses the issues and drafts the language of the ballot question, thus facilitating the response that the governor wants. Such authority gives the Rhode Island governor an extraordinary ability to mobilize the public behind his position. The legislature has similar power, but it is much more difficult for the legislature to agree on a ballot proposition or its wording. The governor has used this power; the legislature has not.

Governors can target their audiences more effectively than legislatures. As part of their appeal to the public, they can direct their message specifically to key groups. Bob Taft of Ohio, for example, had proposed an additional $253 million for higher education in the budget he submitted in 2001. The legislature, however, was not about to accept that level of spending. Taft urged university trustees to accelerate their lobbying efforts to protect his budget proposal. When Gov. George Pataki and the Democratic assembly and Republican senate of New York were at odds on his 2003 budget proposal, he tried to get business leaders to persuade the legislature to go along with him. He also rallied Republican leaders in the state, the most conservative of whom threatened to challenge incumbent senators in the 2004 primary elections if they supported tax increases.[9]

A governor can choose not only to go over the heads of the legislature but also to attack or blame the legislature for its failings. Ventura's approach was verbally to abuse legislators, whom on occasion he referred to as "gutless cowards," and also to castigate just about anyone else who came into his sight (calling a Christian Coalition lobbyist a "fat load," for example, and local government officials "stupid" and "thick as a brick").[10] In the tripartite budget negotiations during 2001, Ventura's strategy was to remind the public that he had done his job as governor but that the legislature was failing to do its job. A typical press release from the office of the governor read:

> This process had gone on too long and is now dangerously close to causing a government shutdown. I don't think that the legislature should be playing this game of chicken. It is difficult for me—and I'm sure for the people of Minnesota—to understand why this could not have been done in the five months of the regular session. . . .[11]

As the legislative session was nearing its constitutional end, Ventura on his weekly radio show or elsewhere would vent against the legislature, likening its members to children playing "a game of marbles" or "wanting to take their ball and go home." [12] His aim was to whip up public dissatisfaction and put heat on the legislature.

The legislature is no match whatsoever in a communications battle with a governor. Individual legislators may manage a good press. The institution seldom does, especially if it is under assault. Minnesota legislators were furious with their treatment at Ventura's hands, but there was little they could do. He had them over a barrel. One Democratic-Farmer-Labor (DFL) senator commented: "To the extent that the legislature doesn't do something, it's good for him. He's got us politically." Another acknowledged: "We can bash the governor all we want, but he can bash us worse."

Another threat governors employ during tough budgetary negotiations is the government shutdown. Gov. James McGreevey of New Jersey, for example, threatened such a shutdown in order to bring senate Republicans to a budget agreement, while the Republicans were trying to position themselves in as favorable a light as possible vis-à-vis the Democrats. During the difficult budget year of 2003 several governors made use of the government shutdown tactic. Ventura certainly had done so during his struggle two years earlier. Late in the session he announced that if legislators did not reach agreement, he would let state government just shut down for a while. With regard to calling a special session, Ventura indicated on his weekly radio show in mid-April:

> Well, I can tell you right now I'm not calling it and I'm the only one that can. If they don't finish that work on time, look for a government shutdown come June 30.

At that point, there were five weeks left in the regular legislative session.

Few governors are as unremitting in their public disdain for the legislature as Ventura. But Virginia's Republican governor, James Gilmore, was known rarely to pass on an opportunity to publicly bash his antagonists in the senate, even accusing Republican senators of allowing themselves to be manipulated by minority party Democrats. The senators fought back, however, pooling about $40,000 in campaign funds to hire a public relations firm to help them counter their governor's assaults.

For the most part, governors do not take on the legislature as directly and as vehemently as did Ventura. Nor do they single out legislative opponents, as did Gilmore. They use the bully pulpit positively, to build general support for themselves and more specific support for their agendas. And their efforts in this respect generally succeed.

The Power of Agenda Setting

State constitutions provide for the initiation of policy by governors. Article V, Section I of the New Jersey Constitution is illustrative of this point, stating that "The Governor shall . . . recommend [to the legislature] such measures as he may deem desirable." Nowadays, custom dictates that governors fashion and present a program for the legislature to enact. By means of the State of the State address and special messages, governors offer their agendas and then have major items drafted and introduced as bills. As a former speechwriter for California, governor Pete Wilson explained: "The state of the state speech is to a governor what a strong serving game is to a good tennis player. It is a chance to put the ball in play and determine the location and move his opponent." [13]

Governors have a great advantage over the legislature in being able to focus on an agenda; they can pick and choose. Focus is possible, but much tougher, for a legislature in which practically every member has an agenda of one sort or another. Legislatures manage to sort things out, separating the wheat from the chaff. They even develop legislative priorities. But it is a longer, more arduous process than that in which governors engage, and the agendas with which they deal are far larger than those of the governor.

If governors focus on a limited number of initiatives, chances are that these items will be given top billing by their legislatures as well. If they attack too many issues, legislators have a more difficult time sorting among them and the governors' agendas are likely to suffer. Governors might not get everything they want in exactly the form they want it, but they generally achieve much of what is on their agenda. It takes skill and it takes work. Gov. Zell Miller of Georgia was a master at agenda setting, with one or two issues constituting his primary thrust, his area of concentration. By focusing his efforts, he was able to accomplish a great deal. Gov. Ned McWherter of Tennessee also got what he asked for, and over his eight years in office he concentrated on a limited number of major issues, all of which passed. As one legislator confirmed: "He'll have his package of bills every year, and we always pass them." [14] Pataki of New York was much the same. He would stake out a few legislative objectives each year and then stay on message in pursuit of them.

It helps, of course, if governors start out with initiatives that are popular with the electorate. Ventura's tax overhaul in Minnesota, with the state taking on a larger share of financing E–12 education, was such an initiative. He managed to get a lot of what he wanted, despite DFL opposition in the legislature. Georgia's Miller also chose issues that were popular with the public, thereby increasing his support in the legislature.[15] Few governors have been as successful as Maryland's Glendening, however. During the 2001 session he chose to focus on fifteen administration bills, including collective bargaining for higher education employees, smart growth, and the outlawing of racial profiling. Virtually everything that Glendening wanted he got, although he left it to the legislature to work out many of the details.

Not all governors stress their role as "chief legislator." Vermont's Howard Dean, during his last years in office, had little of an identifiable agenda. He did offer proposals in his State of the State address, but his follow-through was rather casual. He had campaigned against Act 60 in 2000, yet he did not come up with a plan to modify it, leaving the initiative to the Republican house. By contrast, Madeleine Kunin, one of Dean's predecessors, had ambitious agendas (some would say too ambitious).[16] Like other governors, she would pick and choose the issues and then devote herself to them.

The governor's role extends beyond that of fashioning an agenda for the legislature to enact. The governor is also a participant in the legislative process, even if most of the crafting is being done by the legislature. The president of the Kansas senate, Bud Burke, acknowledged that while Gov. Mike Hayden was not continuously involved in the session's policy making, "every time there was a kink in the hose, he was there to straighten it out." [17] Sometimes governors are dragged into legislative fights because each side believes the governor's weight may tip the scale in its favor.

The Power of Budget Formulation

Although the legislature has the power to appropriate funds, in truth, when it comes to the budget, the governor has a distinct advantage, at least in most states. This is primarily the case because the executive formulates the budget and submits a budget bill or bills to the legislature. The state's budget is where priorities are set not only by deciding how state revenues are raised and expended but also by introducing new substantive policies. "The governor's power to propose budgets," writes Tom Loftus, "is what really gives the governor the tiller when it comes to setting the course of policy." [18] In the budgetary arena, according to one Connecticut analyst, the governor is the "ringmaster." It is with the governor's formulation that the legislature has to work, while "the governor, his policies, and his budget staff are in the center ring." [19]

Not all governors have such an advantage over the legislature. In perhaps ten states the executive shares responsibility for budget formulation with the legislature. In Colorado, for instance, the legislature's Joint Budget Committee is the driving force. "The governor develops a budget and the legislature ignores it," a former JBC chairman said. The 1997 JBC chair observed of Gov. Roy Romer's budget: "her first inclination was to toss it into the trash." [20] But in about forty states the governor's budget formulation shapes the discussion that follows. This enables governors to spend somewhat more (or to cut, if necessary, somewhat less) on the programs they favor rather than on those favored by the legislature. When there is a surplus, governors will allocate all of it, leaving little or no funds to the discretion of the senate and house, which are then obliged to try to substitute their preferences for the governor's.

In Vermont, for instance, in 2001 Governor Dean selected new initiatives to fund, such as increased health benefits for teachers and paid family leave—a total budgetary increase of over 5 percent. At the same time Dean felt that he could underfund some programs, knowing that the legislature would increase the budget in these areas. The legislature, and particularly the Republican house, had an uphill struggle to challenge Dean's priorities. New York's governor Pataki also entered negotiations with the senate and house with the advantage of formulation, including detailed priorities on how the money was to be spent and on reimbursement rates to nursing homes under Medicare. Pataki's budget also lumped projects together to give himself more discretion in dealing with the legislature. And the legislature had to respond to the governor's formulation.

One budgetary advantage possessed by governors in eleven states is that of estimating revenues from taxes, fees, and other services. In the rest of the states the legislature, as well as the governor, makes its own estimates of revenues for the fiscal year. In a number of states the executive and legislative staffs come together in formal sessions to reconcile the differences in their estimates through what is known as a consensus process. The purpose is to reach agreement so that the executive and legislative branches can at least start with the same numbers. Projections are part science, part art, and part politics. No one can know for certain where the economy will go, and, thus, whether tax proceeds will rise or fall. But revenue estimates are critical to the budget process, so those who determine them begin with an advantage. Exaggerating revenues will allow for higher spending; minimizing revenues will require belt-tightening. Governors can use revenue estimations to control how much will be spent and when. For example, Pataki had reason to lowball estimated revenues when formulating the budget in 2001. To hedge against an economic downturn, he indicated that he wanted as much money to be saved in the budget as possible. The assembly Democrats wanted to spend $2.3 billion and the senate Republicans $1.1 billion more than the governor's $3.6 billion. The speaker, Sheldon Silver, maintained that the governor was underestimating revenues not for economic reasons, but in order to spend an accumulated surplus just before the November 2002 election. "The governor is running for reelection next year," Silver said, "and he doesn't want to spend the money this year." [21]

Probably no other governor has as much budgetary power vis-à-vis the legislature as does the governor of Maryland. Here the General Assembly is constitutionally proscribed from increasing items in the governor's budget, or even switching funds around. All the legislature can do is cut. If the legislature wants something, that means it has to persuade the governor to insert a legislative priority either in the budget itself or in the supplemental budget that is dealt with separately. Thus, the governor's priorities dominate the process; yet the legislature still is in the game. It is a game in which, as Sen. P. J. Hogan put it, "all we [the legislature] have are pawns. I want bishops and knights." [22] In response to such domination, at the end of the 2001 session Sen. Bobby Neale took the senate floor and asked to be removed from the Budget and Taxation Committee because of the legislature's powerlessness in the budget process. No legislature—not even Maryland's—is powerless in budgeting, but few legislatures—and certainly not Maryland's—can quite match the thrust of the governor's priorities.

The Power of Provision

With the New Jersey senate split 20–20 in 2002, Democratic governor James McGreevey could not ignore the need for Republican help, particularly for his budget. He showed what a governor had to offer members of the legislature, even those of the opposition party. In building support, McGreevey traveled from one end of the state to the other, bearing gifts of state funding for local projects and lavishing praise on Republican senators William Gormley in the south and Robert Littell in the north. The governor accompanied Littell in his district on a visit to a dam, where he promised to restore $5 million in funding for its repair. Together with the senator, the governor grabbed a shovel and broke ground on a project to improve traffic at a busy intersection. The governor visited Atlantic City, Gormley's constituency, and offered proposals to make New Jersey's gambling resort the nation's "premier destination" for family vacations. The governor also promised to push the senator's plan to streamline casino regulations and to provide funds for transportation, boardwalk, and neighborhood improvements. One deal in particular helped McGreevey obtain a vote he needed for his proposed corporate business tax, which was part of the budget settlement. Sen. Walter Kavanaugh, a Republican, gave the governor his vote in return for the reappointment of a constituent as county prosecutor. "They needed certain things and there were certain things that were important to me," Kavanaugh said in defense of trading his vote. "To serve your constituents well, you have to make agreements that will be beneficial to your district." [23]

McGreevey's largesse may not have been a quid pro quo, as such, but it did lay the groundwork for successful dealings with two key legislators. His largesse with a third was more demonstrable. Because of their positions and the resources at their disposal, governors can give individual legislators much of what they want—for themselves and for their districts. Legislators desire acknowledgment, the kind that McGreevey heaped on the two Republicans he was courting.

Governors have what legislators want and need. They want a bill passed, a gubernatorial visit, and as much attention as possible. In Ohio Governor Taft travels to Republican members' districts to sign bills and attend fund-raisers and other events where they are featured. But gubernatorial provision extends beyond visiting legislators where they live. Gary Taffett, McGreevey's chief of staff, explains why this is so: "People just want that phone call; they want to be in his office." [24] It is tough for legislators to say no to a governor who invites them in and strokes them. "They're not all heavy lifts," Taffett states, "they're not all big asks."

Nearly everywhere legislators seek funds and projects for their districts; they want to be able to bring home the bacon. In Vermont the major commodity with which legislators are wooed is transportation projects. A governor will ask a lawmaker who may be on the fence: "What can I do for you in your district?" Legislators want the governor's support for their legislative priorities. If the governor endorses a bill they introduce, its prospects will brighten. And the governor can quietly or more loudly help move the bill along. Legislators also need the help that governors can provide in direct benefits to friends, constituents, and campaign contributors. A low license plate number, an appointment with a member of the governor's staff—favors like these enhance the local reputations of legislators.

Perhaps most important are appointments for legislators' constituents, which range from membership on boards, commissions, councils, and task forces to salaried positions as judge or prosecutor. In a state where legislators are term limited, like Ohio, legislators not only want appointments for their constituents, but also for themselves when their legislative terms expire. One of the reasons that house Republicans could not override a Taft veto was that a number of them did not want to hurt their chances of securing a gubernatorial appointment after their house careers ended.[25]

Nearly every governor learns quickly how to use the resources available. The chief executive exploits such resources to shape the expectations of legislators. And legislators expect the chief executive to take into account their needs, if they take into account what he or she wants from them. Zell Miller was extremely effective in his approach as governor of Georgia. As one legislator described:

> He is not bashful at all about using the personal power of the office to meet with members of the general assembly. When you are called down to the governor's office, it is a very impressive office, you're talking to the governor, and you know that he controls things that could be good or ill for your district. He controls grants, he controls roads, and other things.[26]

Governors also draw on their power of provision specifically, when they are trying to influence a few votes. In such instances one or a couple of legislators may be targeted, and they usually are offered a carrot rather than threatened with a stick. "You have to know what they [legislators] want, what they really want," said Taffett.[27]

The governor may call a legislator with an invitation to deal: "Let me know if there's anything I can do for you." It does not happen on many issues or with many legislators, but it may prove decisive on a few votes each legislative session. Michael Torpey, a former chief of staff to New Jersey's governor Christine Todd Whitman, explained how he managed the legislature on the most important issues: "There wasn't a single big vote I went into that I wasn't negotiating with appointments." [28] Not often, but occasionally, governors have to point out to lawmakers just what they will be missing if they do not go along. Usually it is implicit, but sometimes governors are more direct. Taft's message to Ohio legislators, communicated through his aides, was that unless they supported his line-item vetoes on the budget, they could forget about any help from him in the future—no appointments for constituents, no projects for the district, no nothing.[29]

The Power of Denial

If governors are able to bestow and reward, they are also able to deny and punish. Governors may withhold carrots from legislators, but only on special occasions do they actually try to use the stick on those who cross them. Occasionally, though, a governor will dismiss friends and relatives of lawmakers from patronage jobs or end funding for a local project. Pataki did not hesitate to go to whatever lengths he felt necessary in order to prevail. Among others things, he tried to have Joe Bruno replaced as senate majority leader, and he threatened personally to campaign against lawmakers who supported tax increases that the legislature put into the budget during its 2003 session.[30]

The veto is the executive's principal weapon of denial, and it is a powerful one indeed. The governor can veto any bill the legislature passes, and in all but six states it takes an extraordinary majority by both houses to override. Governors use the veto with varying degrees of frequency, depending on the governor and the state. Gary Johnson, New Mexico's Republican governor, set a record for a session by vetoing almost half—200 of 424—the bills passed by the Democratic legislature.

Despite the efforts of the Maryland legislature to reach a compromise on a law to require gun-safety education for public school students, Gov. Parris Glendening objected to students in grades 7 through 12 traveling to shooting ranges to handle rifles, shotguns, and handguns in programs that included one run by the National Rifle Association. Glendening vetoed the legislation. The case of Minnesota governor Jesse Ventura's veto in 2001 of an "informed consent" or "right to know" amendment to an appropriations bill for health and human services illustrates the decisive power of the governor on a controversial issue such as abortion. The amendment would have required that women seeking an abortion receive specified information at least twenty-four hours in advance, including possible medical risks and medical assistance available for prenatal care, childbirth, and neonatal care. Ventura had vetoed a similar bill the year before, so his position on the issue was known. Proponents of the measure hoped to avert a veto by including it in an omnibus spending bill, which the governor would be less likely to veto for fear of jeopardizing funding for health and human services agencies and programs. But the governor was insistent, writing to the house and senate leaders that "as I have previously communicated to you and the public, I will veto the Omnibus Health and Human Services bill and any other bill containing Right to Know provisions." [31] Meanwhile, the governor's spokesperson suggested that abortion-related legislation should be in a separate bill—which would have made it even easier for the governor to veto—not in a finance bill. The "informed consent" provision was backed by a substantial majority in the Republican house and by a closer majority in the DFL senate. [32]

When the bill passed both houses, Ventura vetoed it. But the battle continued with the house putting the provision in a separate bill and the senate passing a health and human services budget bill with no abortion language. The issue was not resolved until the health and human services bill was reported out of the conference committee held during a special session of the Minnesota legislature. Because of Ventura's threat to veto the conferees' bill, no provisions that would restrict access to abortion appeared in the final bill. However, as part of the compromise, the governor and the senate gave up a teen pregnancy prevention proposal that they favored. [33] Ventura's actual veto and his threatened veto, along with a compromise, held the pro-life side at bay, even though it had majority support in the legislature.

In the executive-veto arsenal, the regular veto is supplemented by the line-item veto. Governors in forty-three states have the power to veto sections or items of appropriation bills, usually proposed expenditures, without having to reject the entire bill, as Ventura had to do to excise the anti-abortion provision. (In Maryland, where the legislature cannot add to the executive budget, the governor does not need and does not have a line-item veto or any veto on the budget.) The line-item veto allows governors to use a scalpel rather than a meat axe, and to reduce an amount or remove a very specific activity that they do not want funded. Its usage varies greatly. In New York, for instance, line-item vetoes have been rare, since the governor and the two top legislative leaders normally negotiated budgets on which they all signed off. From 1983 through 1997 New York governors cast no budget vetoes. In 1998, however, Governor Pataki refused to negotiate a budget with senate and house leaders; instead, he reviewed the budget the legislature sent to him and cast 1,300 line-item vetoes (and in fifty-five instances vetoed language as well). [34] In 2003, in a major executive-legislative confrontation, Pataki vetoed 119 items. To override Pataki's line-item vetoes, the legislature would have had to summon up a two-thirds vote in both the assembly (100 of 150 members) and the senate (41 of 62 members) on each line that was struck out by the governor. And the governor would be able to target legislators and apply pressure, trying to win over the votes he needed to deny an override.

After a difficult budget process in the 2001 legislative session, Ventura cast thirteen line-item vetoes. Despite the fact that his party controlled both houses, Republican Taft in Ohio used the line-item veto forty-nine times, the most since Gov. James Rhodes vetoed seventy-two items in the 1975 budget. Most important, from the legislature's institutional point of view, he vetoed a provision that would have exempted legislators and their staff from liability in civil lawsuits and protected them and their internal communications from being subpoenaed. [35]

On occasion, the governor has to use the line-item veto with the consent of the legislature to put the budget in balance. For instance, the Washington legislature during its 2002 session could not get enough votes to raise taxes on liquor, leaving a $30–40 million imbalance in the budget that the Washington Constitution does not permit. The legislature willingly left it to the governor to figure out what items to veto in order to balance the budget.

Some governors have additional veto powers, usually called conditional or amendatory vetoes. The conditional veto in New Jersey allows the governor to take a piece of legislation and negotiate a change with the legislature without having to start the process afresh. Partly because of the veto power, which includes the ordinary veto, the line-item veto, and the amendatory veto, the Illinois governor can impose his or her policies on the budget. This is one reason why Illinois is considered a strong executive state.[36]

Use of the veto is not necessarily an indication of gubernatorial power. The very fact that the governor has the veto or a gubernatorial threat to employ it on a measure makes a great impression on the legislature and legislators. Ventura's threat of a veto with respect to abortion language worked in Minnesota. Taft threatened to veto a concealed weapons bill if it was not supported by Ohio law enforcement. He threatened to line-item the budget bill if it included a provision for video lottery terminals at racetracks. He also indicated that he would not approve of general tax increases to pay for school funding. By threatening a veto Ventura managed to persuade a conference committee to abandon a provision that applied to the governor the same ethics code that covered other state employees. The governor's top lobbyist wrote to the committee that the governor and other constitutional offices are not employees of the state and that the state and ethics language could "jeopardize the entire bill" that funds a number of state departments. "If this is the matter that's going to in effect shut down government," said Sen. Richard Cohen, the senate's chief negotiator on the bill, "discretion is the better part of valor." The section was removed.[37]

Gov. Carroll Campbell of South Carolina used the veto during the first year of his administration, mainly to establish a dominant position in his relationship with legislators. He wanted to show them that he carried a big stick and was willing to swing it. During his first legislative session he used the line-item veto 276 times, with a majority of his vetoes sustained. Even though some were overridden by the required two-thirds vote of members present, the dynamics changed in his favor. Campbell described his changed relationship with lawmakers:

> From that point on I haven't had to do that [veto] very often because most of the time if there is something that they are in doubt over what I am going to do, they'll come and ask me. Then it is a much better process because they'll say, "Are you going to veto this?" And I'll say, "Yes, I have to veto it." So they'll say, "Well, what will you take, or what do you want?" When you get into that type of process, it is a much better process, but you have to establish the willingness to veto or to stand up when you think something needs to be done. I do that but I don't try to overdo it; but I've done quite a bit.[38]

Gubernatorial vetoes and veto threats are used in the battle over the budget bill and major legislation; they are also used to win over members whose support on particular measures the governor needs. If the governor threatens to veto a legislator's pet bill or item in the appropriations act, that legislator will weigh his or her position most deliberately. "Both the item veto and the simple veto," writes William K. Muir Jr. with respect to executive-legislative relations in California, "could be used to break an individual legislator's resistance." Imagine the governor telling a legislator that he would kill his bill, a bill the legislator had worked for several years to pass, unless the legislator helped him elsewhere.[39] The line-item veto, in particular, can—and occasionally is—used to punish members who withhold their support when the governor asks for it. In New Jersey, for instance, governors are expected to line-item veto projects of legislators who refuse to vote for the budget on which the governor and the legislature have already agreed.[40]

The veto is probably the most obvious manifestation of gubernatorial denial, but governors can also take action that virtually denies legislators their careers. They can refuse to give financial and other assistance to legislators in their own party; they can work to defeat legislators they target in the other party. Occasionally they threaten—and may even carry out such threats—to campaign against legislators who oppose them, as did Gov. Paul Cellucci of Massachusetts with legislators who voted the other way on death penalty legislation in 1998.

Probably no governor has denial power equivalent to that of Maryland. That is the case because the Maryland governor can affect legislators where they live—in their districts with regard to their reelection. While most governors do participate in the decennial legislative redistricting process, the initiative is usually with the legislature. Governors, of course, can veto a plan on which the legislature agrees. But in terms of where lines are drawn, the influence of most governors is relatively slight. However, in Maryland the initiative for legislative redistricting is with the governor, not the legislature. Under the state constitution the governor must submit a redistricting plan to the legislature every ten years. If the legislature cannot agree on an alternative plan within forty-five days, the governor's plan becomes law.

Gov. Parris Glendening's power to draw lines for legislators' districts in 2002 was certainly a factor in the legislative session that year and the previous one. Glendening was confident that the plan that would go into effect would be his, because the legislature would not be able to agree on one of its own.[41] He playfully reminded legislators that their district contours were in his hands. On the opening day of the 2001 session he made courtesy calls to the house and senate chambers, carrying with him a rolled-up map he told members was his redistricting plan. He meant to be amusing, but also to convey a message, which is exactly what he did. The general attitude, as expressed by one legislator, was: "This is no time to annoy him." [42] Legislators who visited the governor in his state house office would invariably find him leaning over one of two maps sitting on an easel: a map of senate districts if the visitor was a senator and a map of house districts if the visitor was a delegate. He would smile and point to the member's district. The member would not know whether Glendening was serious or kidding, nor would the member care to find out.[43]

The Difference That Party Makes

The governor benefits, at least with his partisans, by virtue of being leader of the state Democratic or state Republican Party. Members of a political party share a disposition to be loyal, if they possibly can. They have a strong basis for going along with one of their own. They share beliefs and interest group supporters. In elections, they run on the same slate. If the governor is running for reelection, he or she will be at the top of the ticket. The governor may not have coattails onto which legislators can hang, but an unpopular governor may cost legislators' votes. Why do something to make the governor unpopular? The tendency of legislator members of the governor's party is to back the governor.

In the words of one Georgia senator, the governor is chair of the party: "It is his party." A Georgia representative agreed; the governor can count on a great deal of party support: "That is sort of his ace in the hole." Although many Georgia Democrats have differences with the governor, "when it comes down to it, ultimately, the speaker, the lieutenant governor, and most of the leadership will go along with him.[44]

Loyalty to the governor extends to legislative leadership. A former speaker of the Wisconsin assembly writes that party affiliation largely determines the legislative leader's role. "If the governor is of the same party, the Speaker becomes the governor's *lieutenant* [emphasis added] in addition to his or her role as a legislative leader." Similarly, if the governor's party is not in the majority, the minority leader becomes a *lieutenant* to the governor. When Democrat Tony Earl was governor of Wisconsin, Speaker Loftus, both as a friend and a member of his party, wanted him to succeed. The speaker's deal with the governor was that he would try to push his agenda and prevent bad bills from getting to his desk so he would not be faced with having to veto them. In return, he would have to supply Democrats some bacon to bring back to their districts. Loftus's role was "to broker the needs of the Democrats in the Assembly as well as serve as the governor's lieutenant in the legislature." [45]

Leaders may have disputes with governors of their party, but they still try to protect them from harm that might only benefit the opposition. Ohio's house Republicans, for instance, wanted to put a provision for a video lottery in the budget, even though Governor Taft was against it. Legislators stood ready to override Taft's veto if, as was expected, he cast it. Senate President Richard Finan, however, counseled against splitting with his party's governor on the issue. "I have to think about the politics," he told the Republican speaker of the house. "I hate to embarrass the governor." Mike Miller, Maryland's Democratic senate president, went even further for his Democratic governor. Despite the fact that

Beretta, the gun manufacturer, was located in his district, Miller supported the governor's antigun legislation in 1999. The legislative leader was not happy with the situation, but his greater concern was not allowing a Democratic governor to lose a priority bill.[46]

Thus, when a governor's party is in control, the legislature tends to be somewhat less of a balancer and somewhat more of an enabler. The coincidence of partisan inclinations and interests acts to interfere with the balance between the branches. In an essentially one-party system, however, party loyalty to the governor matters less. There is no threat from a partisan opposition that brings the executive and legislature together. It means more when the minority party is a serious challenger for seats in the legislature. That is why the surge in Republican legislative strength in the southern states has actually given governors a slightly greater edge. Take Georgia, for instance. Today Democrats work together better than they had in the past. According to one Republican senator, Johnny Isakson, in the early 1980s the Georgia governor and speaker were at odds, each a dominant force in the Democratic Party. By 1994, however, Republicans in the legislature had a significant number of votes and Democrats could no longer afford to fight among themselves. "They've got another enemy, so to speak, which is the Republican party," he said. A decade earlier, Democrats could afford to split with a governor of their party.[47] Now they cannot, and the governor's partisan support and strength is greater.

But the governor does not always prevail, even with members of his or her own party. In 2003 Pataki and the Republican senate were on a collision course over the budget. Still, Republican legislators were reluctant to confront their own governor and wanted the governor and the senate majority to undertake serious negotiations. According to one of them Joe Bruno, the majority leader, had been trying to approach Pataki, but "then he ripped us." Bruno knew how firm his caucus was in its position, and he offered to let the governor speak to the caucus as a group or individually. There was no accommodation, however.[48]

For governors the most favorable situation is one in which both chambers are controlled by their party—and where the legislature is reasonably competitive. During the 2001 legislative sessions that was almost the case in Ohio, under Republican control, and Maryland, under Democratic control—in both places by comfortable margins. It was very much the case in Washington during the 2001 session, where Democrats had the governorship and controlled each house of the legislature by the narrowest of margins. Less favorable, from the executive vantage, is where the governor's party controls one chamber and the opposition party controls the other.

Divided government undoubtedly accounts for some of the aggressiveness of state legislatures. Over recent years the incidence of unified government has been on the decline. As of 2003 in twenty-nine states at least one chamber was controlled by a party other than that of the governor. In some states, as a matter of fact, unity is rare. In Nevada, for example, from 1905 on the governor's party has controlled both houses of the legislature less than one-fifth of the time. In

New York Democrats have had a lock on the assembly and Republicans on the senate, so under a succession of both Republican and Democratic governors control in New York has been split almost continually since the 1960s. In California, government was divided in 1966–1968, 1970–1974, and 1982–1998—all told almost three-fourths of the time until Gray Davis was elected governor in 1998 and became divided again when Republican Arnold Schwarzenegger replaced him in 2003. During the 2001 session that was the case in Vermont, where Democratic governor Howard Dean's party had a majority in the senate but had just lost its majority in the house. Earlier, Madeleine Kunin as governor had the advantage of a Democratic legislature.

The least favorable situation, from the executive's perspective, is where the opposition controls both houses of the legislature. In such circumstances rivalries between the two branches are reinforced by competition between the two parties. One reason that the Colorado legislature has appeared powerful vis-à-vis the executive has been the division of party control since 1974, when Democrat Richard Lamm was elected governor and the Republicans controlled the legislature.[49] For about a quarter of a century that situation continued until Republican Bill Owens's election as governor in 1998. Other examples of partisan division acting as limits on gubernatorial powers occurred in Connecticut, Massachusetts, and Rhode Island, where Republican governors have had to deal with Democratic legislatures during recent years. In all of these cases governors managed with the constitutional and political powers at their disposal. They had to bargain somewhat harder and perhaps ask for less and compromise more, but if they persisted they certainly were matches for their legislatures.

An unusual case occurred in Minnesota during the legislative sessions of 2000–2002. In this instance a governor, who had won as a third party candidate, faced a Democratic senate and a Republican house. Only one legislator was a member of the governor's Independence Party (IP): Sen. Bob Lessard, who had switched to IP from DFL in 2001 and became a one-man caucus carrying Jesse Ventura's banner.[50] It might be assumed that with virtually no partisan allies in the legislature, the governor's power would be severely curtailed. As we have seen earlier, such was not the case. The governor was still a force to be reckoned with. Senate DFLers and house Republicans shaped their agendas to win Ventura to their side in negotiating with the other chamber and other party. In tripartisan government, as well as divided government, two against one was deemed critical. Here too the governor's role was practically anything he wanted it to be.

Party loyalty helps, but even without it the governor is the dominant figure. Take the case of Louisiana.[51] Here, with few modern exceptions, governors have determined who was chosen speaker in the house and president in the senate. They have even been involved in naming the chairs of standing committees. Both Republican and Democratic governors have had their way with the legislature because the legislature allows them to, not because the constitution prescribes it. Rep. Charles McDonald described the system in Louisiana:

It is assumed that when you assume a leadership position, along with that goes some loyalty to the administration. . . . It is understood that on issues important to the administration you will vote with them.

The two sides here are not Democrats and Republicans but the governor's or administration's side and the other side. Louisiana's governor is so strong mainly because the legislature is content being weak.

NOTES

1. Tom Loftus, *The Art of Legislative Politics* (Washington, D.C.: CQ Press, 1994), 63.

2. Alan Rosenthal, *The Decline of Representative Democracy* (Washington, D.C.: CQ Press, 1998), 293–294.

3. Based on Table 6-5 in Thad Beyle, "The Governors," in Virginia Gray, Russell Hanson, and Herbert Jacob, eds., *Politics in the American States* (Washington, D.C.: CQ Press, 1999), 210–211. I have excluded from Beyle's index the "party control" item. Although party control greatly affects the executive-legislative balance, it is a factor that can change from election to election and is of a very different nature than constitutional (or statutory) powers.

4. George W. Scott, *A Majority of One: Legislative Life* (Seattle: Civitas Press, 2002), 55–58; Thad Beyle, "The Governors," 224.

5. Ember Reichgott Junge, unpublished manuscript, 2000.

6. Ibid.

7. *Washington Post,* March 31, 2001.

8. Laura A. Van Assendelft, *Governors, Agenda Setting, and Divided Government* (Lanham, Md.: University Press of America, 1997), 198.

9. *New York Times,* April 17, 2003.

10. Virginia Gray and Wyman Spano, "The Irresistible Force Meets the Immovable Object: Minnesota's Moralistic Political Culture Confronts Jesse Ventura," in Stephen R. Graubard, ed., *Minnesota, Real and Imagined* (St. Paul: Minnesota Historical Society Press, 2001), 195.

11. Press release, office of Gov. Jesse Ventura, June 7, 2001.

12. *Minneapolis Star Tribune,* June 2, 2001.

13. *New York Times,* January 7, 2004.

14. Van Assendelft, *Governors, Agenda Setting, and Divided Government,* 89, 108.

15. Ibid., 87.

16. Interview with the author, April 9, 2001.

17. Burdette A. Loomis, *Time, Politics, and Policies: A Legislative Year* (Lawrence: University Press of Kansas, 1994), 151.

18. Loftus, *The Art of Legislative Politics,* 75.

19. Carol Lewis, "Connecticut: Prosperity, Frugality, and Stability," in Edward J. Clynch and Thomas P. Lauth, eds., *Governors, Legislatures, and Budgets* (Westport, Conn.: Greenwood Press, 1991), 41, 46.

20. John A. Straayer, *The Colorado General Assembly* (Boulder: University Press of Colorado, 2000), 214.

21. *New York Times,* April 3, June 1 and 18, 2001.

22. *Baltimore Sun,* February 28, 2001.

23. *Newark Star-Ledger,* May 26, 2002; January 13, 2003.

24. Lecture at Eagleton Institute of Politics, Rutgers University, December 4, 2002.

25. *Columbus Dispatch,* June 13, 2001.

26. Van Assendelft, *Governors, Agenda Setting, and Divided Government,* 71.

27. Lecture at Eagleton Institute of Politics, Rutgers University, December 4, 2002.

28. Lecture at Eagleton Institute of Politics, Rutgers University, December 5, 2001.

29. *Columbus Dispatch,* June 20, 2001.

30. *New York Times,* May 1, 2003.

31. Letter from Gov. Jesse Ventura to Rep. Steve Sviggum and Sen. Roger Moe, May 1, 2001.

32. The abortion provision, it should be noted, could not be removed by a line-item veto because the governor was only able to use such a veto for spending items, not policy items.

33. *St. Paul Pioneer Press,* June 29, 2001.

34. *New York Times,* July 11, 2001.

35. *Columbus Dispatch,* June 7, 2001.

36. Irene S. Rubin et al., "Illinois: Executive Reform and Fiscal Conditions," in Clynch and Lauth, *Governors, Legislatures, and Budgets,* 17, 20.

37. *St. Paul Pioneer Press,* June 30, 2001.

38. Van Assendelft, *Governors, Agenda Setting, and Divided Government,* 180.

39. William K. Muir Jr., *Legislature: California's School for Politics* (Chicago: University of Chicago Press, 1982), 169–171.

40. Lecture at Eagleton Institute of Politics, Rutgers University, December 5, 2001.

41. Interview with the author, March 23, 2001.

42. *Baltimore Sun,* March 30, 2001.

43. Interview with the author, March 23, 2001.

44. Van Assendelft, *Governors, Agenda Setting, and Divided Government,* 74–75.

45. Loftus, *The Art of Legislative Politics,* 63–64, 68.

46. Interview with the author, March 23, 2001.

47. Van Assendelft, *Governors, Agenda Setting, and Divided Government,* 74.

48. *New York Times,* May 8, 2003.

49. Straayer, *The Colorado General Assembly,* 240.

50. Among Ventura's three line-item vetoes in 2001 was a $100,000 appropriation for the district of Lessard, his only Independence Party member in the legislature. The governor showed no favoritism here. *Minneapolis Star Tribune,* July 11, 2001.

51 . This paragraph is based on material in the *Lafayette Daily Advertiser,* March 24, 2004.

9 BALANCE: HOW GOVERNORS AND LEGISLATURES DEAL WITH ONE ANOTHER

Constitutional, statutory, and political factors set the stage for the governor's exercise of power vis-à-vis the legislature. But how the drama gets played out hinges on how the executive approaches the legislature and vice versa. The balance in practice between the two branches depends in part, indeed in large part, on the attributes of the individual governor. That is to say, governors generally have the wherewithal to match or outmatch their legislatures—if that is their desire and if they have skill. Most have both.

That is why some governors manage to be effective legislatively despite having weak executive systems. Richard Riley, for example, had minimal formal powers as governor of South Carolina, although he furnished strong leadership in policy making. Florida's governors had been constitutionally constrained by a cabinet system of government, but both Reuben Askew and Bob Graham proved to be strong governors in a weak governor state with a powerful legislature. And Jeb Bush continued the tradition after the state had turned from primarily Democratic to primarily Republican. In contrast, a few governors turn out to be weak even though their offices are endowed with substantial authority. David Treen of Louisiana was one of them; he was uncomfortable with the legislative process and not disposed to wield power. Maryland's Harry Hughes was another; he believed that it was the responsibility of the legislature to take the lead in policy making. During the Hughes administration the legislature gladly did so. Other Maryland governors—Marvin Mandel, William Donald Schaefer, and Parris Glendening—interpreted their executive role very differently and exercised strong leadership vis-à-vis the legislature.

How the Governor Sees the Legislature

"I've learned [by being in the legislature] what I think many a governor learns," said Vermont's Madeleine Kunin, "and that is a successful governor means one who works well with a legislature." [1] Most governors share Kunin's understanding of what it takes, and most share her respect for the legislature as a coequal branch of government. Zell Miller of Georgia had a sense of the legislative institution and its dynamics, and he also realized that tension between the governor and the legislature was inevitable. Ned McWherter of Tennessee, a veteran of the legislature, understood the legislative process. He realized that as governor he might want to order members of the legislature: "This is really what needs to be done, let's get it done." But, instead, McWherter let the legislature put it together.[2] Both Miller and McWherter respected the legislative institution and process, which helped in their dealings with the legislature.

Other governors believe that the legislature is parochial and petty and that its members are self-serving. These governors have disdain for the legislature. They may or may not articulate such feelings publicly, but legislators cannot help but be aware of them. Robert Ray, an extremely popular governor of Iowa, exemplified the executive who could not stomach the legislature with which he had to work. "The legislature was one thing that really got to him," one of his aides recalled. It could not be controlled and it was hard to deal with. "He'd have been happy if the legislature never met.... His Christmas present was when we adjourned," said a legislative leader. On one occasion a delegation of Shriners dressed in brightly colored attire that might have resembled circus costumes entered his office, prompting Ray to exclaim: "Oh, I thought the legislature adjourned already." No admirer of the legislature he faced in Des Moines, Ray also was critical of the species generally. If one lined the fifty legislatures up against the wall and blindfolded fifty governors, according to him, it would not matter which legislature was selected. All were equally unattractive.[3] George Pataki, during his three terms as governor of New York, kept his distance from the legislature and many times simply refused to recognize the role of the legislature in policy making. For Pataki, the governor was supreme. Neither Howard Dean of Vermont nor Parris Glendening of Maryland had great regard for their legislatures. In their view, legislatures were obstacles to be overcome in order to achieve good policy and good government. To the chagrin of legislators in Vermont, the governor would portray the legislature as the negative force. "The governor's office should be treated like an abusive ex-spouse, and you have kids" is the way the executive was characterized by a legislator of Dean's own party. Relationships, however, had to be maintained, and the executive and legislature had to get along.

Few chief executives, however, have had as negative an approach to the legislature as Jesse Ventura. Elected as a third party candidate in a campaign that exploited the Minnesota public's negative attitude toward political institutions, political parties, and political people, Ventura had a simple message—"I'm not one of them"—and that message apparently appealed to nearly two out of five voters.[4] As one senator characterized Ventura's attitude: "He has utter disdain for the legislature and utter disdain for us."

A governor does not have to hold a legislature in high regard in order to work with it effectively. But gubernatorial respect for the institution tends to facilitate executive-legislative relationships, which in turn help governors get what they want. Disrespect tends to make it more difficult for governors, even if—like Ventura—their approval ratings were faring well in state public opinion polls. If their ratings drop, as Ventura's did, chances are that the legislature will try to strike back at a governor who has a habit of dissing them. The verbal abuse Ventura heaped upon house, senate, Republicans, and DFLers alike proved to be a barrier to resolving the issues. It probably served to drive participants in the lawmaking process further apart. "He has no reservoir of good will in the legislature," said Roger Moe. "He has spent three years berating the legislature. In this process, you have to have some capital." [5] Ventura ended his four-year term with little or no capital in reserve, and little that he had expended. Nonetheless, he was far from powerless in his dealings with the legislature, both because he was governor and because the DFL controlled the senate and the Republicans controlled the house. The power of being the deciding vote in such an alignment was considerable.

The Governor's Style and Techniques

A governor's style and techniques regarding the legislature obviously derive from the governor's orientation toward the legislature. Governors can be positively or negatively inclined, and their styles can range from amiable and deft at one end of a continuum to confrontational and heavy handed at the other. Kid gloves rather than boxing gloves, however, would appear to be a more effective way to handle the legislature and legislators. Yet that still allows governors to be firm. Governors, it would appear, can reap advantage from a number of factors.

First, it helps to have friends in the legislature. Ned McWherter served as speaker of the house in Tennessee and had been responsible as speaker for the appointment of many legislators who held leadership positions during his subsequent terms as governor. He continued to maintain close ties with legislator friends. A Republican leader, Ben Atchley, explained that, because of his close relationships, McWherter had sometimes been accused of "being Speaker of the House as opposed to governor." [6] Tom Loftus discusses his relationship as speaker with Gov. Tony Earl:

> Tony and I were in the best position for cooperation to get something done. We were of the same party, we were newly elected, we wanted to establish a good record, and, most importantly, we were friends. We could talk without thinking the other had a hidden agenda.[7]

Second, legislators are happier with governors who provide them access— that is, governors whose doors are open to the rank and file as well as to the leaders of the legislature. Zell Miller had Georgia legislators out to the governor's mansion for luncheons, not to lobby them but rather to express his appreciation for their support. Moreover, during the legislative session he freed time in his schedule for legislators to come to his office about anything they wished to discuss. The governor dealt with their agendas, not his own. Tennessee's McWherter also had an open-door policy. "I can call him at his residence any hour of the day or night and he'll return my phone calls, or he'll take the call immediately," a Republican member of the legislature reported.[8] Maryland's Glendening also wooed lawmakers, although perhaps less successfully than his southern governor colleagues. He would invite legislative leaders and other members to breakfast at the mansion from time to time. He calculated that during a legislative session he spent about two-thirds of his time in meetings with legislators. He would ask members what they thought and what they wanted. One legislator requested a traffic light in her community, to which the governor replied that if it could be done it would be—and he immediately called his secretary of transportation to expedite the matter.[9]

Governor Ventura offers a sharp contrast in both leadership style and personality. Sen. Reichgott Junge recalls that she tried to help Ventura relate personally to legislators. "Governor," she said, "this isn't about deals. This is about access. If you want legislators to be interested in your issue, they want the chance to know you and perhaps talk with you about an issue of interest to them." Ventura agreed to meet with legislators individually to the extent his schedule allowed. But she doubted that he had met with anyone but those who already were in his camp on an issue. "This governor just doesn't do one-on-one relationships with legislators," she concluded.[10]

Third, legislators relate better to a governor they can trust. Although Glendening tried to make legislators feel appreciated, they were not sure that they could rely on him or his word. "The problem in my committee," one chair said, "is that nobody trusts the governor." Members of the Minnesota legislature were never entirely sure whether Ventura would stand by commitments made by his staff and commissioners. Those who supported a "woman's right to know" bill in the 2000 legislative session thought they had an agreement with the governor's staff. Ventura vetoed the measure, however, whereupon the speaker of the house announced that he was considering any further agreement with the governor would have to be in writing.[11]

Fourth, a governor who invites legislators to participate in the process of executive formulation is likely to be more favorably regarded by them. McWherter was a model in this regard. He worked with legislators to develop his agenda. He would meet with them and listen to their ideas in order to develop consensus before he took a public stand. And after taking a stand, he left it to legislators to refine his proposal to their liking. When the governor's initiative finally got enacted, legislators felt fulfillment that derived from their participation. Few governors are that consultative. More typical is the behavior of Ohio's governor Bob Taft in 2001, who developed a major school-funding proposal in response to a decision of the state supreme court. He did not consult with legislators. As a consequence, the senate majority developed its own plan without waiting for the governor to reveal his in the State of the State message. Later the speaker of the house developed his own plan as a counter to those of the governor and the senate.

Along with consultation goes a willingness on the parts of governors to share power and credit. McWherter had no problem in this regard, recognizing the legislative desire to be an equal partner. According to the governor's press secretary, legislators "want to be consulted, they want to be informed, and they want to participate." [12] Ventura was the opposite. McWherter could let go without any threat to his ego. Ventura, however, held tight personally. "All I could remember was the Governor announcing the day after the last session that 'I won,' " recalls

Reichgott Junge. "It wasn't 'we won,' or 'Minnesotans won.' I guess there's only one winner in a wrestling match." [13]

Fifth, most legislators prefer a governor who works at building consensus within the legislature rather than going public to pressure the legislature. Clearly, governors are expected to stand firm on some issues. It helps rather than hurts for them to be tough when that is what is called for. Legislators respect that kind of backbone. That is very different than gubernatorial confrontation, unwillingness to negotiate and deal, and going over the heads of the legislature. Howard Dean of Vermont could be confrontational and given to public displays of temper when the legislature proved recalcitrant. But usually he would come around. Parris Glendening, when circumstances required, would be flexible and accept amendments to bills in his legislative program. Jesse Ventura, however, was constantly in the legislature's face. According to the house speaker, Steven Sviggum, the governor's attitude was "My way or the highway." Kirk Fordice of Mississippi, a Republican governor dealing with a Democratic legislature, was also not the type to work at coalition building. He was firm in his convictions, confrontational in his approach, disposed to go public, and willing to use the veto. Carroll Campbell of South Carolina, another Republican governor dealing with a Democratic legislature, was different. He could be tough and confrontational, but he preferred to engage in consensus building. McWherter always went first to the legislature before going outside, understanding that the inside game was the way to build consensus.[14]

Governors may ride high without cultivating good legislative relationships. But, when the opportunity arises, the legislature will rebel. George Pataki was uncompromising with the New York legislature; and he could be needlessly punitive in how he behaved toward it. For example, he refused to approve a pay raise for legislators unless they agreed to enact a law that withheld their paychecks every day that the budget was late. The effect was that legislators in succeeding years had to wait for their pay for weeks and months because they could not reach a budgetary agreement by the deadline date. In his ploy, Pataki succeeded only in generating ill will, for which he paid a price in the budgetary struggle in 2003.

The Governor's Engagement

Minnesota legislators complained that Jesse Ventura did not understand the legislative process, did not grasp the details of state issues, and did not work very hard at governing. For example, he exited a press conference in the capitol early to make tee time at a charity event. He also left a meeting in which his department heads were explaining details of the budget compromise that had been worked out with the legislature.[15] Sen. Reichgott Junge recounts Ventura's disengagement during the 2000 session, often traveling out of state and turning his sights to national issues and politics. "He's basically disengaged himself from the process and has the whole session long," said Speaker Sviggum. Majority Leader

Moe agreed: "He's as removed as any Governor I've ever worked with." [16] Dean of Vermont eventually also seemed to lose his focus, having served term after term upon succeeding to office on the death of Gov. Richard Snelling in 1991. Ten years after becoming governor, he appeared bored. By 2001 he was not viewed as a heavyweight in the legislature. In contrast, Maryland's Glendening came across as too heavy a weight for legislators to accept. As the end of his second term approached, Governor Glendening was concerned about his legacy.[17] That meant that what he wanted to be remembered for in Maryland would receive a disproportionate share of state funds in the budget, while the base would be underfunded. Legislators understood; as Sen. Barbara Hoffman put it: "Every governor is into legacy-building." [18] But lawmakers did not like it, and they thought Glendening went too far, and with negative effects. The Maryland governor, however, could hardly be accused of being disengaged, lacking focus, or not being taken seriously by the legislature.

Gubernatorial Lobbying

Legislators want the governor to ask them for their votes. They like to be asked. They expect governors to lobby legislators on behalf of their agendas and not leave it to legislative leaders of their party or their own aides. Ventura refused to engage in this aspect of the job. In 2000 he proposed the creation of a unicameral legislature. Speaker Sviggum agreed with the proposal and introduced a bill for a unicameral legislature. But at the outset, by a vote on the floor of 76–54, the speaker's bill was referred to a hostile committee. Sviggum gave up. "I pushed very hard for the governor's marquee issue," he said, "and I've received very little push back." One legislator commented on the governor: "The guy pushing it doesn't give a damn about it, why should we?" [19]

Few governors are as personally hands-off as Ventura, the hands-on wrestler. Dean's lobbying efforts in Vermont decreased over time. He started out his tenure by hanging out in the legislature. When that approach did not work and he lost some issues, he went to the opposite extreme, pretty much secluding himself and relating to the legislature through the press. In a state as small as Vermont and a capital as intimate as Montpelier, this was a rather unusual way of doing business. From time to time the governor would engage with members, as during the 2001 session when he telephoned—not visited with—every Democratic member of the Appropriations Committee to ask them to support his priorities. Perhaps Dean called on legislators when he sorely needed them, but that did not appear to be often. One member of the house recalled that in five years Dean had solicited his support on exactly two occasions—the only times he ever met with the governor.

Most governors are willing to work legislators at close quarters, personally lobbying their bills. Washington's Gary Locke, for example, spent the last day of the session lobbying on both the senate and house sides of the legislative building. "I've been putting out brush fires on behalf of House and Senate members on virtually every issue imaginable," Locke said.[20] Glendening was also one who got into the trenches. During the Maryland legislature's 2001 session he had to work hard on members of the Senate Judicial Proceedings Committee in order to get a gay rights bill reported out. The same bill had died in the committee in earlier years and was finally approved, thanks to the governor's lobbying. Not all legislators got handled in the same manner by Governor Glendening. "Some legislators you treat with respect, some you have to kneecap," the governor said.[21]

Part of a governor's lobbying effort has to do not only with satisfying legislators' material needs but also with satisfying their psychological needs. Recognition and small favors can mean a lot to legislators, as can visits by the governors and praise for them in their home districts. Nelson Rockefeller of New York was a master at stroking legislators—in his office, at the governor's mansion, or at his beautiful Pocantico estate on the Hudson River. Lawmakers wanted to stay on the right side of Rockefeller partly in order to ensure invitations to Pocantico.

The lengths to which a governor has to go in lobbying legislators is revealed in a story that Ralph Wright, the former speaker of the Vermont house, tells in his memoirs. In lining up votes on a bill important to Gov. Madeleine Kunin, Speaker Wright asked one of his lieutenants why legislator Frank DaPrato was not among them. He was told that DaPrato was mad at the governor, whereupon the speaker went looking for him, eventually tracking DaPrato down in the capitol cafeteria. Wright recounts their meeting and subsequent events as follows:

"Frank, I gotta talk to you about a problem I understand you have with the governor. What is it?"

"I don't have the problem. She does," he answered. "She can go to hell, and if you're here to get me to change my mind, just forget about it. I ain't going to do it."

"Now wait a minute, Frank," I pleaded. "Tell me, What's the problem?"

Frank took five minutes, non-stop. The governor seemingly had snubbed him several months earlier and he had not forgotten it. Of course, Kunin had no idea of the affront, thus she had gone on about life in the State House without ever being aware that DaPrato was angry at her or that the anger had grown to giant proportions.

"I won't forget it. What goes around comes around. Let her cook, I don't want her God damned four number license plate," he spouted out, getting angrier all the time. . . .

"What about the license plate?" I asked nonchalantly.

"She can stick that, too. I'm never gonna ask her for another thing."

I broke away with the parting I'd be back to him and headed for Bankowski's [the governor's chief of staff] cubbyhole, just off the governor's office. "Liz, can I see ya a minute?" and she immediately got up and huddled with me in the corner. "Look, Liz, I think I can get the vote we need, but it's gonna take a conversation with one of the members and the governor. She's going to have to apologize to DaPrato," I said hurriedly.

"Apologize for what?" Bankowski was willing, but wondering.

"Well, I'm not sure exactly what she did to him, but just have her apologize, ya know, sort of generically." Listening to my own conversation, I was beginning to realize how stupid this was all sounding. . . .

Liz mulled over what I had described as the problem. She thought she knew the solution.

"Mr. Speaker, that's what he wants? The plates, not an apology. How am I going to tell a governor she has to apologize for some unknown infraction to a Rep from up on the Canadian border? We'll do it. I'll find a way, and I'm sure she'll do it as we've got to have this bill, but let's try the number plate first, and then we'll get them together and she can apologize for whatever."

It worked. He got his plates and an audience with the governor. Though she didn't have to apologize, she was forced to schmooze with someone with whom she obviously didn't have a helluva lot in common, and we got our bill, by a margin of victory that totaled one.[22]

Relating to Legislative Leaders

How governors fare in the legislature depends in large part on how they relate to legislative leaders. How they relate, of course, varies according to partisan lineups; nonetheless, some governors have a way with legislative leaders of either party; some do not.[23]

Many governors make it their business to interact with legislative leaders on a regular basis—weekly or biweekly when the legislature is in session. Others meet with them less often. As governor of New Jersey, Christine Todd Whitman did not hold regular meetings with legislative leaders, although she met with them from time to time on specific issues. She did not feel comfortable with lawmakers, and engaging in small talk with them was not her style. Ventura, too, stayed as removed as he could, not committing himself to regular scheduled get-togethers with either DFL or Republican leaders in the legislature.

Most governors, by contrast, cultivate the leaders in the senate and house. Zell Miller of Georgia got together with his floor leader every morning and Ned McWherter of Tennessee had a breakfast meeting with the leadership every Wednesday.[24] Gov. Richard Snelling of Vermont had Friday morning meetings for house leaders and other meetings for senate leaders.[25] Howard Dean would meet with Democratic and Republican leaders separately. In Ohio meetings were held every week of the "Big Three," the house speaker, the senate president, and the governor. Once a month the leadership group was broadened.

Parris Glendening paid special attention to legislative leaders, hosting breakfasts for house and senate leadership teams every two or three weeks. For example, at the March 16, 2001, breakfast meeting, Glendening and his lieutenant governor, Kathleen Kennedy Townsend, met with fifteen members of the house leadership team. (They had breakfasted with the senate leadership team the day before.) The committee chairs reported to the governor on the status of the administration's package of bills, informing him of which of his bills was stalled and asking him what he thought they should do. He especially thanked each chair for his or her help.

In addition to such institutional sessions with leadership, governors target individual legislative leaders for special attention. Sen. Walter Baker chaired the Judicial Proceedings Committee, which had jurisdiction over several of Glendening's priority bills. The governor treated Baker with great respect, and at the start of each year's legislative session he would visit Baker's hotel to have breakfast with him. During the 2001 session Glendening's attention paid off. His gay rights bill was stalled in Baker's committee. The governor pleaded, but Baker replied that he could not let the bill out, for it would kill him back home. In any case, the committee was against the bill by the narrowest of margins. So the governor prevailed on the senate president, Mike Miller, to change the membership of the committee. Miller pulled a conservative off the committee, put on a liberal in his place, and managed to persuade another member to vote to report the bill out. As chair, Baker could still have prevented gay rights from advancing to the floor. But, perhaps as a result of the governor's solicitous treatment, Baker relented; the bill was reported, passed the senate, and was enacted into law.[26]

Two public officials could not have been further apart philosophically than California's Republican governor, George Deukmejian, and Democratic speaker of the assembly, Willie Brown. But Deukmejian, a former legislator, learned that the key to Brown was in helping him protect his position as assembly speaker. The governor understood that the speaker would "be willing to negotiate and try to resolve differences, provided he did not lose the confidence of his caucus." Furthermore, the governor recognized that Brown could be handled as long as he shared in the credit or, better still, got all the credit, and as long as he was permitted to be the key player. With these guidelines in mind, within four months of taking office Deukmejian managed to form a durable working relationship with Brown. They began meeting for lunch every week, an appointment they kept regularly for the duration of Deukmejian's eight-year tenure in office.[27]

The Governor as Negotiator

Legislative leaders expect that the governor will be in the trenches with them when it comes to heavy negotiations. "Heavy" usually refers to the budget. Some governors delegate negotiating to staff, and others would rather let their veto power do the talking for them. Either way, the legislators cannot ignore the governor's interests.

California is an example of a state where the governor is expected to join in budget negotiations. During the administrations of George Deukmejian and Pete Wilson, these "Big Three" would meet and negotiate from their different perspectives. To get anything accomplished the Republican governor and the Democratic speaker and president pro tem had to come to agreement. In California a two-thirds vote of each house is required to pass a budget. More recently the negotiations—now referred to as the "Big Five"—have come to include the majority and minority party leaders from each house, as well as the governor. Reaching a deal can take days or weeks of negotiations involving the legislative leaders constantly checking with the rank and file. Particularly because so many of California's public policy decisions are wrapped up in the budget process, these negotiations are probably more significant than anything else done during the legislative session.[28]

In New York the tradition was for the governor actively to broker an agreement on the budget. Before 1998 these agreements were made priority among the governor, the senate majority leader, and the assembly speaker. In that year a different and more open procedure went into effect. The governor did not involve himself; rather, the assembly and senate passed their own version of the budget and worked out differences in a conference committee. The problem, however, was that Gov. George Pataki then used the line-item veto with great abandon. After that, Speaker Sheldon Silver insisted on a three-way agreement on the size of the budget before details were ironed out, with the assurance that the governor would not rely so heavily on line-item vetoes. This process worked in 1999 and 2000, but the following year Pataki again refused to negotiate with the assembly and senate leaders. Democratic legislators accused him of failing to exercise customary executive leadership, while he responded that he had performed his constitutional obligation by submitting a budget. It was then up to the two houses to make whatever changes they deemed desirable, pass their bills, and reach an agreement.[29]

Different governors do so differently, depending largely on their personal chemistries and their political calculations. Gov. Mike Lowry of Washington played a big role in budget negotiations. His successor, Gary Locke, was less involved personally but delegated the job to his budget director. Vermont's Kunin left much of it to her chief of staff, as did Dean years later. Ohio's Taft, in contrast, spent almost two full days negotiating the 2001 budget bill.

Ventura, as has been noted, preferred to keep the Minnesota legislature at arm's length. He did not consider it his job to try to broker an agreement on the budget between the DFL senate and the Republican house. The governor had formulated his budget and he had presented it to the legislature. That was his job. "This is their job. I've done mine," he said. Although he stood back from negotiations, Ventura took various opportunities to criticize lawmakers for failing to reach agreement. On the governor's regular radio program, one caller accused Ventura of not doing enough to broker a deal on the budget. The governor responded: "It's not my job to go in there and hold their hands. Am I teaching kindergarten here?" [30] Legislative leaders Sviggum and Moe thought that the governor should have been involved during the tough negotiations. Had he been, the thinking is that he could have helped the contending houses reach agreement earlier.

The governor, even as he kept his distance, did become involved—and not only in his public denunciations of the legislature. Four days after the regular session ended on May 21, he cut a "tentative" deal with Sviggum and Moe. But it fell through when the details on specifics could not be worked out. Perhaps even more important, Ventura delegated the job of negotiating the budget to his commissioner of finance, Pam Wheelock. She had full authority to deal with the senate and house on his behalf; she had been in charge of crafting the governor's budget and then shepherding it through the legislature; and at the end she was spending sixteen-hour days in the capitol bargaining with house and senate leaders on broader issues and with chairs of legislative conference committees on more specific points in the nine major spending bills that had to be enacted. Between these sessions with legislators, she would brief the governor on what was happening and confer with agency heads and staff on strategy. "We all refer to her as Governor Wheelock," said Rep. Alice Hausman. "She's their gyroscope, the most important instrument on the ship," said the House Ways and Means Committee chair, David Bishop. And for Roger Moe, Wheelock was "the epicenter of the administration." Even without the governor's direct involvement, the commissioner of finance succeeded in figuring out compromises both sides could accept.[31]

Indeed, Wheelock may have been more effective as a negotiator than the governor himself would have been. Most legislators were critical of the way the governor handled the process. But as DFL senator John Hottinger admitted, his staff did a super job, and "maybe that's good enough." The governor wound up with much of what he wanted—property tax reform and no restrictions on abortion and benefits for the same-sex partners of state employees. Whether due to his particular role or to the talent of his staff, Governor Ventura came out ahead. He had been proven a skillful "triangulator." He positioned himself nearer the senate DFL on one issue and nearer the house Republicans on another, and eventually it was the executive's weight that broke the deadlock.[32]

Arnold Schwarzenegger's attitude toward the California legislature at the outset of his administration in December 2003 stands in sharp contrast with Ventura's. When the Democratic legislature voted down the new governor's budget proposals, Schwarzenegger appealed to the people over the heads of the legislature. This public relations blitz, according to some, was intended to persuade both Democratic and Republican members that he was serious. The governor then followed up personally, negotiating with legislative leaders and finally reaching a compromise agreement after a session with assembly speaker Herb J. Wesson Jr. that continued until 1:30 in the morning. A week later, however, Schwarzenegger invoked emergency executive powers to cut spending in California, declaring that "Since the legislative leadership refuses to act, I will act without them."[33] The new governor apparently was willing to deal, but he was also willing to confront the legislature. There would still be a long way to go before California's fiscal problems would be resolved, however. Schwarzenegger had much more work to do with the legislature.

An instructive example of a legislature's refusal to follow the lead of the governor is the defeat of a proposal to legalize slot machine gambling in Maryland. The new Republican governor, Robert Ehrlich, wanted legislation to put 11,500 slot machines at the state's racetracks, both to help the horse-racing industry and to improve the state's fiscal situation. The new Democratic speaker, Michael Busch, opposed the slots and campaigned against the governor's proposal both inside and outside the General Assembly.[37]

Legislative influence is also felt through the confirmation process, which allows the legislature to accept or reject gubernatorial nominations for judgeships and other positions. Rejection is relatively rare, but normally its threat can cause the executive to reconsider an appointment. In Minnesota the senate has to consent to the governor's choices for cabinet appointments. The confirmation process had not presented such a problem for over fifty years until Ventura's nominee, Steve Minn, was rejected by the senate. The governor had ample warning that the nomination would be rejected and could have asked Minn to withdraw. Instead, he attacked Majority Leader Moe and other members of the senate. "Minn has a character flaw," Moe explained, "but the real tragedy is the incompetency of the Governor's administration. The Governor had so many opportunities to fix this, to get out of this, and he didn't take them. He wants the fight." [38] The legislature's power to confirm may be used only on rare occasions. But it is there, and it affords legislators, individually, and the institution, more generally, influence with the governor and the executive branch.

Working over the Budget

It is impossible to measure legislative versus gubernatorial power; such power simply covers too many areas. Even if we focus on policy making alone, the issues involved are too many and varied. Probably the best place to look in order to compare the respective powers of the governor and the legislature is the budget. How do the two institutions match up here? On the basis of his experience as speaker of the Wisconsin assembly, Tom Loftus acknowledges that legislatures routinely deny governors things they want. In his view, the legislature is coequal when it comes to saying no. However, the state budget bill or a solution to the crisis of the moment must pass, and it is here, on the most important issues, where the governor calls the shots. When you brush aside the ifs and buts, what remains is an unequal relationship between legislatures and governors.[39] From another perspective, two scholars point out how executive and legislative influence over budget decisions varies from state to state, but "in no state can the governor completely monopolize legislative budget actions." [40]

It may be the "governor's budget," but nearly always significant parts of it are contested in the legislature. The processes of deliberation and negotiation between the governor and legislature are normally intense and often contentious. When economic times are tough and tax revenues lag, contention over the budget increases, as happened in the 2003 executive-legislative struggles. Whether the governor is the dominant partner or not, as in Georgia, the partnership is one in which the legislature cannot be ignored. Even in states with strong executives budgetarily, "executive hegemony" is less than complete.[41] Sometimes the two branches are at loggerheads on issues that have high visibility, as was the case when New Hampshire's governor, Jeanne Shaheen, pushed for a broad-based tax and the legislature resisted, or when Virginia governor Jim Gilmore and the legislature clashed over a car-tax reduction that proved to be twice as costly as anticipated. More often, however, the executive and legislature are in contention over less visible issues.

Strong executives may come out ahead, but a handicap does not prevent the senate or the house from insisting on its own spending and revenue-producing preferences. Take Illinois, where it is recognized that the governor's power exceeds that of the legislature in budgetary decision making.[42] The Republican senate and Democratic house leaders agreed on an alternative plan to Republican governor George Ryan's fiscal year 2002 budget. They cut the governor's proposed increases in human services spending and outlays for bond-funded building projects and proposed instead bond money and general funds for the local projects of Illinois lawmakers. In the end, however, Ryan got most of what he wanted, leading one student of the process to observe that even when legislative leaders try an end-run on the chief executives, governors usually have their way on the budget.[43]

The Maryland governor is stronger than others because, as already noted, the legislature's power over the budget is limited. The legislature can only cut items and amounts; it cannot increase expenditures, move items, or make substitutions. The Maryland legislature, thus, is at an enormous disadvantage vis-à-vis the executive. The only recourse the Maryland legislature has is to persuade the governor to include some of its spending priorities in a supplemental budget, which is part of the negotiations that take place. Whereas the budget amounted to $21 billion, the supplemental was $158 million, or less than 1 percent of the regular budget. It was what legislators needed, but it was not very expensive, in the opinion of the governor.[44] Glendening agreed to the funding of a bare-bones prescription-drug program for seniors; a renovation and expansion of the house office building and renovation of one of the senate office buildings; and more money for general health care, mental health, and various local projects desired by legislators. Glendening's consent to include these legislative items in the supplemental was in return for the legislature's agreement to restore some of the funds that had been cut from his mass transit, higher education, and antisprawl initiatives.[45] While the regular budget reflected the governor's priorities, the supplemental budget reflected those of the legislature. There is little question, however, as to whose priorities dominated monetarily.

In states other than Illinois and Maryland the legislature has substantially greater influence over the final shape of the budget. In Minnesota, for example, the contest between the DFL senate, the Republican house, and the Independence Party governor had been fairly equal. The 1999 settlement wound up with each deciding how to spend one-third of the monies in contention. The 2001 settlement was also relatively balanced. But since the governor and the house were closer than the governor and the senate on some major items, the governor and the house appeared to come out slightly ahead, while the senate was probably fortunate not to come out further behind. In Ohio the legislature was compelled by the state supreme court's ruling on school funding to raise additional amounts to level the disparity between high-wealth and low-wealth districts. Governor Taft proposed $800—all he thought the state could afford without raising taxes—and presented it in his State of the State address. Immediately, the senate developed its own plan, and the house followed suit. The senate's plan was $1.3 billion, and the house's was substantially higher than that of the governor. The house and senate then came into agreement. "The house and senate are 95 percent on the same page, but Taft isn't even in the same library," said one legislative negotiator. In order to fund increases for the schools Taft's budget drew heavily on the state's billion-dollar rainy-day fund, an account set aside for economic downturns or emergencies, rather than cut state services. Speaker Larry Householder and President Richard Finan refused to go along.

Taft soon came around to the legislature's plan on K–12 funding, agreeing to spend $1.4 billion over two years, about $600 million more than he had originally proposed. After seven hours of meetings the governor, legislative leaders, and their staffs got together on trimming $1 billion from the administration's budget proposal and funding another $400 million by closing tax loopholes, postponing tax credits, and using the state's rainy-day fund. Still, there was a gap of $60 to $80 million between projected expenditures and revenues. The question was where the money would come from. The legislative leaders wanted further budget trimming but Taft objected, insisting that additional cuts would endanger state services. He would have gotten the funds needed to balance the budget by drawing a larger amount from the rainy-day fund. Householder and Finan felt that would be irresponsible, however, because there was no economic emergency.

The Republican legislature had not been daunted by the Republican governor's funding plans; they were virtually ignored by the senate. Indeed, within hours of Taft's public announcement, Finan said the senate would move forward with its own plan, which would devote nearly twice as much money to education. Householder upped the ante, but he soon came around to the senate plan. The final compromise saw the governor giving in for the most part but insisting that gambling not be expanded to raise revenues.[46] From there on, it was up to the conference committee to determine further details and to put the budget in balance; the governor was no longer a major factor. But the situation changed again at the end of the process when he used his line-item veto power forty-nine times on the biennial budget bill that the legislature had passed.

Gubernatorial Success

As long as the governor wants to lead, he is in a good position to do so. As a student of policy making in California observed:

> The office has tremendous potential to achieve and concentrate power in the hands of a strong executive. But you have to understand the process, you have to have an agenda, you have to have an administrative way of imposing your will and consistency of purpose. Otherwise you get lost.[47]

Parris Glendening fits the bill. He happily acknowledged that the governor of Maryland was the most powerful in the nation, and that was the way he liked it.[48] However, a governor does not need that much power to get what he wants, or much of it. A governor with reasonable goals, who makes the effort, and who has a modicum of skill is practically guaranteed a good run in the legislature.

Even if governors are lacking in abilities considered requisite for dealing with the legislature, they can come out ahead as long as they put their minds to it. Ventura is a perfect example. Legislative leaders and legislative rank and file overwhelmingly agreed that he did not work the process well and did not use his powers effectively. Nevertheless, in general Ventura emerged successful and ought to get credit for the budget that was adopted in 2001. He trumpeted what he declared to be a victory in the budget battle: "It may not be a grand slam, but it's a home run with a man or two on base." Ventura exaggerated, but he did succeed in giving Minnesotans a tax rebate and property tax relief, and he got a proposal for light rail through the legislature.[49] His only big loss was on his proposal for a unicameral legislature, which went nowhere. Not a bad record for a governor with no partisan allies and an antilegislative approach.

Not many governors are as successful legislatively as was Parris Glendening during his eight years in office in Maryland. During 2001, for example, he largely controlled the shape of the budget. The legislature cut funds from his priorities and he agreed to fund, at low levels, some of the legislature's priorities. "I've never had a budget this awful," complained Barbara Hoffman, chair of the Senate Revenue and Taxation Committee. Like it or not, the legislature signed off on most of Glendening's requests. His legislation priorities did just as well. Nearly all the fourteen bills on his "Administration Legislation—2001" list passed. His top choices—a ban on racial profiling, gay rights, a 25 percent set-aside for minority businesses, and the right of staff to unionize at public institutions of higher education—were enacted into law, pretty much the way he wanted them. Only his proposal to guarantee buyout money for Maryland tobacco farmers underwent major change. In his eight years as governor Glendening lost only a few administration bills, but he got one of them on a second try.

Still, governors have to live with modification by legislatures of their proposals. And legislatures have to live with vetoes by governors of their proposals. With the veto power, and particularly the line-item veto of budget bills, governors have the last word—unless the legislature can muster the extraordinary majority required for an override. Only occasionally are legislatures able to overcome the veto. In Minnesota the DFL senate and the Republican house managed a number of overrides of Governor Ventura's vetoes, making him by far the most overridden governor in the state's history. Indeed, he suffered more veto overrides in a few hours than all other Minnesota governors had accumulated since 1939.[50] It must be remembered, however, that Ventura was an anomaly—a third party governor with only one member of his party in the entire legislature. Normally, Republican governors can expect Republican legislators to vote to uphold their vetoes and Democratic governors can expect Democratic legislators to vote to uphold theirs.

Ohio demonstrates the power of a governor in hand-to-hand combat with the legislature. When 2001 came to a close Governor Taft had signed eighty-five bills into law while vetoing one. (Meanwhile, California's Democratic governor Gray Davis vetoed more of his Democratic legislature's bills—169—than Taft had signed.) But Taft did veto forty-nine line items in the budget passed by the legislature earlier that year. This was the most line-item vetoes cast by a Republican governor since James Rhodes's seventy-two in the 1975 budget. On his first biennial budget, Taft had vetoed fourteen line items. His predecessor, George Voinovich, used the line-item veto thirty, thirty-one, eighteen, and seventeen times on the four biennial budgets during his two terms in office.[51]

Taft's vetoes amounted to a tiny percentage of the $45.1 billion biennial budget for 2002–2003. But the governor felt strongly about legislators earmarking money for pet projects and telling his administration how to spend money. Three of the vetoes concerned an ongoing dispute between the administration and Ohio's nursing homes. One veto was of a provision protecting internal legislative staff communications from being used as evidence in court. Speaker Householder and conservatives in the house would have liked to have overridden every one of the governor's vetoes, but it was clear that that was out of the question. Since an override vote on the budget must begin in the house, the speaker's strategy was to focus on six of the forty-nine vetoes. These were items on which Householder felt he could get the most support.

The speaker needed sixty of the ninety-nine members of the house—a three-fifths vote—to override. With fifty-nine Republicans, he would need at least one Democrat to achieve this end. But all the Democrats had voted against the entire budget, so if any were going to switch it would require getting something in return. According to Finan, the Democrats wanted $2 million in capital projects for their members and passage of eighteen of their bills in the house. They were offered $1.5 million and twelve bills. The deal was not consummated, however, and the override attempts were dropped. After the failure of the house to override, a plan was fashioned to take a few of the vetoed items and put them in a separate bill that legislative Republicans could pass. House and senate Republicans crafted a budget corrective bill, restoring money for several social service items, and the governor agreed to let the bill become law.

Over Taft's objections, the legislature had cut programs that the administration had already pared down. The governor would have wanted the legislature to close tax loopholes, rather than cut further. But the legislature was insistent and took control. Not until he redlined forty-nine items did the governor regain control, but even then he was willing to cede several items to the legislature.

Even a somewhat weak governor in a state with a tradition of legislative assertiveness is a major force. And in those instances in which the governor and the legislature come into direct conflict, the governor's veto power provides the weapon that can decide the outcome. Take a critical legislative issue that occurred in 2001. A provision was inserted in the budget bill at the insistence of Ohio senate president Finan that granted legislators, legislative staff, and legislative documents immunity from subpoena by the courts. This would protect certain legislative documents from public access and protect members of the legislature's staff from having to testify on how they developed legislation. The issue had arisen when the Ohio supreme court ordered the state to hand over internal documents to a coalition of school districts that was suing the state over its system of funding public education. The court also ordered legislative staff to be deposed by the coalition's attorneys. Finan believed that this was an assault on the institutional integrity of the legislature.[52]

The pressure by the Ohio press on the governor to veto the so-called "shield" provision was intense. While every newspaper in the state was twisting one of the governor's arms, Finan was twisting the other. Finan spoke strongly in a meeting with Taft and then passed the word through the grapevine that he would be angry and would boycott the weekly meetings of the "Big Three" if the governor cast a veto. It was hardly an equal contest; with an election looming the next year, Taft felt that he could not afford to alienate the press. He vetoed the provision, explaining that he believed that it was unconstitutional and that such a matter should not have been included in a budget bill. Furthermore, Taft had written a letter to Finan, which the senate president made public, in which the governor stated:

> If I let it become law as "the legislature's doing," I will be convicted in the press as an aider and abettor. They are on a tear, as you know, against the "secrecy" of "one-party rule." I hope this decision will not permanently damage the good relationship we have enjoyed.[53]

Finan was furious and countered: "Being the hero for a day to the newspapers may help the governor in the short term, but by doing this there will be serious long-term consequences for the legislature."[54] But there was not much the senate president could do. The governor had prevailed; the legislature had lost. Tempers cooled, and the senate, house, and governor would again do business.

Not only Finan but other Ohio legislators rallied around their institution on the "shield" provision. But the minority Democrats were opposed and not all the Republicans would be able to stand the heat from their local newspapers if they voted to override the governor's veto. When push came to shove, the legislature backed down, as tends to be the case where institutional prerogatives and power are concerned. Legislators have few incentives to get into a battle with the governor for something as abstract as the legislature's institutional prerogatives. They are more inclined to let their power erode than to run the political risks that are associated with trying to hold on to power and taking responsibility for its exercise. For example, during its 2002 session the Washington legislature ceded a big chunk of power to the governor. The issue was collective bargaining for state employees. Prior to this time, the legislature determined the amount of wage increases for state employees. Governor Locke's proposal extended collective bargaining rights to state employees, which meant that the administration would do the negotiating with state employee unions and the legislature would have to approve or reject the package as a whole. The legislature thus would cede control of about one-fifth of the state budget.[55] The Washington legislature was willing to relinquish power. Democrats did not want to take on their governor; nor did they and a number of Republicans want to antagonize labor. The power of the legislature as an institution was an abstraction; the power of the executive and the unions was very concrete.

Sometimes the legislature is willing to contest power with the executive. But on these occasions it is difficult for the legislature to win. The 2001 struggle in Maryland to give the legislature greater budgetary authority is an example. A measure was introduced that would have put a constitutional amendment before the voters to allow the legislature to increase and shift funds within the governor's proposed budget. The impetus for constitutional change came from members of the Senate Budget and Taxation Committee and the house speaker, Cas Taylor. The basis was the fact that the Maryland General Assembly had the least amount of budget authority of any state legislature in the country. In addition, Maryland legislators were ready to challenge the governor because he had submitted a budget that ignored the state's basic needs, as the legislature saw them. The proposed constitutional amendment had thirty-three cosponsors out of the forty-seven members of the senate. Glendening fought the amendment, arguing that the governor can focus and prioritize, whereas the legislature cannot. In order to get agreement, the legislature has to give everyone something, argued the governor, thus reducing the efficiency of the state budget. Glendening certainly did not want the institutional power of the governor to be diminished on his watch.[56]

To pass the senate the proposed constitutional amendment needed a three-fifths majority, or twenty-nine votes. It got only twenty-five, and thirteen of its cosponsors wound up voting against it. Several proponents attributed the defeat to the tactics used by the governor's staff in lobbying against the bill—the arm-twisting and the offers of projects in exchange for votes.[57] A few senators probably were persuaded by gubernatorial largesse. Some were allies of the governor and supporters of his policies and were more interested in product than process. Some simply were loyal. Some did not want to see the power of the Senate Budget and Taxation or the House Appropriations Committees increased. Some felt that too many risks would accompany budgetary change; Maryland had a reputation for sound fiscal management, so why jeopardize it? And some legislators did not want additional responsibility. Under the current system, when constituents or groups lobbied legislators to get something in the budget, legislators could not say yes, but they did not have to say no. They had a constitutional excuse for not trying to get such requests included in the budget.

After they finished their session in early April the Maryland General Assembly again turned to a plan to increase its budgetary power. The legislative leadership indicated its intention to study the issue during the interim period with the possibility of revisiting it during the 2002 session. Glendening, however, was not overly concerned. He was confident that, with his power to draw the legislative redistricting map, lawmakers would be reluctant to go against him on such a defining issue.[58] The governor was correct. No attempt was made by the legislature in 2002 to redress the budgetary imbalance of power. The next year brought a new governor, Republican Robert Ehrlich, to Maryland. The legislature made still another effort to redress the budgetary power imbalance, and the senate passed a proposed constitutional amendment on second reading. But by the time the measure came up for third reading, Ehrlich had managed to persuade a few Democrats, along with all the Republicans, to oppose it. Once again—even with a governor of the other party—the Democratic-controlled Maryland General Assembly failed to muster the necessary votes to remedy an extreme imbalance of budgetary power.

Duking It Out

The New York Constitution gives the governor budget primacy. Redrafted in 1927, the constitution shifted responsibility for the budget from the legislature to the governor. It provided that the legislature could not alter appropriation bills except by striking out an appropriation, reducing it, or adding spending on a separate line. The governor then could veto any legislative additions. In a 1938 revision of the constitution the legislature was prohibited from passing other appropriations until it took final action on the governor's bill.

In recent years, New York's governors have used descriptive language in the budget to shape or reshape programs, without seeking legislative authorization.[59] The legislature found the practice objectionable. But in 1993, in *New York State Bankers Association v. Wetzler,* the court ruled that although the legislature could change numbers in appropriation bills, it could not alter descriptions of programmatic purposes. Thus, in the 2002–2003 budget, Governor Pataki proposed changes in the Medicaid reimbursement rate for nursing homes and collapsed several school-aid formulas into a single grant.

Despite constitutional provisions, the legislature has managed to play a role in budgeting. In the 1970s and 1980s, a time when legislatures were being strengthened nationwide, the New York legislature asserted itself, striking a balance with the governor by negotiating among the "Big Three," also known as "three-men-in-a-room." The three in this case were the governor, the senate majority leader, and the assembly speaker. Over the twenty-five years in which this process was followed the legislature changed some of what the governor wanted and tinkered with other items. But in 1998 the governor opted out of this negotiating system, while the senate and assembly also switched gears, resolving differences in public conference committees and not involving the governor. After the legislature sent the budget bill to the governor, Pataki had the last word. He vetoed 1,300 items, or about $1.6 billion in spending, that had been added by the legislature. On the basis of this experience, it appeared that if the governor were not part of a budget deal, he would resort to the veto, thereby frustrating the legislature and legislators.

The long-running power struggle between the governor and the legislature in New York had become a battle between the two institutions. According to the governor, negotiated budgets were an unwarranted exercise of legislative power in defiance of the state constitution. According to the legislature, descriptive language did not belong in the governor's budget bills. The conflict came to a head in 2001 when assembly Democrats and house Republicans joined forces against the Republican governor and passed a bare-bones budget that omitted executive language of purpose and asked that it be submitted as legislation. It was intended to force the governor to negotiate.[60] Two weeks later Governor Pataki brought suit, charging that the legislature had "unconstitutionally acted in a way that diminishes the executive's power." The governor was challenging the balance that the legislature had to work so hard to achieve.

It was up to the New York courts to referee between the two branches. A justice on the state supreme court—the first level of state courts—ruled that the governor, not the legislature, possessed the authority to alter language in appropriation bills. Article VII, according to the ruling, gives the governor the option of including policy changes in the budget bill. The legislature, as prior court decisions specify, can only strike out an entire appropriation, reduce its amount, or add a new appropriation; or it can reject the budget entirely. It cannot, however, change descriptive language. By the conclusion of 2003, a five-judge panel of the Appellate Division had rendered a similar opinion. According to the New York Constitution, the governor's practice of inserting changes to current law in language accompanying appropriations cannot be altered by the legislature.[61] Until the New York Court of Appeals, the state's highest court, ruled on an appeal, the governor and the legislature would negotiate as best they could—with no punches pulled.

Meanwhile, war broke out between the New York governor and legislature once again, this time over the budget during the 2003 legislative session.[62] The budget for the approaching year was like the budgets elsewhere. It had to address a substantial shortfall in revenues. In New York's case the amount was $11.5 billion. Governor Pataki had one approach to closing the gap—with borrowing and cuts in aid to education and Medicaid, but no additional taxes. The governor's budget was unacceptable to a bipartisan legislature. It restored $1.9 billion in cuts to education and Medicaid that the governor had made and added about $2 billion in new spending. And it proposed a sales tax increase and a personal income tax increase paid by those in the highest income brackets.

Both legislative leaders, Democratic speaker Sheldon Silver and Republican senate majority leader Joe Bruno, on behalf of their caucuses, opposed a cut in local school aid, which would have resulted in a rise in local property taxes. The impact would be too great on their constituencies. They chose instead to raise other taxes in order to support state services. Remarkably, the governor's cuts had the effect of uniting Bruno, a conservative upstate Republican, and Silver, a liberal New York City Democrat, as well as bringing together assembly Democrats and senate Republicans.

Pataki, however, stood firmly against tax increases. He stood on principle as well as on his record of having cut, not raised, taxes in the past. He was unwilling to compromise and broke off negotiations, wanting no responsibility for the product. He threatened a veto and launched a public relations campaign that portrayed the legislature as irresponsible.

The legislature passed its budget in defiance of the governor's assault. The vote on the revenue bill, which was the hardest budget vote that legislators had to cast, was 102–45 in the assembly and 55–5 in the senate, more than the two-thirds majority that would be needed for the override of a gubernatorial veto. Nevertheless, Pataki vetoed 119 items, including the entire revenue bill. The legislature overrode all of the governor's vetoes, achieving unanimous overrides of each in the Republican-controlled senate. The legislature also overrode Pataki's veto of an aid package for New York City. The last override of a governor occurred more than twenty years earlier, in 1982, when Democrat Hugh Carey had been overridden by the Republican senate and Democratic assembly.

The New York governor and the New York legislature disagreed. It was not mainly a partisan matter. Governor Pataki had a position in which he believed and a statewide Republican and conservative constituency that he wanted to serve. No increases in taxes. The legislature, whatever the varying beliefs of members, was responding to what they perceived to be the preferences of constituents for the taxes rather than severe cuts in school aid and state services. Given the differences in both conscience and constituency, a compromised settlement was not possible. The executive and the legislature branches duked it out, with the legislature in a rare show of unity winning the battle.

NOTES

1. Address to the Center for American Women and Politics, Eagleton Institute of Politics, Rutgers University, delivered in San Diego, California, November 19–22, 1987.

2. Laura A. Van Assendelft, *Governors, Agenda Setting, and Divided Government* (Lanham, Md.: University Press of America, 1997), 76–77, 187.

3. Alan Rosenthal, *Governors and Legislatures* (Washington, D.C.: CQ Press, 1990), 69–70.

4. Virginia Gray and Wyman Spano, "The Irresistible Force Meets the Immovable Object: Minnesota's Moralistic Political Culture Confronts Jesse Ventura," in Stephen R. Graubard, ed., *Minnesota, Real and Imagined* (St. Paul: Minnesota Historical Society Press, 2000), 194–198; and John E. Brandl, "Policy and Politics in Minnesota," in Graubard, *Minnesota, Real and Imagined,* 171.

5. *Washington Post,* May 1, 2002.

6. Van Assendelft, *Governors, Agenda Setting, and Divided Government,* 103–107.

7. Tom Loftus, *The Art of Legislative Politics* (Washington, D.C.: CQ Press, 1994), 118.

8. Van Assendelft, *Governors, Agenda Setting, and Divided Government,* 76, 110.

9. Interview with the author, March 23, 2001.

10. Ember Reichgott Junge, unpublished manuscript, 2000.

11. Gray and Spano, "The Irresistible Force Meets the Immovable Object," 201.

12. Van Assendelft, *Governors, Agenda Setting, and Divided Government,* 109, 112–122.

13. Reichgott Junge, unpublished manuscript, 2000.

14. Van Assendelft, *Governors, Agenda Setting, and Divided Government,* 160, 180–181.

15. *St. Paul Pioneer Press,* June 23, 2001.

16. Reichgott Junge, unpublished manuscript, 2000.

17. Interview with the author, March 21, 2001.

18. *Washington Post,* March 12, 2001.

19. Reichgott Junge, unpublished manuscript, 2000.

20. *Seattle Post-Intelligencer,* March 15, 2002.

21. Interview with the author, March 23, 2001.

22. Ralph Wright, *All Politics Is Personal* (Manchester Center, Vt.: Marshall Jones Company, 1996), 122–124.

23. For more on this subject, see Rosenthal, *Governors and Legislatures,* 82–92.

24. Van Assendelft, *Governors, Agenda Setting, and Divided Government,* 76, 110.

25. Wright, *All Politics Is Personal,* 34.

26. Interview with the author, March 23, 2001.

27. James Richardson, *Willie Brown* (Berkeley: University of California Press, 1996), 299–300.

28. John Jacobs, "The Governor: Managing a Mega-State," in Gerald C. Lubenow and Bruce E. Cain, eds., *Governing California* (Berkeley: Institute of Governmental Studies Press, University of California, 1997), 30.

29. *New York Times,* June 1, 2001.

30. *St. Paul Pioneer Press,* May 19 and 20, 2001.

31. Ibid., June 30, 2001.

32. *Minneapolis Star Tribune,* June 2, 2001.

33. *New York Times,* December 12 and 20, 2003.

34. Interview with the author, Washington, D.C., May 11, 2001.

35. Wright, *All Politics Is Personal,* 117–118.

36. Loftus, *The Art of Legislative Politics,* 74.

37. *Washington Post,* April 13, 2003.

38. Reichgott Junge, unpublished manuscript, 2000.

39. Loftus, *The Art of Legislative Politics,* 75.

40. Edward J. Clynch and Thomas P. Lauth, "Conclusion: Budgeting in the American States—Conflict and Diversity," in Clynch and Lauth, eds., *Governors, Legislatures, and Budgets: Diversity Across the American States* (Westport, Conn.: Greenwood Press, 1991), 155.

41. Thomas P. Lauth, "Georgia: Shared Power and Fiscal Conservatives," and Edward J. Clynch and Thomas P. Lauth, "Conclusion," in Clynch and Lauth, eds., *Governors, Legislatures, and Budgets,* 55, 152–153.

42. Irene S. Rubin et al., "Illinois: Executive Reform and Fiscal Condition," in Clynch and Lauth, eds., *Governors, Legislatures, and Budgets,* 24.

43. Charles N. Wheeler III, "After Weeks of Dire Warnings, the Budget Is Even Bigger Than Requested," *Illinois Issues,* June 2001, 42–43.

44. Interview with the author, March 23, 2001.

45. *Washington Post,* March 29, 2001.

46. *Cincinnati Enquirer,* May 14, 2001.

47. Jacobs, "The Governor: Managing a Mega-State," 25.

48. Interview with the author, March 23, 2001.

49. *Newsweek,* July 9, 2001; Brandl, "Policy and Politics in Minnesota," 171.

50. Reichgott Junge, unpublished manuscript, 2000.

51. *Columbus Dispatch,* December 31, 2001; June 7 and 25, 2003, as reported by Lee Leonard.

52. Ibid., June 7, 2001.

53. Ibid.

54. *Cincinnati Enquirer,* June 7, 2001.

55. *Seattle Times,* March 13, 2002.

56. Interview with the author, March 23, 2001.

57. *Baltimore Sun,* February 28, 2001.

58. Interview with the author, March 23, 2001.

59. This section relies on reporting in the *New York Times,* August 16 and 22, 2001; January 18, 2002.

60. *New York Times,* August 22, 2001.

61. Ibid., December 12, 2003.

62. This section relies on reporting in the *New York Times,* March 26, April 15, May 3, May 11, May 15, and May 20, 2003.

10 DOES LEGISLATIVE LEADERSHIP
MAKE A DIFFERENCE?

What element is key to the job performance of the legislature representing, lawmaking, and balancing the power of the executive? The question is difficult to answer, because the legislature is a complicated operation, involving many people. Legislators, legislative staff, interest groups, lobbyists, constituents, the governor, and executive officials all play parts in the process. Although no one runs the legislature as such, legislative leaders are the fulcrum on which much of the work of the legislature hinges. It would be difficult for the legislature to do its job without leadership. The leadership that is central to how the legislature functions, particularly in terms of lawmaking and balancing the power of the executive, is that provided by the speaker of the house and the president, president pro tem, or majority leader of the senate and their respective leadership teams. Individuals holding these top positions have dual responsibilities—first a responsibility to the entire chamber, and second a responsibility to the majority party (although in unusual cases it could be the minority party).

Varieties of Leadership

The way leadership operates runs the gamut. It differs from the senate to the house and varies from one session to the next, depending on the size of one's majority, who is serving as governor, and the issues that arise. It also varies by setting. In Vermont, for example, the senate's top leader, the president pro tem, serves on two standing committees, just like other senators. The Finance Committee meets mornings, the Transportation Committee meets afternoons. The president pro tem has less time to perform leadership duties than does the speaker, who is not a member of any of the standing committees of the house. The senate in Vermont, as elsewhere, is more collegial and power is more dispersed than in the house. Thus, house leaders have been able to exercise more control than have their senate counterparts.

Political personality also is important. Ralph Wright, who served as Vermont's speaker, was especially strong, as well as confrontational and combative. He would not hesitate to bend the rules to achieve the results he wanted. He delighted in wielding power, as he wrote in his memoirs: "I satisfied my need for love and acceptance by accruing power. It was power to do good things as I saw it, but nevertheless it was there for all to see." [1] Wright's successor as speaker, Michael Obuchowski (also a Democrat) was straightforward, but Wright was given more to Machiavellian stratagems. Although an effective leader, Wright engendered partisan bitterness.[2]

Like Wright, Vern Riffe, speaker of the Ohio house, was a strong leader. His philosophy was simple: "If you're the leader, you're the leader. If you're strong, everyone wins, and if you're weak, they all lose." [3] Riffe's counterpart in the Ohio senate, Stanley Aronoff, never could establish similar control. His successor, JoAnne Davidson, a Republican, had an entirely different approach. Whereas Riffe held the reins tightly, Davidson gave her members far greater leeway. She opened up the process, made it more inclusive, and abandoned some control. Her successor, Larry Householder, also a Republican, reasserted control even though he was a junior member constrained by term limits that had just gone into effect. Meanwhile, under Richard Finan, senate leadership had become more centralized, only to become further decentralized under Finan's successor, Doug White. Another contrast in leadership styles is that between house speaker Cas Taylor and senate president Mike Miller in Maryland. The former was involved in the substance of policy as well as the politics of the process; the latter engaged with few policy issues *per se*. According to one observer of the legislature: "For Miller policy is a distraction between elections." [4] The variation in these leaders' styles appears to be considerable. Yet all of those mentioned above appear to have been effective in their jobs. Political scientists generalize about leadership, reducing variation to manageable dimensions and categories.[5] This may be a worthy endeavor, but there is still a wide range in styles that serve to get the job done.

The nature of the leadership job is more circumscribed. Ralph Wright employed a metaphor, asking people to envision the Vermont house chamber as Boston's Symphony Hall:

> Where [the legislators] sat was where the 150 members of the orchestra sat. As the Speaker at the Podium, I was merely the conductor. The talent sat where they sat. There were strings and horns and it was my job as the conductor to know where the various musicians sat and when to bring them in. If I did right, and anticipated timing and talent, this orchestra produced a symphony of sound, music to the ears, so to speak. If, on the other hand, I as Speaker, brought in the wrong players at the wrong time, all that occurred was noise. It was no different with the peoples' legislation.[6]

If one has a well-trained ear and eye, and a facility for hearing and reading between the lines, Wright's characterization contains an element of truth. But leadership brings to mind other metaphors as well. On the basis of his eight-year stint as speaker of the Wisconsin assembly, Tom Loftus recalls the job in the following way:

> On some days I was like the teacher in front of the classroom. I was the font of real knowledge, and I decided what we did during the day, including when we took recess. On other days I was like someone in front of a firing squad who is fumbling with his blindfold and last cigarette in order to buy time. If leaders are lucky, they will have more days like the former than the latter.[7]

Legislative leaders pursue a number of objectives, not the least of which is getting members of their party elected and winning or retaining control of the senate or house. One of their principal objectives is the enactment of legislation, especially that favored by legislators of their party. How they go about the management of lawmaking in the legislature is the subject for examination here. It entails the building of capital, collaborating in the shaping of legislation, and working to achieve results.

Leadership Resources

In doing their jobs in the legislature leaders have several advantages. The first and foremost is that they have been chosen by their colleagues—usually their party colleagues—to fill the top positions. With the position go a number of prerogatives, depending on the state and chamber. The selection of the leadership team and the appointment of members to chair and serve on standing committees afford leaders influence. If members hope to get ahead, or stay ahead, it is better to be on the right side of the house speaker or senate leader than on the wrong side. Leaders also have something to say about whether members fare well in securing benefits for their constituencies or achieving their legislative agendas. Finally, on matters that might appear minor but clearly affect the quality of legislator life, leaders have a big say. Office assignments, parking spaces, authorization to use legislative funds, travel to legislative conferences, and the like come within the purview of legislative leaders.

Just as important, leaders nowadays are in charge of their legislative party's election campaigns. Through leadership and caucus political action committees, leaders in about three-fourths of the nation's legislative chambers raise and allocate monies for the conduct of campaigns. Some also engage in the recruitment of candidates and the formulation and implementation of campaign strategy. Some members, primarily newer ones, may owe their seats to leadership efforts. The legislative party as a whole may owe its majority, in part at least, to the work of leadership.

Somewhat like governors, legislative leaders may provide or withhold benefits to members, and may actually punish them. Members often rely on leaders to raise funds for their campaigns, and leaders are obliged to allocate what they raise to the competitive races where such investments are most likely to pay off. Whether leaders do or do not make much use of the resources at their disposal to persuade members, on their parts legislators operate as though leaders might. Other things being equal, or relatively equal, members give their leaders the benefit of the doubt and cooperate with them and their caucuses whenever they can.

Despite their edge, leaders have to work to persuade members when occasions demand. Threats and intimidation are rarely employed, most likely because they do not work. What legislative leaders require—and what constitutes their principal resources—is a stock of capital that may be drawn upon in times of need. That is because leaders depend on members for their cooperation.

They need members to show up, to work with their colleagues, and occasionally to vote in favor of a closely contested proposal. Whether the leader succeeds or not hinges on many factors, one of which relates to the political capital the leader has built and how much has been depleted along the way. There is only so much to be expended. As Maryland's Cas Taylor observed with respect to a tough issue: "I'm using up too much capital on this. . . . Now best to distance myself."

Legislative leaders are constantly building capital upon which they can later draw. The first rule of legislative capital formation for leaders is to be sensitive to the mood of the members. Vermont's Wright, whose occupation was classroom teacher, paid close attention to this aspect of his job. "As in a classroom," he wrote, "I had to be ever observant as to the mood of members, not simply as a group, but as individuals. I had to constantly remind myself these people had other lives which involved spouses, children, jobs, and more." [8] A leader like Mike Miller also is aware that building relationships is what leadership is about, and for Miller that means conviviality, schmoozing, constant stroking, and never being out of touch with members of the Maryland senate.

Not all leaders are as personable as Miller, but all do know that one important aspect of their job is ministering to members. Their doors are wide open to their colleagues, who have access at practically any time. Legislators come to them with problems that run the gamut—from the highly political to the intensely personal. One needs an appointment for a constituent and asks the leader to intervene with the governor. Another needs more school aid for her district. Still another wants the leader to intervene with a committee chair to have his bill scheduled for a hearing. As Wright notes, any day is filled with dozens of occasions for the leader to be helpful to other members. Wright himself followed a rule never to let even the most mundane request go unanswered: "My criteria to judge just how far I would go to help a member was simple and straightforward. As long as it wasn't against the law, didn't require that I go to confession, or wouldn't break up my marriage, I did it." [9] Thus, Wright built his stock of capital, on which he drew when appealing to members for their help in the lawmaking process.

Leaders have to be able to bring members together, not primarily with carrots or sticks but by dint of their abilities to persuade. Years ago, a member of the Minnesota house was unhappy because he was about to cast a vote at odds with the speaker, Martin Sabo. He disagreed with his leader's position on an issue. The legislator's troubled mood stemmed not from any punishment he might suffer or rewards he might forego, but rather from having to vote against an individual for whom he had the greatest affection and respect. When members are inclined to follow because they hold their leaders in high regard, leaders have a much better chance of effectively doing their jobs.

Collaborating in the Shaping of Legislation

Leaders cannot do it alone. They rely on the membership—the entire senate or house, the members of the standing committees, their leadership teams, and their party caucuses—to craft and manage important legislation through the lawmaking processes.

Leaders and Committees

Standing committees are the vehicles by means of which legislation is shaped. Thus, the membership of each committee is important for policies within that domain. Leaders have major responsibility for the appointments of committee chairs and committee members. The presiding officer has the appointment power in about three-fifths of the chambers, while in thirteen chambers a committee on committees names the chair. In the South Carolina house the chair is elected by members of the committee, while in the Alaska senate and house, the Hawaii house, and the Nebraska unicameral a vote of the full body is required. But just about everywhere the top leaders have considerable say in who chairs the standing committees. Within limits, they can distribute talent as they choose. They may be limited by considerations of seniority, geography, ideology, and demographics, but they try to wind up with committees upon whom they can rely politically, especially on the relatively few occasions when the team has to pull together. Some leaders try to stack committees, as did Ralph Wright, while others balance out ideological persuasions, as did Walter Freed—both of whom served as speaker in Vermont. The advantage of the former approach is that the leader can get what he or she wants out of a friendly committee; the advantage of the latter approach is that a representative committee's reports have a better chance of getting the support of the chamber's membership.

It is important for leaders to appoint competent legislators to chair committees, particularly the major committees such as budget, appropriations, or finance. Maryland's Miller put excellent legislators in these positions, although a few may not have been his strongest political allies. For example, even though Thomas Bromwell challenged the senate president in an abortive run for the top leadership post, Miller kept him on as chair of the Finance Committee. He did so because Bromwell was a capable chair and popular among his colleagues. Also important is giving members an opportunity not only to advance their own agendas but to share in crafting some of the priority items of legislation. Those on the budget committees have this opportunity, and this is one reason why budget committees tend to be larger than others. More members thus get a piece of the budget action. The practice of the Minnesota senate is to have every member serve on the Finance Committee's division or subcommittee that corresponds with his or her substantive committee assignment. Members' tendency to demand a piece of the action is one reason why the Maryland house created subcommittees, first in Appropriations and then in the other committees. Just about everywhere leaders want to use the talents of members and include them in the lawmaking process.

The appointment of committee chairs is critical because leaders themselves cannot run the committees. They cannot screen through the bills referred to each. They delegate subject-matter leadership to the committee chairs and pretty well leave it in their hands. They have to trust members of their team, since they cannot monitor everything. Leaders do urge committees to kill bills that are generally considered "bad." These may be bills that have been introduced and reintroduced for years, ones that cannot be passed but that will force members to vote against powerful interests, or ones that clearly are fiscally irresponsible. The tendency among many committee members, however, is not to reject a colleague's proposal, lest the colleague at some point reciprocate in kind. Therefore, it is the chair's responsibility, according to leadership, to hang tough on bills that ought not to become law—to dispose of them in some way without bringing them to a vote. Normally the committee is on its own, but on occasion the leader will lean on the chair to get something done that the chair might otherwise fail to do. Responding to the chamber membership, the caucus, or perhaps the governor, the leader will intervene.

In Maryland, for instance, the speaker had to convince the chair of the House Ways and Means Committee to do a few things she did not care to do and also lobby the Judiciary Committee chair to get votes on a death penalty moratorium. The senate president had to go further to satisfy the majority of his members and the governor. In order to get a gay rights bill reported in the 2001 session, Miller had to change the composition of the Judicial Proceedings Committee by replacing Sen. Norman Stone with the more liberal senator Perry Sfikas. That made a 6–5 vote possible in the committee. Miller also had to persuade the committee chair, Walter Baker, to let his members vote on the death penalty moratorium bill. Baker had indicated that he was not thinking of scheduling it, whereupon a number of senators sought help from the senate president. Miller told them the bill would be voted on in committee. Afterwards Baker explained why he finally brought the bill up: "We all have a boss." [10]

Leaders are hardly the "boss," however. For the most part, they have to leave things up to the committee. They stay informed, but they exercise little control. When they do intrude upon a committee's operation, they have, at least implicitly, a mandate from a majority of the chamber. More often than having to pressure the chair or a committee, leaders and chairs are on the same wavelength. Then the issue is one of strategizing together, with leaders supporting and encouraging the committees on specific issues. One illustration is provided by a discussion in the speaker's office among Cas Taylor, the speaker, Michael Busch, who chaired the Economic Matters Committee, and Democratic majority leader John Hurson. The subject was a pharmaceutical drug program for senior citizens. The chair explained the proposal being developed in committee. Taylor supported the committee's work, despite the fact that the matter was controversial and the senate had an entirely different take on pharmaceuticals. "You guys ought to move forward, just do it," the speaker advised. "Draft it, take it into a voting session. Then, all hell's going to break loose. So what!"

Another example of the leadership role is the meeting of the Minnesota senate majority leader, Roger Moe, with the Democratic members of the E–12 division of Senate Finance on the education budget in 2001. What he needs, Moe told the chair, LeRoy Stumpf, and the members, is a bill that is balanced geographically in providing state aid for public schools. It is their job as committee members to achieve a balance between the inner cities, Minneapolis and St. Paul, and the surrounding suburbs. The committee chair indicated that they were still short of funds to devote to equity and wondered where the funds would come from. "If only we could free up some money," added a member, "but by this stage of the game everything's locked in." With more funding for the cities, the northern and western suburbs represented by Democratic-Farmer-Labor (DFL) members were losing out. "How can we mitigate that a number of our people will be put in a tough position on the floor?" asked Moe. Because of their constituencies, DFLers were split on school funding. The task, according to Stumpf, was to get money to suburban districts that were not eligible for equity funding. Building a consensus within the senate DFL on school funding would not be easy. But the majority leader charged his members: "I expect you all to get this worked out." It was clear to all that when the bill was reported out of committee and got to the floor, they could not afford to lose any votes.

The school funding issue split DFL senators and representatives alike. The suburban areas felt that they were being short-changed, while the cities believed that they merited special equity assistance. Stumpf needed his leader's help in arriving at consensus within the budget division. And the majority leader did his best to help. Indeed, providing support for the chair's efforts is a big part of the leadership job. Committee chairs turn to their leaders. In Vermont the House Appropriations Committee chair turned to the speaker: "I'll need your help on this." The leaders offer committees assistance. The president pro tem addressed the Finance Committee chair: "I'll help you on the committee; just tell me who to talk to." On some of the tough issues the chair cannot do it alone. As chair of the House Ways and Means Committee put it with regard to the revision of Vermont's school finance Act 60: "We're making progress. Now, I'll let the leadership deal with it."

Leadership Teams

Once a bill has been reported out of committee, leadership is ready to provide its persuasive powers, if they are needed. At a meeting of senior house leaders in Maryland, for instance, the majority leader asked the Judiciary Committee chair whether any of the bills coming out of committee were "so close on the floor that you think that you are going to need assistance?" The answer was no. More broadly, at the same meeting the speaker asked if there was anything on which the committee chairs needed leadership assistance. If so, the leadership was prepared to "whip" any bill—by which he meant get a tally of likely "yea" and "nay" votes. In one form or another, the house speaker and the senate president operate in conjunction with a leadership team or leadership teams. The team can consist of a few members—say, the top leader and a few of his or her most trusted associates, or the top leader along with other party leaders and the chairs of major committees. The team may be differently composed according to the issue at hand. House Republicans in Minnesota counted the speaker, Steve Sviggum, and the majority leader, Tim Pawlenty, as their principal leadership team. The two shared in strategizing and negotiating, in part because house Republicans were concerned that the speaker had been too willing to compromise with Senate Majority Leader Moe in the end-of-the-session budget negotiations in 1999 and 2000. Pawlenty could serve as a brake on Sviggum's eagerness to get a deal and a reminder that in negotiating they were not to deviate from the agenda of the Republican caucus.[11] And just to make sure, house Republicans established an executive board to work with the two principal leaders to guarantee that caucus views were represented.

Leaders feel free to organize their teams as they wish. Maryland's senate and house leadership teams have always been relatively large. On the senate side, Miller consults with his leadership team of about twenty people, listens to what they say, and then tries to bring other members into the fold as he works from the bottom up. Only where there is a possible breakdown or where a divisive issue threatens the senate community does Miller step in and try to cool things down.

On the house side Maryland leadership teams have varied in size. As speaker, Marvin Mandel had a team of thirty-five, but his successor, Thomas Hunter Lowe, employed an eight-person leadership group. John Briscoe, who followed, expanded the group's size, and then Ben Cardin built it up to about thirty-five. Cardin consulted regularly with his leadership group, also dealing with legislators one-on-one in order to reach consensus positions. The next speaker, Clay Mitchell, relied on only a few key leaders, was far less consultative, and insisted on discipline.

A larger leadership team means that more legislators feel a stake in the success of its efforts. The more who feel included, the greater the likelihood that they will make a contribution to the collective work of the legislature and not simply to their own legislative agendas. The more they are included, the more they can be expected to buy in when consensus is being built by leadership. This at least partly explains why in many legislatures the number of standing committees equals or occasionally exceeds the number of returning majority party members. It also explains why appropriations committees have grown larger and why subcommittees have been established in many legislative bodies. In Washington, for instance, the Ways and Means Committee includes half the Democrats in the senate, with most of the other Democrats also part of the leadership team.

Cas Taylor's large leadership team consisted of about forty-five members, almost one third of the total membership of the Maryland house. Included were the chairs of committees and subcommittees, the whips, even the minority leader, and a few others. Full leadership meetings were held from time to time to keep members informed and to line them up on key issues that were about to be reported to the floor. (Maryland senators joke about everyone being in house leadership, while senators have to earn leadership.) Top leadership in the house is smaller. It is presided over by the speaker, is referred to as the senior leadership, and consists of the majority leader, the committee chairs, and a few others—about sixteen people in all.

The team serves a number of purposes. First, leadership meetings enable the committee chairs to share information with one another and with the speaker. This is how top leadership keeps abreast of what is happening in the committees and how the chairs learn what is occurring in committees other than their own. Second, the speaker may indicate the direction he or she wants taken, which the chair of the particular committee then has to work out with committee members. Third, leadership meetings allow the speaker to mediate jurisdictional, or other, disputes among committee chairs. Fourth, leadership meetings enable the speaker and the chairs to build support on key measures. "We sure would like you to stick with us on that one," said Maryland's chair of Ways and Means to her colleagues. The expectation is that members of the team can be depended on to stick together and encourage associates to do the same. And so they do, with rare exceptions. As Howard Rawlings, the chair of Appropriations, recalled: "I wasn't the sponsor of the bill. I didn't like it. But I voted for it. It was a leadership bill."

The Politics of Inclusion

Good leaders work to be inclusive, at least within their own parties, so that as many people as possible have meaningful assignments. Committees serve this purpose, as do leadership teams. But inclusion extends beyond these assignments to more general operations. It is necessary to get agreement on contentious or difficult issues. For Tim Ford, the speaker of the Mississippi house, this meant giving as many of the most capable members, who represent different factions, a piece of the action. That way, a large percentage of the membership feel that they have something at stake. "By and large, members who have an opportunity to express themselves on a bill are much more likely to compromise when the time comes," he said.[12] In that way settlements can be reached. Similarly, in Minnesota Moe tried to appoint as many DFL senators as possible to conference committees on the budget. However, no matter how inclusive a leader is, not everyone can become involved in everything. In some legislatures, such as that in New York, the role members play on major issues is a relatively limited one. Here, leaders take into account their members' views and interests, but it is they and their staffs who call most of the shots, not the members themselves.

No matter what their involvement, some members will feel excluded. John E. McDonough writes of a conversation with one of his Massachusetts house colleagues, who had started off as a rebel (like McDonough himself) but was on the slow path to leadership under Speaker Charles Flaherty. The colleague recalled his early days in the house

> watching from my seat [in the house chamber] as the top leaders would huddle on the rostrum trying to finagle something through. Then a few months ago, as I was standing up on the rostrum with Flaherty and his lieutenants, I realized all of a sudden I had *become* what I once abhorred! I was now one of *them*.[13]

Legislative leaders have to know where members stand on issues, what they want, and somehow coordinate the wants and needs of as many individuals as possible. Leaders try to avert blowups. Speaker Ford and his lieutenants in Mississippi, for example, work hard to prevent dissension. The processes of the house can be stopped by a member insisting on reading a bill, so Ford tries to find out what the problems are and deal with them in advance. As a colleague observed: "We're a collective bunch of ego-filled individuals and a collection of special interests here. He puts them all together." [14] Maryland's Miller put it simply: "You have to listen to everyone's point of view—to make the place work."

The principal agency for membership inclusion is the party caucus. There are exceptions, of course. When one party is dominant, no majority party caucus may meet other than at the start of a session for purposes of organizing the chamber. For example, in the Maryland house the large leadership team substitutes for a Democratic Party caucus. That is because successive speakers felt much more comfortable with this mechanism than with the Democratic caucus. On the senate side, the president held caucus meetings every two weeks during the session because members had complained that they had not been sufficiently informed of what was going on. Miller brought members together, but he kept divisive issues off the agenda. On occasion, a leader chooses not to convene caucuses on a regular basis. As speaker in the Ohio house, Vern Riffe believed that bringing members together could only cause problems for leadership, so he scheduled few caucus meetings. Normally, however, the caucus is the setting where the most extensive discussions of issues and strategy take place, with all majority (or minority) party members assembled in the same place at the same time. At these sessions leaders confer with members, state the position of leadership on legislation, garner the support of committee chairs who are part of the leadership team, and determine which members are uncomfortable with a caucus position. They call on the loyalty of their partisan colleagues on those issues where the vote might be close. Sometimes members and leadership are in agreement; sometimes members are divided, as they often are on budget issues.

Probably the greatest challenge facing leaders is that of "representing" their caucus colleagues. First, the caucus can be very diverse, such as the Republicans in the Minnesota house. They run the gamut, according to Tim Pawlenty, from almost Democratic to almost Libertarian.[15] No speaker could dictate to such a body, so power among the Republicans is rather diffuse. Members keep their leaders on a short rein. Ohio's senate Republicans held frequent meetings so that their leader could get a sense of where his colleagues were on the issues of the day. "We've given Dick [Finan] an idea of what he can negotiate and what he can't with the governor," said Doug White, a senior member.[16] Second, the caucus, especially in a term-limited legislature like Ohio's, may need education from time to time. For Speaker Householder, the biggest job in the 2001 session was educating new members on the budget and the legislature's role in shaping it. In working the caucus, the job of leaders is to listen, encourage, prod, invoke loyalty, and bring members along to where they collectively appear to want to go.

That can be difficult to know. As the majority leader told his caucus in the Vermont house: "I need you to tell us [the leadership] where we are and where we are going to go." It is by no means an easy task to lead, when one is not sure of the exact direction in which colleagues want to go. Members have to have room to come together. JoAnne Davidson, as speaker in Ohio, gave her Republican colleagues rather free rein but told them they needed to reach agreement by a certain time. Her successor, Larry Householder, also knew how to allow his members adequate leeway and then bring them together on an issue and expect their votes. Davidson did it with a light hand, Householder with a heavier one. Leadership is a business that requires a good ear, an impeccable sense of timing, an ability to persuade, and great patience.

The Leadership Agenda

Leadership has to make choices among issues to handle, and then it has to handle them. Leaders play a significant role on relatively few issues that come to the floor. For the most part, they leave matters to standing committees and rank-and-file members to sort out. Leaders cannot *control* anything, and they can *manage* only a limited amount. They have to save themselves—their influence and their persuasiveness—for what they, and others, deem to be the important matters. Otherwise, they leave it to their members, and sometimes no decision is reached until an issue or an amendment is fought out on the floor. Speaker Taylor, for instance, made sure of majorities on a small proportion of all the bills; on the others, it was up to the house. The leadership was not in control and the committee may not have been in control; the chamber majority ultimately worked its will. And in the course of a legislative session, there would always be some surprises. Leadership in the Maryland senate was even less directive and more likely to let issues be worked out or fought out. For example, Miller knew that a floor fight was looming on a cigarette stamp bill. He and his Democratic colleagues took no collective position on the issue, choosing instead to let the senate work its will. That was the way that bill and many others were handled.

Leadership takes over from time to time, either in killing what it regards to be "bad" bills or putting together the votes to ensure that "good" bills are passed. To a large extent, the speaker of the house and president of the senate can rely on a committee to sidetrack a bill that most members would rather not decide on directly. This can be done in various ways. By referencing a bill to a hostile committee, giving it a dual committee referral, or requiring consecutive referrals, a leader can increase the odds that it will not receive favorable action. Bills can get lost or misdirected, so that by the time they reemerge it is too late. Leaders can use their referral authority to play for time, as Tom Loftus in Wisconsin did when he opposed a National Rifle Association (NRA) bill. With only about three weeks left in the session, and most attention directed toward passing the budget, Loftus referred the bill to the Finance

Committee in addition to the standing committee where it had originally gone.[17] Similarly, when the question of how to dispose of a campaign finance bill came up at a Maryland house senior leadership meeting, legislators devised a way to sidetrack the issue. To get to the floor the bill would have to make its way through two committees, Commerce and Government Matters on the one hand and Appropriations on the other. One chair commented that somewhere between these two committees, "there *has* to be a hole." The bill, in short, would be lost in transit.

If a bill is reported favorably by a standing committee, the presiding officer has considerable discretion over whether it reaches the floor for a vote.[18] Indeed, the calendaring power, by which a bill is scheduled for consideration on the floor, may be the foremost power of legislative leaders. In only a few chambers do bills go directly to the calendar in the order in which standing committees report them. More often they get to the calendar by way of the presiding officer or a rules or calendaring committee. Either way leaders normally can make a determination. But in exercising their calendaring powers, just as in exercising their referral powers, they do not go beyond where most of the members of the chamber, or most members of the caucus, want to go. Some bills arouse emotion and controversy, and no one wants to vote on them. A vote would serve little purpose, where divisions are sharp and compromise out of the question. Since one of the jobs of the legislative leaders is to protect members— usually members of their own party but sometimes colleagues on both sides of the aisle—leaders try to divert contentious issues that are likely to see more losers than winners.

A leader's primary responsibility is not the promotion of his or her personal agenda but, rather, that of a broader legislative agenda. This does not mean that leaders are without policy or other goals. At the very least, leaders want to do whatever they can for their constituencies by way of bills, projects, and local aid formulas. Beyond that, some leaders have relatively limited policy goals; instead, they work to advance those of the members and perhaps of the governor. Vern Riffe of Ohio had no strong commitment to particular policies *per se*. He wanted to get the job done to the satisfaction of as many of his colleagues as possible. Willie Brown of California had a similar approach. His best work, according to his biographer, "was in negotiating legislative deals for others." Yet Brown did have general objectives in mind throughout his speakership: expand liberal Democratic programs where possible and soften the fall when a program was under attack by moderates and conservatives.[19]

But some leaders have strongly held policy objectives, and insofar as possible they try to promote them. Peter Shumlin, president pro tem of the Vermont senate, arrived in Montpelier with three goals in mind: to equalize local tax burdens; to pass a stalking law; and to improve health care. He carried these goals into his leadership position. Roger Moe's ideological commitments grew stronger during his years as majority leader in the Minnesota senate. When pro-life legislation came before the senate Moe actively tried to convince his colleagues to oppose it. He also felt strongly about guns and gun control but was in a minority on these issues in the DFL senate caucus.

In many legislative bodies there is a general rule that a house speaker and senate leader get some of the things about which they feel strongly.[20] The smaller the item, the more likely a leader will prevail. On more important matters leaders take their chances. When JoAnne Davidson, a pro-choice Republican who succeeded Riffe as speaker in Ohio, was faced with an anti-abortion bill, she did not try to waylay it on its journey to the floor. She might have been able to do so, even though the bill had fifty sponsors. She only went so far as to try to discourage her caucus from taking a party position. Or, as Senate President Finan recalled about a provision in the omnibus budget crafted in the 2001 session, "I opposed the item, but once it goes in it's mine." In New Jersey a proposal to require school children to recite part of the Declaration of Independence had been pushed for more than a decade. The speaker of the assembly was an ardent proponent and made a personal appeal for legislators to pass it, but it failed by two votes to win the forty-one needed for passage.

According to Roger Moe, legislative leaders have to be able to see the bigger picture, which Moe likened to a jigsaw puzzle in which each legislator has a piece. In order to fit the pieces together, the leader has to look at the picture on the cover of the box—and only the leader has the box cover. When leaders assemble the puzzle, they are usually responding to what their members want. They ordinarily do so on an issue-by-issue basis, although occasionally a leadership agenda will emerge. Such an agenda will bear the fingerprints of top leaders and of the leadership team, and it will be one that will serve the interests of most legislators in the chamber or in the party.

An example of such a leadership package is that of Cas Taylor during the 2001 session of the Maryland house. Fifteen bills were on the leadership list.[21] They were developed in the aftermath of the discussion at a leadership meeting preceding the session. The leadership team, along with Tom Lewis, the speaker's chief of staff, put together various ideas members thought should be in the mix. A few were of concern to Taylor, others to other members of the team, some were carried over from previous sessions, and just about all were likely to start out with considerable legislator support. The package appeared to make good political sense. It was generally progressive. The reason, Republican minority leader Robert Kittleman observed, was that in the 1998 election six conservative Republicans had lost house seats to liberal Democrats. As house Democrats got more liberal, so did their leader. "A lot of that stuff on his agenda doesn't reflect his personal philosophy at all," Kittleman noted. "That's not wrong, that's the way the body works."

Several of the measures were not divisive, so building consensus would be a matter of fashioning agreement on details. One bill, on education, was a natural. A task force had identified needs and the only difficulty in trying to meet them was the tightness of the budget. Another bill would have changed the standard for drunken driving from a 0.10 to a 0.08 percent alcohol level. Unless Maryland stiffened the standard, it would lose some federal highway funds. The bill had been before the legislature for six years and had passed the house before. In view of the financial incentives and the positive media coverage of the issue, this too was a natural. Given several scandals involving lobbyists, an ethics measure was also included in the leadership package. Prescription care for seniors was obvious. It was on many state legislative agendas, including Maryland's. The legislative women's caucus pressed for a measure to establish a women's health office, and the leadership adopted this proposal. Del. Sandy Rosenberg was able to get his measure offering an environmental tax credit in the mix.

In reflecting the views of his members, Taylor was well on the way to developing consensus in the house. Taylor's basic beliefs were more conservative than the package he and the leadership were proposing; but the state of Maryland was more liberal than either Taylor or his district, and that is what got his attention. Taylor's efforts paid off and a former governor and current comptroller of Maryland, William Donald Schaefer, paid a tribute to him: "If you had to have a permanent speaker, he'd be it." Taylor's colleagues would have agreed. But not much is permanent in politics. In the 2000 elections, targeted by Republicans, Taylor lost by a narrow margin in a district more conservative than the house speaker and the rest of the state.

Getting the Job Done

A large part of the leader's job in lawmaking is to know what to push and what to leave alone. The agenda of the speaker and the house leadership team in Maryland was carefully crafted to respond to members' desires and needs and to exploit opportunities. So having the judgment to make good choices is critical for legislative leaders. Then—and really simultaneously—leaders have to build consensus for what appear to be the right measures, the ones that have a chance of passage and will not boomerang politically. Building consensus requires enormous patience and skill, which have to be applied throughout the lawmaking process.

An important part of the consensus-building enterprise is calming things down. Disputes have to be settled. Standing committees contest jurisdiction. The chairs fight it out, but at some point the leader steps in. Individuals have to be soothed, because when tempers flare divisiveness can arise within the chamber or caucus. And many issues split the members, anyway. One such issue is concealed weapons, which so divided the senate DFL in Minnesota that several members boycotted a meeting of the Finance Committee. "This is getting too divisive," said Moe, who stepped in to bring the principals together for a heart-to-heart. Wherever possible, splits within the party are played down. In an unusual occurrence the Maryland House Appropriations Committee had an amendment on nursing homes beaten by a voice vote on the floor. The chair and members, not about to suffer a loss, sought recognition to ask for a roll-call vote. But the speaker would not recognize them because he did not want the vote to lead to more division than there already was.

With so many transactions in the works, problems pop up constantly. On a session day, leaders move from caucus to floor to members to lobbyists to constituent delegation to press conference to radio talk show, while handling other matters by telephone. Anything can go wrong along the way, and something usually does. For instance, in New York a bill for insurance on rental cars had the backing of the leaders. It breezed through the senate, but in the assembly a Democratic member objected, arguing that the bill would drive up auto insurance rates. It became evident that the bill would be defeated, so the speaker quickly had the sponsor pull it in order to avoid embarrassment.[22] "We just put out one fire after another," characterized Ohio's Finan of much of his leadership job.

Leadership Strategizing

While doing everything else at once, leaders are at the center of strategy making. This activity is a constant in their lives, beginning even before issues are raised and bills introduced and ending only with the legislative session itself. Strategy of one sort or another is part of practically every conversation leaders have.

The key to an effective strategy for leaders is to have an endgame in mind— that is, to know what the end result ought to be and then build backwards from there. In that way leaders can adjust in light of events, but their direction and destination remain constant. This requires steadfastness and patience, both of which tend to come with experience. On the budget and other issues, the endgame is likely to involve negotiations with the other body, whether in a conference committee or between leaders, and also with the governor. Either way, the strategy in drafting and passing the bill requires that items be included that can be traded in the negotiating process. Each side wants flexibility and resources with which to deal.

Along the way, strategies change, adapting to new circumstances. The leader is always in the thick of it, however. Referring a bill to a friendly committee, collaborating with partisan allies in the other chamber, or designing persuasive approaches to one's immediate colleagues—all call for strategic thinking. Nothing is out of the question, as far as figuring out how to prevail is concerned. In trying to defeat the concealed weapons bill in Minnesota, for instance, the majority leader suggested that senators step aside and let law enforcement officers, who opposed the bill, do the lobbying.

Strategy affects the legislative schedules. Some leaders keep members on the floor for long hours, in the belief that consensus can emerge out of discomfort. "When the members are grumpy and tired and want the issue to be over," said Scott Jensen of Wisconsin, "is when a deal can be made." [23] The Rhode Island legislature takes this principle to an extreme degree. The legislature's chambers have not been air-conditioned, it is said, because of the need to resolve budget disputes at the end of the session in June or July. Legislative leaders feel that if they air-condition the capitol building members would not mind "hanging around," and thus would never be able to reach agreement on a budget.[24] "If we get started, we'll go on into the evening," the senate president told the house speaker in Ohio. "I work on the empty stomach theory." The Minnesota senate, operating on the same premise, does not break for lunch on the assumption that hunger would make things move faster. Additionally, big bills are taken up on Friday; and the process goes faster, because members are eager to get home for the weekend. Once there seems to be an agreement, leaders try to get it endorsed as quickly as possible. Finan indicated that "a conference report was not like fine wine, it shouldn't be deferred." The longer it hangs around, he added, the more cause members have to call and complain.

Leaders are the chief strategists when it comes to lawmaking. But their strategies have to extend also to providing political protection to their members. Legislators, of course, look out for themselves electorally; but their legislative party leaders are concerned as well. One of their principal responsibilities is to help their legislative party colleagues get reelected and retain or win a majority in the senate or house. Not only do they raise funds for the campaigns of legislative party members, but they also protect them politically while they are engaged in lawmaking. They encourage members to check out controversial issues with their constituents when they are home in their districts. They figure out ways to shield members from having to cast votes that could hurt them. They devise strategies to give members political cover in order to fend off the opposition's attacks. And they let members off of tough votes whenever possible. For example, in Ohio Finan let two senate Republicans vote for one of several Democratic amendments to the budget bill, and he allowed another Republican off on another amendment. All had been targeted by Democrats in their districts and faced tough races.

The 2003 vote in the New Jersey senate on the budget and taxes is an excellent illustration of legislative strategizing—in this case to provide cover to as many party members as possible. Twenty-one (out of forty) votes are required to pass a bill in the senate. Democrats and Republicans each had twenty members. Several bills increasing taxes were part of a package that had generally been agreed to by the Democratic governor, the Democratic assembly, and the tied senate. The challenge facing senate (as well as assembly) leaders was to pass a budget, but at the same time to protect their members from competitive districts from having to vote in favor of higher taxes. The Republicans committed to delivering one vote for each of several tax bills, to go along with all twenty Democrats. The Democrats would have liked more Republican votes on taxes, so that they could let three of their members who faced tough elections off the hook; but they had to settle for one safe Republican voting for an omnibus fee bill, another for a realty transfer fee, another for a hotel tax, and still another for a cigarette tax. One of these Republicans also provided the twenty-first vote for the budget bill. The leaders obtained the votes they needed and the governor got a budget without an increase in the two most politically dangerous taxes, income and sales.[25]

Building Consensus

Reaching agreement on an issue is an important objective of leadership strategy, one that can only be done if the combatants meet and hash out their disputes. Not anyone can bring this about, at least not the way a house speaker or senate president can. "My job is to bring people together," said Miller in Maryland. Moe in Minnesota expressed a similar idea: "Get all the passion in the same room." Speaker Taylor wanted to address the issue of the horse-racing industry in Maryland. "We need to get John Franzone, Joe Bryce, and Sheila Hixson in the same room—with no weapons," he said, adding after another moment's thought, "include Tiger Davis and John Hurson." On a dispute between committees, Taylor told his chief of staff: "Find time to get Guns and Busch in the same room." Only a legislative leader—such as the speaker or the president—could get four or five important people to a meeting on short notice. And in the legislature there is no time for other than short notice. Getting people to show up at a meeting may not appear impressive, but it attests to a leader's power.

When a leader brings different parties together his or her role may be that of facilitator. A bill in Ohio to give townships a greater voice in annexation had been blocked by representatives of cities. Speaker Householder insisted on a compromise being reached among township officials, municipal officials, county commissioners, developers, real-estate brokers, and a few other interests. What emerged, because of Householder's insistence, was a balanced, delicate compromise. (That measure was reported favorably by the committee and rushed to the floor by the speaker before any opposition could mobilize.) When the gun safety bill was in trouble in Maryland, the speaker intervened to work out a compromise acceptable to the NRA on the one hand and Marylanders Against Handgun Abuse on the other. In each of these negotiations, the respective speakers were crucial in forcing agreement. California's Willie Brown as speaker could bring together several major interest groups in California for a series of meetings in his private cloakroom and at Frank Fat's restaurant in Sacramento. The culmination of these sessions was what became known as the "napkin deal," which led to compromise legislation changing the state's liability laws. As described by James Richardson, the speaker's involvement was essential:

> As plates of chicken wings and pea pods were shuttled to the tables, the representatives of the warring industries scribbled on legal pads, trying to work out a political truce. They were joined by Democratic State Senator Bill Lockyer and eventually by Willie Brown. The night wore on, and Brown shuttled between the tables, talking with each participant, probing for trouble spots. The talks nearly broke down when the trial lawyers balked over a detail. "Are you going to trust me?" . . . "Are you going to let me deal for you?" Brown closed the deal.[26]

Negotiating

Much of the negotiating done by leaders is with other leaders or with the governor. Not everyone can be involved, and only the leaders are authorized to negotiate on behalf of their colleagues. If they are to represent their caucuses effectively, leaders have to keep in close touch and have a good sense of where their members are, how far they can go, and what they can surrender in arriving at a deal. Not every leader has the same latitude. Depending on the chamber, the caucus, and the leader's standing, some can go further and others have to tread very carefully.

Realistically, only one or a few people can do the job. Negotiating requires enormous skill, patience, and, often, stamina. The negotiator has got to know what he or she needs, as well as what others need—not only with respect to the particular issue at stake but out of the entire process. New York's assembly speaker, Sheldon Silver, is supposedly one of the best negotiators in the business. He is said to be brilliant at finding what his opponents need and then blocking it to get what he wants.[27] Especially toward the end of the session, when the two chambers are trying to resolve differences, rank-and-file legislators have to wait for their leaders to arrive at settlements. They may caucus from time to time, as leaders check back and bring them up to date, but the heavy lifting is done only by a few.

Take, for instance, negotiations over the budget in Minnesota, involving the DFL-controlled senate, represented by Roger Moe; the Republican-controlled house, represented by Steve Sviggum, the speaker, and Tim Pawlenty, the majority leader; and the governor, Jesse Ventura of the Independence Party, who was usually represented by his commissioner of finance. At the most basic level, leaders of the senate and house had to reach agreement on bottom-line numbers, as well as on how much tax relief there would be. More specifically, negotiations extended to many specific items. The top leaders had to decide when to begin deciding on budget targets. They had to figure out whether to keep certain issues out of the budget, such as Profiles in Learning, an education program, which caused a sharp partisan split. They had to align different senate and house budget divisions into nine or so conference committees. They also had to decide whether leaders themselves would serve on conference committees. And so on. Whenever an issue arose that the work groups—established as conference committees in the special session—could not settle, it was referred to leadership. It was the job of the leaders to reach agreement between them and with the executive.

Rounding up Votes

In order to get the job done, leaders are also responsible for putting together majorities. Negotiations that broaden the appeal of a measure or lessen the downside are designed to net votes. But leaders use other means as well. They round up votes one by one. This requires that they know how many votes they have and, thus, how many more they need to have a majority. Vote counts by leaders and their staffs are an important part of leadership work. The house minority leader in Vermont described his efforts: "We don't break heads, we count them." Ralph Wright as speaker worked hard reviewing the numbers, trying to figure out where to get the seventy-six votes he needed to pass a bill.[28] A committee chair will have some idea in reporting a bill favorably whether it will command a majority in the chamber. At a senior leaders' meeting in Maryland, the chair of the Environmental Matters Committee informed the speaker: "You might want to get a straw vote. I don't think you can pass it." It was then in the hands of leadership.

In writing of his experiences in the Massachusetts house, John E. McDonough recalled how George Kevarian as speaker and Charles Flaherty as majority leader went about rounding up votes. Kevarian owned a set of colored markers with which he kept track of his lobbying efforts. He used one color for his solid "yes" votes, another for his "yes leaners," one color for solid "no" votes, another for "no leaners," still another for "maybes," and one more for those who might take a walk on the vote.[29] The leader has to know which members to approach. Some are at the base of a bill's support, already committed—the solid "yes" members. Wright seldom had to appeal to liberals; they were already on his side. "Whenever we got into counting on issues that were anticipated as being a battle royal," he wrote, "we could merely sit down and check off the members whom we were aware of who would agree with the intent of the bill. They were like money in the bank." [30] Some members are on the other side, opposed to a bill for reasons of conscience, constituency, or otherwise. Leadership seldom solicited their votes.

Those in the middle, who are essentially undecided, are the legislators susceptible to leadership persuasion. Not all have to be approached or persuaded, just simply enough to get the necessary majority. "There's an Annapolis axiom," reports Maryland delegate Sandy Rosenberg, "that you don't buy a landslide. That is, don't incur more obligations than needed to get the bill passed." [31] But the job of rounding up support is not completely done until the votes are cast. Wright describes the process on a particularly emotional issue in Vermont:

Within 24 hours, I was in the mid-sixties. Passage required a majority of those present. If there was full attendance, 75 votes would do it. The Speaker, as one of 150, only voted to break or make a tie, which in the latter case meant the bill failed. No one ever could guess correctly what the attendance would be on any given day, but our exercise as a leadership team was to begin a running count the day of the vote. This would begin early in the morning and be updated constantly as to who was there and who wasn't, right up to the moment the roll call began. Missing members would be tracked down, assuming they were going to vote with us, and calls would go out to their home, business or car phone. We were diligent about it and this extra effort often made the difference.[32]

Rounding up votes is tough work. William Bulger, a former president of the Massachusetts senate, characterized the challenge facing legislative leadership as follows: "You come into the Senate every day with a wheelbarrow of 33 cats. Your job is to get the wheelbarrow with 17 of those cats to the other side of the chamber." Leaders can choose from a variety of approaches to members whose votes they want. They can use their whip operation, call on the governor's office for help, assign the job to particular colleagues of the targeted member, or turn the job over to an interest group. Most likely, they will work a member in multiple ways. But there is no substitute for the leader's personal efforts. A leader has to be able, as said by Rep. David Evans of Householder in Ohio, "to visit with those members who were way out there and bring them in." [33]

When members do what leaders want them to do, usually it is not because of arm-twisting or threats. Discipline is rare; punishment does occur, but it is the exception. Even Riffe of Ohio, who was reputed to be a strong leader and strict disciplinarian, over the course of twenty years resorted to punishment only on a few occasions. Some committee chairs were relieved by Riffe of their positions and some were denied reappointment for having deserted the legislative party on key issues. Years later Ohio's senate president, Doug White, removed Kevin Coughlin from the Senate Finance Committee because he would not vote with his Republican colleagues to raise the sales tax. New at the job and term limited, White had to demonstrate to the caucus that he was in control. Coughlin, however, continued as chair of a committee and managed to get a project for his district in the budget bill. Thus, the discipline, while embarrassing, was quite tolerable.

Elsewhere, too, discipline is invoked, but infrequently. The lone Republican assembly member in New York who voted with the Democratic majority on two budget bills in 2003, after being told what was expected of him by the minority leader, lost his position as ranking minority member on a committee. With that he lost a $9,000 stipend that went with such a leadership position.[34] Even in a state like Massachusetts, where leadership is powerful, sanctions for disloyalty are rare. Voting "off," or against the leadership, once carried a substantial price. Now opposition is simply accepted.[35] Contemporary leaders subscribe to the dictum as articulated by Wisconsin's Scott Jensen: "If you punish them today, they'll punish you tomorrow." [36]

While it is rare for leaders to threaten, members can never be sure of what will happen to their bills or pet projects if they refuse their leader a vote. They may not get what they aspire to, such as appointment as committee chair, if they do not go along; they don't know. While punishment in Vermont is extremely rare, members discuss its possibility. "As long as the threat's there," said an official of the executive branch, "that's what you need." Members' fears of what leaders might or might not do for them or to them tend to induce the undecideds to go with leadership if asked.

Occasionally, leaders offer inducements. But "buying" or "trading" votes is not done frequently. When necessary, however, leaders will accommodate members whose votes are sorely needed. Wright was always willing to deal in Vermont, depending on the price. According to him, a number of house members drove a hard bargain. They did not care about the bill in question, but they wanted something in return for their support. If they did not ask the speaker at the time, he knew that they would come around and make their requests later on.[37] By contrast, Roger Moe in Minnesota rarely made such deals. He would try to help senators if they went along, but he usually did so without agreeing to a quid pro quo. One of the tough issues Moe handled in the 2001 session concerned a "woman's right to know" amendment to the budget. He had to get three or four DFLers to change their votes, and he knew that two of them wanted to be appointed to one of the conference committees on the budget. That was not a heavy demand, and Moe was willing to entertain it; but he still could not convince these DFLers to switch their votes.

The main technique that Moe and other leaders use is simply to ask members for their votes, invoke loyalty, and try to persuade them. Members do not want to be taken for granted; they want to be asked. Wright remembers requesting a house member's support for a gay rights bill. Their delightful exchange, reported by the Vermont speaker, runs as follows:

"Billy, can I talk to ya for a minute?" I said, as we bumped into each other just outside the Speaker's office. (Billy is a fictitious name.)

"Sure, Mr. Speaker," came the less than enthusiastic reply. Billy sensed he was about to be buttonholed.

"C'mon in the office for a second," I said. He followed like a kid headed for Mother Superior's shed.

"Now, Billy, you know I've been working my ass off trying to get enough votes to pass this gay rights bill and I need your help. I wouldn't ask you, but it's going to be an extremely tight vote. What do you say, can I count on you?"

"Geez, Mr. Speaker, I just can't give you a hand on this one," he said. "My district is dead set against me voting for something like this." He was nervous.

"Oh, for Chrissakes, Billy, you know as well as I that by the time next election comes around no one's going to remember this vote. We're a year and a half from the next time you have to put your name on a ballot," I argued.

"They'll remember this one, Mr. Speaker. I've been getting a lot of mail and calls. This is a tough one." He said it with the confidence of a man winning an argument.

"C'mon, Billy, I really need you on this one," I pleaded.

"Mr. Speaker, you know I'd do anything to help you out if I could but you know it isn't just my folks back home. Frankly, the bill just isn't right." That was the killer. He spoke now with the conviction of a used car salesman closing a deal for a lemon with sawdust in the transmission. He repeated this plea.

"It's just not right." Now at his best, his was the voice of an innocent altar boy.

Suddenly my mind flashed back to a rather famous "Tip" O'Neill tale and I ended the conversation by lashing out at him, paraphrasing the legendary U.S. House Speaker from Massachusetts:

"Billy, you ass, I don't need you when I'm right. I need you now."

I was up to 66.[38]

Asking a colleague for a vote is serious business, even for leaders. They have to know their members and just how to approach them, and how some of them will follow particular colleagues. When Moe was trying to get votes in caucus for a collective bargaining provision, one senator agreed to change his vote if two others did the same. "If Doug, David, and Sam change, we'll have thirty-five," said the leader. "We can defend it as a labor issue." Moe got the votes. The leader must know how to ask, and the answer most often will be yes.

But not always, as McDonough recounts:

In one of his many drives to assemble eighty-one votes in favor of a tax package, Keverian reached out in late November to Sal DiMasi, a likeable, wisecracking attorney and rep from the North End section of Boston. DiMasi had recently been released from the hospital after suffering a heart attack and was recuperating at his home, only a five-minute drive from the capitol. Keverian called to ask if he would consider making a special trip to the State House to vote for the tax package. "You don't understand, George," he said. "I had a heart attack, not a lobotomy." [39]

Holding Up under Fire

It is difficult to imagine how the legislature could hope to match the executive without the benefit of effective leadership. It is almost as difficult to imagine how lawmaking would take place without leadership to manage the process. It is almost impossible, in short, to conceive of the legislature doing the heavy lifting it does without leadership. Effective leadership is critical, but the burdens are heavy. Leaders are under great pressure; and by the end of the legislative session even the most weathered leader may be near the breaking point. With negotiations over the Minnesota budget coming down to the wire, the leaders were feeling the strain. Speaker Sviggum and Majority Leader Pawlenty blew off steam by jogging during a break in the legislative schedule for the day. Majority Leader Moe wore a tie bearing a reproduction of *The Scream,* the Edvard Munch painting of a figure suffering an anxiety attack on a bridge. "This is a deliberate pick," Moe said. "I'm getting ready to scream." [40]

NOTES

1. Ralph Wright, *All Politics Is Personal* (Manchester Center, Vt.: Marshall Jones Company, 1996), 201.

2. David Moats, *Civil Wars: A Battle for Gay Marriage* (New York: Harcourt, 2004), 149.

3. Interview with the author, February 23, 1996.

4. Interview with the author, March 16, 2001.

5. See Malcolm E. Jewell and Marcia Lipman Whicker, *Legislative Leadership in the American States* (Ann Arbor: University of Michigan Press, 1994).

6. Wright, *All Politics Is Personal*, 4.

7. Tom Loftus, *The Art of Legislative Politics* (Washington, D.C.: CQ Press, 1994), 47.

8. Wright, *All Politics Is Personal*, 5.

9. Ibid., 24–25.

10. *Baltimore Sun*, March 21 and 23, 2001; *Washington Post*, April 4, 2001.

11. *St. Paul Pioneer Press*, May 27, 2001.

12. Bob Gurwitt, "Good Old Boy, Circa 2001," *Governing*, May 2001, 31, 35.

13. John E. McDonough, *Experiencing Politics* (Berkeley: University of California Press, 2000), 190.

14. Gurwitt, "Good Old Boy, Circa 2001," 36.

15. *St. Paul Pioneer Press*, May 27, 2001.

16. *Columbus Dispatch*, April 11, 2001.

17. Loftus, *The Art of Legislative Politics*, 196.

18. This paragraph is based on Alan Rosenthal, *The Decline of Representative Democracy* (Washington, D.C.: CQ Press, 1998), 259–260.

19. James Richardson, *Willie Brown* (Berkeley: University of California Press, 1996), 365. See also the discussion of Brown's legacy in James Richardson, "Talk About a Legacy," *California Journal* (December 2003): 12–17.

20. Loftus, *The Art of Legislative Politics*, 126.

21. This paragraph relies on the report by Sarah Koenig, "House Speaker Casts Wide Net," *Baltimore Sun*, March 11, 2001.

22. *New York Times*, June 22, 2001.

23. Interview with the author, July 24, 1996.

24. Maureen Moakley, "The Rhode Island Legislature: The Center Still Holds" (paper prepared for delivery at the annual meeting of the American Political Science Association, San Francisco, August 29–September 1, 1996).

25. *Politifax*, vii (July 9, 2003), 1, 3.

26. Richardson, *Willie Brown*, 348.

27. *New York Times*, February 11, 2003.

28. Wright, *All Politics Is Personal*, 177.

29. McDonough, *Experiencing Politics*, 137–138.

30. Wright, *All Politics Is Personal*, 177.

31. Diary of Del. Sandy Rosenberg, March 20, 2001.

32. Wright, *All Politics Is Personal*, 24.

33. *Cincinnati Enquirer*, December 30, 2001.

34. It was believed that the punishment was mainly the governor's decision. *New York Times*, May 6, 2003.

35. John Powers, "Altered State: It's a New Era on Beacon Hill, with New Players, New Rules, and New Attitudes," *Boston Globe Magazine*, June 16, 1996, 31.

36. Interview with the author, July 24, 1996.

37. Wright, *All Politics Is Personal*, 176, 181.

38. Ibid., 25–26.

39. McDonough, *Experiencing Politics*, 142.

40. *St. Paul Pioneer Press*, May 20, 2001.

11 WHAT IS A "GOOD" LEGISLATURE?

In light of the discussion in the previous chapters, it is hard to imagine a legislature without leadership. In such a legislature power and responsibility would be equally distributed among members. No one would have principal responsibility. Leadership, however, is critical for the legislature to perform at least two out of three of its major jobs: lawmaking and balancing. We have seen that the work of representing, lawmaking, and balancing the power of the executive is not easy. It is "heavy lifting," indeed. Exploring the way legislatures do this work has been necessary in order to address the question we set for ourselves at the outset: What is a "good" legislature? Performance, not product or structure, has to be the principal standard in assessing legislatures. How well, then, do these institutions do their job representing, lawmaking, and balancing?

The Legislature's Job Performance

Public opinion polls provide an indication of what people think about the legislature's performance, but it is usually not an informed assessment. Some years ago, I examined statewide polls in New Jersey to see whether there was any explanation for the public's ratings of the legislature. The only pattern I could discern from a dozen years of data, collected on a quarterly basis, was that positive approval ratings were higher in July and August than they were during the rest of the year. That is because the New Jersey legislature was generally in session from January through June, while it was in recess during the summer months of July and August. Apparently, when the legislature is not meeting it looks best, but when it is doing its job it looks worst.

The public cannot be expected to make an informed judgment on something as elusive and complex as the performance of a legislature, and certainly not in the dimensions set forth here. But the opinions of legislators themselves about how their institutions function deserve attention. During the era of legislative modernization, and as part of comprehensive studies of legislative organization and procedure from 1967 through 1971, lawmakers in six states were asked to assess the jobs actually being done by their legislature.[1] Did they think that their legislature's performance was "excellent," "good," "fair," or "poor" with respect to each of the following: constituent service; policy and program formulation; and policy and program control (legislative oversight)? The results of these surveys indicated that, overall, Wisconsin legislators rated their institution's per-

232

formance best, while Mississippi's rated theirs worst. More important, however, in every state legislators gave the legislature's performance of constituent service higher ratings than that of policy and program formulation, both of which were rated much higher than policy and program control. "Excellent" or "good" ratings for constituent service ranged from 64 percent to 92 percent, policy and program formulation from 41 percent to 78 percent, and policy and program control from 15 percent to 27 percent.

The current "five-state survey," conducted thirty years later, asked legislators in Maryland, Minnesota, Ohio, Vermont, and Washington questions along similar lines about their legislature's performance: whether they thought that their legislature did an "excellent," "good," "only fair," or "poor" job representing constituencies, lawmaking, and balancing executive power, the results of which are shown in Table 11-1. In each of the states the ranking is the same. The representing function is highest rated, as it was in the earlier studies. Overall, 88 percent of those surveyed think their legislature is doing an "excellent" or "good" job in this respect. Lawmaking comes next, as in the earlier studies, with 69 percent regarding legislative performance positively. The function of balancing the executive is broader than that of policy and program control, which was intended to refer mainly to legislative oversight activity. Here, legislators think that that job is done least well; only 41 percent give their legislature's performance a positive rating.

There are variations among the states, about which one can only speculate. Ohio members are less positive about representation, possibly because of the large size of the districts that senate and house members represent, or because of the instability created by that state's term limits. Vermont and Washington members are least positive in their assessment of lawmaking, while Maryland and Minnesota are most positive. Differences here are difficult to explain. Only in Minnesota do more than half the members assess the job their legislature does balancing executive power positively, possibly because Gov. Jesse Ventura never really engaged with the legislature and his Independence Party was represented by a single legislator out of the total of 201. In contrast, only one out of four Maryland lawmakers think the legislature did an "excellent" or "good" job balancing the power of the executive, which is understandable in light of

Table 11-1 Lawmakers' Assessment of Their Legislature's Performance

Function	Percentage assessing performance to be "excellent" or "good"					
	Total	Maryland	Minnesota	Ohio	Vermont	Washington
Representing constituents	88	87	90	75	89	94
Lawmaking	69	76	77	68	58	61
Balancing executive power	41	28	53	44	46	39
Total n	($n = 258$)	($n = 95$)	($n = 90$)	($n = 44$)	($n = 87$)	($n = 47$)

Source: Data compiled by the author.

the Maryland legislature's weak budgetary powers and the governor's control of redistricting. What is surprising is that only 44 percent of Ohio legislators believe that their institution was a match for the executive, when in fact the Ohio legislature had been dealing with governors on a relatively equal basis for some time—but perhaps not equal enough for the legislators.

Lawmakers' assessment of the job of representation varied little by characteristics such as chamber, party affiliation, majority or minority party membership, or gender. What mattered was length of service; the longer they served, the better job at representation members thought their legislature achieved. Assessments of legislative performance of lawmaking varied greatly with one characteristic—that of majority party status. As might be expected, minority party members were much less positive about their legislature's performance at lawmaking than were majority party members. Among minority party members, 51 percent rated performance positively; among majority party members, 82 percent rated performance positively. Senators and Democrats were more likely than representatives and Republicans to rate their legislature's balancing efforts positively.

The assessments of members are on target, especially in their ordering of the performance of the three functions. As indicated in chapters 2 through 9, legislatures do best at representing, second best at lawmaking, and worst at balancing the power of the executive.

Representing

If representation were their only job, legislatures would deserve high ratings and the "good" legislature would be practically ubiquitous. In representing them, legislators offer constituents a connection to the political and governmental world—that is, if constituents want to take advantage of it. Virtually anyone can gain access to a legislator and even to the legislature; yet relatively few seek it. Most people are preoccupied with their families and jobs, their problems and pleasures, and have little time or incentive for politics. Nevertheless, legislators constantly try to build up their trade, wanting to hear from more people than ever would contact them. Some practically advertise to get business. Their constituents, of course, are potential voters, and that is most significant to the legislators. Beyond that, lawmakers take tasks of representation seriously for various reasons. Service is important to them. They want to do and get as much for their constituency and constituents as they possibly can. Helping individuals who are having problems with governmental agencies or programs, or with most anything at all, is what virtually every legislator does as a matter of course. Some do it more, others less, but the job of serving the folks back home is neglected by few members of state legislatures.

Part of the representational role for the legislature is also to express the interests and views of the constituency. This is more problematic, because the large majority of issues in contest are well under the radar back home. Constituents are unaware, unconcerned, and unaffected—except in the most indirect sense.

They have neither interests nor views on the overwhelming majority of issues. On some issues, constituency members of an organized interest group take sides, but the numbers of voters involved comprise a very small percentage of the electorate. On a few issues a substantial proportion of the constituency does care, as does their representative, and most often the views of the dominant constituency group and those of the representative coincide. Infrequently, however, they clash. When this happens, depending upon the specific issue, representatives either take a Burkean position, voting according to their own conscience, or go along with the dominant views of the constituency.

The system is one in which elected representatives decide on their own when necessary, listen to their constituencies when there is something to which to listen, and only on rare occasion have to worry about conscience and constituency clashing. No matter how they vote, however, some people in their districts are likely to be dissatisfied. Legislators can tolerate this, as long as there are not too many of them. All of this would seem to make for effective representation, especially when the many service aspects of representation are added in. What representation entails is not any single action, but the overall functioning of the system. Representatives are continuously sensitive to the opinions, interests, and demands of their constituents. "There need not be a constant activity of responding," according to Hanna F. Pitkin, "but there must be a constant condition of responsiveness, of potential readiness to respond." For Pitkin, even if most of the time people are unaware of what their government is doing, so long as there is an opportunity for them to initiate action if they desire, the representational system is working.[2] The condition of responsiveness is surely there.

It may be argued, however, that not everyone in the state or district is represented equally. If they were, shouldn't more women, minorities, blue-collar laborers, and younger people be holding seats in the legislature? And what about Republicans who live in heavily Democratic districts and Democrats who live in heavily Republican districts? Are they fairly represented? If an adequate system of representation requires that the characteristics of the legislature mirror those of the population, then the system would have to be deemed inadequate. Our legislative bodies are composed disproportionately of older, white males who are well educated and relatively affluent. Does the underrepresentation of some groups affect how legislatures work and what they work on? This is probably the case, but not to a great extent.

There is evidence that the substantial increase of women in legislatures since the 1970s has resulted in the incorporation of so-called "women's issues" onto legislative agendas—a trend that is less likely to have occurred without women spearheading them in the legislature.[3] The likelihood also exists that larger contingents of African Americans and Hispanics in legislative bodies have also made a difference—not on the overall process but on a few of the issues that otherwise might not have made the legislature's agenda. "Descriptive representation," whereby a legislative body accurately corresponds to or resembles the population that it represents, has had some supporters over the years. The problem, of course, is that the mechanics of achieving such correspondence are daunting, to say the least. Moreover, the question remains which characteristics ought to be proportionately represented—gender, race, income, education?[4] Still, women, African Americans, and Hispanics in state legislatures represent more than the people in their districts. Many—albeit not all—also tend to represent their gender, race, and ethnicity. Similarly, but to a lesser degree, teachers tend to express the interests of teachers, attorneys of attorneys, and so forth.

The system is not only criticized for underrepresenting such characteristics but also for underrepresenting partisan minorities. Without some system of proportionality, in legislative elections in the states the winner takes all. The predominance of single-member districts means that the members of one party win while the members of the other party lose. Except in very few places—most notably Burlington, Vermont—a candidate of a minor party has little chance of being elected.

The problem of losers being unrepresented is exacerbated by the fact that so many districts are safe for one party or the other. Over 90 percent of congressional districts are safe for either Democrats or Republicans. In some states as many as 60–80 percent and in others 20–40 percent of the districts are relatively safe in partisan terms. The noncompetitive nature of legislative districts is reinforced in many places by the decennial redistricting process, which may increase the number of safe districts. And since, as pointed out in chapter 3, legislators tend to see constituency views mainly as those of their supporters, adherents of the district's minority party may feel left out. In a strict sense they are. More broadly, however, their views are represented in the legislature, by legislators from other districts, and to whose party they belong, as well as by interest groups to which they also belong or with whom they share views. That is because political parties and interest groups are also channels of representation, supplementing and overlapping representation by legislators elected from districts. Since most legislatures and legislative chambers are reasonably competitive (while many legislative districts are reasonably safe), many people who support the minority party in a particular district do tend to have their positions represented in legislative lawmaking.

Our assessment of legislative performance representing constituencies is made within the context of the current representational system, not a different one. Given the overall system, legislatures do a good job representing constituencies and constituents. They do the job somewhat differently, depending largely on the number of constituents each legislator must represent, the resources they have to perform the service aspects of representation, the careers they are pursuing, and their constituents' expectations of them. Aside from suggesting that the resource-deprived legislators, such as those in Vermont, receive greater assistance and legislators elsewhere receive additional aid to help them keep in touch, it is difficult to know how their job representing could be significantly improved.

Representing is very much a job for individual legislators, with each member doing much of it on his or her own. Legislators may be limited in what they can do by the size and configuration of their districts and the resources the legislature makes available to them. But such constraints do not prevent them from doing a good job. Securing funding on projects for the district requires help from other participants in the legislative process, as does representing constituency values and interests on public policy. But legislators tend to be entrepreneurial and responsive—and these qualities contribute to commendable legislative performance in representing constituencies.

Lawmaking

The lawmaking part of the legislative job has to be considered in the context of the legislature's representational role. Individual legislators, as was shown earlier, tend to see eye to eye with their constituents on the few issues on which constituents have strong views. But legislators in the aggregate represent people who do not agree with one another. Fundamental to the system of representative democracy is the diversity of the nation and states. The public's values, interests, and priorities differ and conflict. Such disagreements are reflected in how legislatures make law, and they may also be sharpened in the process. Just about all are also channeled by political interest groups, a number of which align themselves with one of the political parties. Finally, some of the more important differences and conflicts are represented by the Democratic and Republican Parties. "They built [the state capitol building] for different ideas to come together and that's what happens," said Minnesota's senate majority leader, Roger Moe, at the close of the legislative year in 2001. The concerns of the electorate, interest groups, political parties, and legislators themselves all come to bear on the lawmaking process in the complex interactions that have been portrayed in this book.

What, then, can be expected from lawmaking as performed in bodies that handle differences and conflict? In other words, what makes for good lawmaking? First, the issues in contest must be studied. The sharper the disagreement, the more information and knowledge are likely to be brought to bear by supporters of various positions. The ability to process information and shape public policy are also requisite. Second, deliberation ought to be a large part of the lawmaking process. This means that proponents and opponents will argue the merits of their case, as they see it. Depending on the issue, these arguments may turn some legislators around and affect others on more marginal aspects. For deliberation to work, legislators must be willing to listen to arguments both for and against.

As discussed, study and deliberation do play substantial roles in lawmaking. At the committee level, especially, both are the key elements of the process. They are not just for show but weigh heavily in the formal and informal proceedings. Study and deliberation continue beyond the committee stage and are infused in the discussion and debate at leadership meetings, party caucuses, on the floor, in conference, and elsewhere. They have major effect on outcomes.

Third, we can expect strategy and negotiation to play a role along with study and deliberation. Whatever a bill's substantive merits may be, it is necessary to put together and keep together the support required to get it enacted into law. For many issues of a noncontroversial nature, building support is relatively straightforward. But on a number of issues, putting together majorities at successive stages of the lawmaking process is extraordinarily challenging business. As legislators calculate how to advance—or defeat—some measure and negotiate for support and strive to achieve agreement, they also anticipate how their constituencies may react to what they do. Legislative responsiveness is not so much specific pressure from the public bearing down on legislators as it is anticipation of public reaction to what legislatures finally enact into law.

Study, deliberation, strategy, and negotiation all take place within an unstable and unpredictable environment. No one ever has firm control of any given situation; in fact, seldom does anyone have much control at all. Things easily fall apart soon after they have been put together for any number of reasons, among them the fact that everyone in the legislature depends, to considerable extent, on everyone else. As the president pro tem of the Vermont senate, Peter Shumlin, pointed out at an orientation for new members: "You can't do anything in this building without needing all 179 other members, at some point or another." Rep. Bill Seitz, a Republican member of the Ohio house, reflected along similar lines on the daunting mission of getting anything done in the legislature: It may seem straightforward, but "when you've got to convince at least 49 other people. . . , that's another matter. What is expendable to some people is extremely valuable to others." [5] The final word in the legislative process is the majority vote—not just one majority vote but several of them. "Democratic government," writes Richard Posner, "allows people to agree to disagree—that is, to acknowledge that there is no better method of resolving many disputes than by counting noses." [6]

So what constitutes better legislative performance at lawmaking? With so many variables operating, it is difficult—if not impossible—to specify. Each legislature engages in lawmaking in somewhat different fashion depending upon the situation, circumstances, and personalities involved. Take the revision of Act 60 in Vermont. The supreme court's ruling and the enactment of an educational finance plan set the stage. The response was the dissatisfaction of districts that wound up paying more in taxes and the Republicans' campaigning on the issue. This had to be taken into account. The difficulties associated with devising a financial aid formula that would do the job and also be politically viable also had to be faced. The leadership furnished by the Vermont House Ways and Means chair, Richard Marron, was also instrumental in the process. All of these factors, combined with others, were critical to the process in the 2001 session of the Vermont legislature. Change several or any one of them and the process itself would have been different.

The process is not the same among legislatures from day to day and issue to issue. Just as there are various ways to skin a cat, so there are various ways to make law. But it gets done one way or another, as Maryland delegate Nancy Kopp observed: "We get there . . . eventually." "Eventually" could mean years later; Marron's revision of Act 60 would not be enacted by the Vermont legislature until 2003. Minnesota's Moe, a legislative veteran, agreed. "I think the legislative process worked. We got the work completed and found common ground," he said after the 2001 session. The Republican speaker, Steve Sviggum, was of the same mind: "It was well worth the product," [7] he said.

Good lawmaking is very much a balancing of ingredients. Study and deliberation are critical. So are strategy and negotiation, which are more likely to get attention because legislators desire results, something to show for their labors. They want a law enacted—something that will help people, groups, or the state as a whole—and will benefit them and their parties electorally. The incentives for investing energies here are powerful and the contest between one side and the other can be exciting. This is not the case as far as study and deliberation are concerned, however. Few legislators are students as such, so the incentives for more study and more deliberation are weaker. Crafting legislation is less stimulating for most members than steering it through the labyrinth of a process. But both have to be done, and both are done.

That is why the standing committee stage of lawmaking is so important. It is when measures are reviewed, shaped, and agreed on in committee that study and deliberation are mainly brought to bear. Committees are said to be the workhorses of the legislature, and they truly are. They are key to the decisions that get made on substantive grounds. Insofar as committees are weak, negligent, or bypassed in the lawmaking process, study and deliberation are apt to be shortchanged. Therefore, strong and effective standing committees probably are requisite if a legislature is to be "good." [8]

This is not to minimize political considerations—that is, how a policy proposal plays in the state and what the public thinks of it. Substance and politics both have to be factored in. In her admirable study of the U.S. Congress, Barbara Sinclair examines the public's contradictory expectations of the national legislature. First, it wants Congress to be responsive and enact laws that reflect the will of the people. Second, it expects Congress to enact laws that deal effectively with pressing problems. These two criteria, which Sinclair labels "responsiveness" and "responsibility," are distinct and may even come into conflict.[9]

Most observers probably would regard input from both the majority and minority to be healthy. Ideally, the two parties ought to take different positions on major issues, but then they ought to negotiate a compromise. The product ought to have input from each party. All that is necessary, then, is the willingness to give ground so that allegedly the public comes out ahead. Minnesota's Sviggum is a proponent of doing so in such a manner:

> If one side or the other—the Democrats, the Republicans, the House, the Senate, or the governor—had totally receded from or caved in on their philosophy, we could have finished this session not only on time, but in March. We need more cooperation. More give and take.[10]

Such bipartisan cooperation may sound fine, but Speaker Sviggum's own house minority leader had another response to the question of why the legislature did not get its work done earlier. "The answer," said Tim Pawlenty, "is we couldn't have gotten our goals if we would have finished this session in late May. We could not have gotten the tax package as big and bold as it is now." [11] In their representational roles the two political parties, or other blocs of legislators, are trying to advance certain values and interests. At what point should they compromise or give in? Does the public really come out further ahead if there is an earlier settlement rather than a later one? It is difficult to know.

On occasion it appears that the opposing sides over an issue get carried away by the gamelike nature of the process. Each side wants to win, in part, just for the sake of winning. Governor Ventura, for example, was critical of this aspect of the legislative process and blamed the process for promoting "poker playing" at the expense of what he believed would be more efficient legislating.[12] There is no doubt that the "game" is important to many members, and some legislators may lose sight along the way of why they are taking a position at all. They are caught up in the competition. Nevertheless, no matter how they proceed or how much they enjoy the game, their adoption of a position initially is grounded in values, partisan affiliation, and constituency.

Shouldn't the minority party play more of a role in the process than it often does? It might be nice for everyone to have input. But other than giving the minority roughly equal resources, the power to appoint its own members of a standing committee, and basic procedural rights, there is no way to ensure that the majority will include the minority on decisions. In a divided legislature, such as Minnesota and Vermont, the minority in one chamber can have its basic views expressed by the majority in the other chamber. On many issues majority-minority status does not matter much, but where it does, relationships vary according to personalities, politics, circumstances, and what each side wants and is willing to surrender.

In Maryland, for instance, what changed over the years was the politics of the situation and the increasing aggressiveness of the minority Republicans. During earlier years, when the Republicans posed no threat, the Democratic majority treated them quite benevolently—indeed, almost as equals. But when they started acting like a competitive party, the legislature became more combative along partisan lines and the minority's role in setting a legislative agenda was diminished. Or take the case of the Republican majority and Democratic minority in the Ohio senate. In 2001, under the leadership of the senate president, Richard Finan, the two parties could not reach agreement on the minority's role in the budget process. Moreover, the Republicans did not need Democratic votes to pass the budget, so they were unwilling to give the Democrats what they wanted in return for minority party cooperation. Two years later, with Finan termed out, the senate presidency was assumed by Douglas White, who kicked off the legislative session in a bipartisan tone. White had a 22–11 majority in the senate, so he did not have to let Democrats into the process, but he did. In the house, because of defections in his own party, the Republican speaker, Larry Householder, had to negotiate for some Democratic votes for the budget; and he did. Partisan (in 2001) or bipartisan (in 2003), either way, the Ohio legislature did its job.

It is easy to second-guess the legislature and the process. There may always be better ways to pass a bill, or to defeat one. More study, more deliberation, more input, and greater efficiency are frequently advocated. Editorial writers seldom hesitate to tell the public how the legislature could better do its job, and the legislature—whether in Maryland, Minnesota, Ohio, Vermont, Washington, or elsewhere—probably could always do better in some way. But the process is not really manageable, depending as it does on contingencies of all kinds. As long as there is disagreement among members, interest groups to deal with, another house to worry about, or a governor who wants a piece of the action, the process can take just about any course, and it does. Everyone and everything is connected, interdependent, and no one is in full control. Lawmaking is truly a collective endeavor, but it is one in which many people pull in different directions.

Balancing

Performing the job of balancing the power of the executive overlaps that of representing and lawmaking, especially the latter. Balancing requires, far more than lawmaking, that the legislature share with the governor the capacity to participate as equals in setting the priorities and policies for the state. Performance here is not mainly a matter of individual behavior, but rather one of institutional will. Here is where legislatures are at their greatest disadvantage. No matter how much staff they have to serve them or time they have to put in the work, the governor ordinarily has the upper hand vis-à-vis the legislature. The governor's unity, and the ability to focus and communicate that stems largely from oneness, can never be matched by the legislature. At the very least, however, legislators need constitutional and statutory power and the resources even to try to balance the governor's structural and political edge. While legislators acknowledge that the balance is not at all in their favor, they believe that power ought to be shared on a relatively equal basis between the two branches.

In a few cases legislatures appear to hold the predominant position, because they are accorded power to draft the state budget or because they traditionally have shaped the budget and the executive has acquiesced. In a few cases governors actually defer to legislatures. For the most part, however, legislatures have to assert themselves if they want to balance their governor, let alone their budget. If the governor is a member of the minority party in the state, while the legislature is controlled by the majority party, legislative assertiveness is likely. Such is the situation in Rhode Island today. Or a governor may have no partisan support whatsoever, as was the case with Ventura in Minnesota. An Independence Party member, like Ventura, who is detached and abusive at the same time, can mobilize the legislature to action as few other forces can.

In some places a spirit of coequality has developed into a legislative norm. For example, during the past twenty-five years, whatever the partisan breakdown and whoever the governor, Ohio's legislature has insisted on a partnership with the executive. While hands-on governors do well with the legislature, over the years a power-sharing tradition has taken root. During his term as governor, if James Rhodes ordered the legislature to jump, the leaders would ask, "How high?" Since then, and even during Rhodes's later terms, the situation changed—at the insistence of the house speaker, Vern Riffe, and senate president, Stanley Aronoff. Gov. George Voinovich initially tried to take control but after six months' struggle realized that he could not. Gov. Bob Taft did not even try.[13] The Vermont legislature is as citizen a legislature as exists, with one of the smallest staffs in the country. Nevertheless, it does credibly at holding its own in a system where governmental powers come into contention. Richard Snelling, by force of intellect and personality, was able to dominate, but Madeleine Kunin and Howard Dean did not even try, nor would the legislature have permitted them to do so.

New York is a state in which the modern governor has been quite strong. Nevertheless, the state's chief executive has had to negotiate on the major issues, since partisan control of government has long been divided there. New York governors have gotten their way more often than not, but they have not been given license to go it alone. When George Pataki refused to deal on taxes and spending with the Democratic assembly and Republican senate in 2003, he was decisively defeated. Not even in New York can the governor ignore the potential power of the legislature.

Maryland is an entirely different case. The legislature's weakness vis-à-vis the governor is not only political, it is also constitutional. The governor's budgetary powers, as well as his control of the decennial legislative redistricting, stand in the way of legislative coequality. During the past thirty years, the legislature took the lead only during the governorship of Harry Hughes. That was the case chiefly because Hughes philosophically believed that the legislature ought to make policy for the state, and also because the speaker of the house, Benjamin Cardin, was more than willing to have the legislature take the lead. Most recently, a Republican governor, Robert Ehrlich, had his troubles with the Democratic legislature in Maryland. The balance of executive-legislative power in the state can be attributed to the budgetary control that the constitution grants the governor. The legislature is by no means without power, but its battle with the governor is an uphill one. If the legislature is to do its job of balancing the executive, what is needed is a constitutional change. The issue had been raised by the legislature, but an amendment has yet to be put to the required vote of the electorate.

There may be other states that require constitutional or statutory change to remedy an imbalance between the governor and the legislature; but after allowing for the governor's structural advantages, the balance of executive-legislative power depends mainly on personalities and politics and, to an extent, on what have become customary ways of doing things in a state. Personalities and politics change rather quickly; customary ways also change, but not with the same speed. Sometimes a legislature is up, sometimes it is down. Balancing executive power is one of the toughest jobs legislatures have, and it is one that they do least well. That is because coequality requires that the legislature have almost the same unity or oneness as the governor. In other words, not much defection from legislative ranks can be tolerated if the legislature is to stand up to the governor. At the very least, what is necessary for the legislature to do its balancing job is a recognition that it ought to do it and have the will to try to do it. In most places that recognition exists; but with so many other problems to tackle, the will may actually get in the legislature's way.

"First, Do No Harm"

What, then, has to be present for a legislature to do a good job? One house or two? Partisan or nonpartisan staffing? An independent ethics commission or not? Probably none of the above. Instead, what appear vital to the legislature's performance are the following:

1. A connection by legislators to their constituencies and a responsiveness to constituency views where they exist. This requires, among other things, that legislators want to remain in office and rely on their constituencies for their political well-being.
2. A balance between the deliberative aspects of lawmaking on the one hand and the political aspects on the other, ensuring that the process takes into account arguments as to the merits of a measure. This ordinarily means that a legislative chamber delegates a major role to its standing committees. Deliberation requires policy expertise, which usually derives from experience in a committee's subject area. It also requires some continuity of committee membership. It is at the committee stage of the process, moreover, that minority party members usually have their maximum input into the process. In committee work groups, a member's party is less important and partisanship is more muted. If the committees—or at least the major committees—are ineffective, the legislature's lawmaking will suffer.
3. Effective legislative leadership, which requires that leaders have substantial experience, skills, and resources. Legislative leadership matters relatively little with regard to representation; legislators do that on their own. But it is hard to imagine the lawmaking process succeeding without both committee and party leadership. Among the many responsibilities of majority party leadership are finding common ground, facilitating compromise, forging consensus, and enabling a legislative majority to find and work its will. It is normally a bipartisan will, although on some measures— significant ones, including the state budget—the will may be that of the majority, not the minority party.

Members need leadership, and leadership depends on the support of members—or, at least, that of the majority party caucus. The caucus, or the chamber membership as a whole, determines leadership positions on policy or sets parameters within which the leadership can try to establish positions with members. Even in a state like New York, reputed to have the most centralized leadership in the nation, leaders have to satisfy rank and file. The granting of strong authority to leaders helps to focus the negotiating process and serves the interests of members. Legislators want a say on policy and they want to get reelected; they get both under the system in New York.[14]

Without legislative leaders, how would agreement be forged? Who would do it? The governor, most likely, increasing that already ample role. Legislative leadership also has to negotiate with the governor on behalf of the senate and house. Only through such leadership can the power of the legislature be brought to bear in negotiations with the executive. Without such leadership, a governor could pick legislators off one by one; there would be little to hold them together, and the balance would shift substantially. On the whole, therefore, the weaker the legislative leadership, the stronger the governor.

It is easier to identify what will make legislatures worse than what will make them better. Term limits will make them worse, and the effects of their adoption in the 1990s are beginning to be felt in the early years of the twenty-first century. These effects vary from state to state, but overall they interfere with the legislature's job performance. The results of a recent survey of legislators in the fifty states are revealing.[15] It was mailed to all 7,399 legislators in 2002 and completed by 2,982—or 40 percent—of them. The bottom line is that term limits had effects that, in the judgment expressed above, were detrimental to the legislature's job performance.

One area that showed significant decline in term-limited legislatures was representation. Legislators in term-limited chambers reported spending less time keeping in touch with constituents, engaging in constituent service, securing state funds and projects for their districts, and being responsive to the demands and views of their constituents. Second, the power of majority party leadership and committee chairs suffered. The survey study indicated that party leaders are weakened as soon as term limits go into effect, whereas the influence of committee chairs holds as long as the old experts are still around but diminishes once they are gone. Third, the power of the governor and the executive-legislative balance shifted. Governors in states with term limits in place were regarded by legislator respondents as stronger than governors in states without term limits. The investigators conclude that "Term limits clearly increase the power of the executive branch relative to the legislature," in part because "the two institutional actors generally regarded as best able to coordinate collective action among legislators—majority party leaders and committee chairs—are debilitated by term limits."

The impact of term limits is being investigated by scholars in a number of states, and the results are starting to come in. For example, the effects of Proposition 140, which brought term limits to California, are believed to have significantly contributed to the trouble in which the nation's largest state found itself in 2002–2003. According to two scholars, the lawmaking process in California is more flawed than it ever was in the past. Legislators bring less experience and expertise to the process, have little incentive to learn about the budget, and do not take their budget subcommittee work seriously.[16]

The first rule for physicians is, "Do no harm." That rule might well be applicable to the efforts of those who are critical of and want to bring substantial change to state legislatures. These institutions are far from perfect, but they seem to be doing what they were intended to—the job of representing, lawmaking, and balancing the power of the executive. The job entrusted to America's state legislatures is extraordinarily tough and, for the most part, thankless. But it somehow gets done—albeit somewhat differently by different people in different states and at different times. If only the public could appreciate how well representative democracy and state legislatures are serving it.

"Second, Tell It Like It Is"

Like it or not, nowadays appearance may be as important as reality. As discussed in chapter 1 and alluded to thereafter, legislatures do not look good because of the very nature of the functions they perform. They channel, express, and try to settle differences and conflicts, and they do so in a complicated, unprogrammed, and human fashion. A most unattractive business to the average eye, legislatures and the process come off as even less attractive as a result of their treatment in the press, in political campaigns, by advocates for one side or another, and because of the misbehavior of some of their own members.

If it is principally a matter of perception, the solution in the judgment of a public relations professional would be to improve the legislature's image. How, then, can it be improved? One way is to present to the public a story that is interesting, appealing, and dramatic. The legislature can do this by having itself scripted, as it might appear in the form of a television series. After all, *The West Wing* has helped the images of the presidency and the White House. Why not an *East Wing* for the legislature? Alternatively, to improve its image the legislature might be advised to abandon much of its job. That is, it could minimize conflict and deliberation—which the public sees as "bickering"—and compromise—which the public regards as "selling out." For a more favorable image, the legislature then might merely sit it out, sidestepping any issue on which serious disagreement and sharp conflict might arise. Either scripting or abdication would probably lead to an increase in a legislature's ratings by the public, but the cost would be that the legislature would be neglecting its job. The problem here is that the public needs and benefits from the legislature doing its job, even though what the public sees it doesn't like.

Instead of trying to change the legislature's looks, we must accept how it looks, warts and all, because of what the legislature is and what it does. Legislatures are not pretty, but neither is democracy. Somehow, the legislature has to involve itself in a drive to persuade the public that representative democracy and legislatures really do work. A state legislature might simply launch a public relations campaign, with brief, catchy radio and TV ads and/or endorsements by celebrities. "The legislature works" is the message that it would want to convey.

However, public relations is not the answer. The legislature must convey a message to its constituencies; it ought to be communicated not by means of institutional advertising, but rather by means of civic education on the subject of representative democracy and the work of the legislature.

The first constituency for the legislature's message is members themselves. Legislators have to understand their institution and devote themselves to its maintenance. This does not mean that they should not try to change their institution or improve the way it works, but that they should take care not to abuse it or sacrifice it for political ends. When engaged in a tight political race, it is easy to run against the legislature; many incumbents—as well as challengers—do. But such posturing inflicts needless damage. When the process does not go one's way, it is easy to blame the system. This too inflicts needless damage, and even minor damage adds up.

The second constituency for the legislature's message is the public. Members individually and legislatures collectively have to take on the task of explaining representative democracy to their constituencies. Explaining in simple terms the basics of a complex system is a huge challenge. But it ought to be taken on as part of the legislature's representational role. Legislators acknowledge their responsibility for explaining their positions on policy issues to people. However, they have yet to accept responsibility for providing civic education; in their view, that is for educational institutions or the media or groups to do. In the "five-state survey," for instance, legislators were asked if it was important for them to educate people about representative democracy. Their responses indicated that they endorsed such a task but did not rank it among the more important in serving their constituents. They had too much else on their plates to devote much attention to civic education.

In a democracy such as ours, people need to know how the system functions—not everything, necessarily, but the basics. That information is more important, perhaps, than any other the legislature provides the public. Teaching about legislatures cannot be left solely to schools and other institutions. They ought to be encouraged and prodded, but legislatures and legislators have to engage and take responsibility.

Like legislatures, democracy in action is not pleasing to the naked eye. It is burdensome and contentious, and it does not always give us what we want or feel we deserve. Appreciation does not come naturally. People have to be taught to see democracy's beauty beneath the crusty surface of the legislature.

There is always room for improving legislatures. They are far from perfect institutions. Yet they are the best we have, and preferable to any conceivable alternatives. Not only that, they actually work, albeit in rather messy and somewhat mysterious ways—representing, lawmaking, and balancing the power of the executive. They deserve more understanding and greater support than they have been given. Without that, the public might not be able to continue counting on them to do the job that they have been doing—and doing well.

NOTES

1. These studies were conducted by the Eagleton Institute of Politics at Rutgers University under contract with the legislatures in Arkansas, Connecticut, Florida, Maryland, Mississippi, and Wisconsin. See Alan Rosenthal, *Legislative Performance in the States* (New York: The Free Press, 1974), 12–13.

2. Hanna F. Pitkin, *The Concept of Representation* (Berkeley: University of California Press, 1967), 221–222, 233.

3. See Susan Thomas, *How Women Legislate* (New York: Oxford University Press, 1994); Cindy Simon Rosenthal, *When Women Lead* (New York: Oxford University Press, 1998); and Susan Carroll, ed., *The Impact of Women in Public Office* (Bloomington: Indiana University Press, 2001).

4. Pitkin, *The Concept of Representation,* 60–91.

5. *Columbus Dispatch,* May 7, 2001.

6. Richard A. Posner, *Law, Pragmatism, and Democracy* (Cambridge: Harvard University Press, 2003), 10.

7. *Minneapolis Star Tribune,* July 2, 2001.

8. An early attempt to gauge the effectiveness of standing committee systems is by Rosenthal, *Legislative Performance in the States.*

9. Barbara Sinclair, *Unorthodox Lawmaking: New Legislative Processes in the U.S. Congress,* 2nd ed. (Washington, D.C.: CQ Press, 2000), 233.

10. *Legal Ledger,* May 24, 2001.

11. *St. Paul Pioneer Press,* June 30, 2001.

12. *Minneapolis Star Tribune,* July 2, 2001.

13. Interview with the author, May 22, 2001.

14. Jeffrey M. Stonecash, "The Rise of the Legislature," in Sarah F. Liebschutz et al., *New York Politics and Government: Competition and Compassion* (Lincoln: University of Nebraska Press, 1998), 86.

15. John M. Carey, Gary F. Moncrief, Richard G. Niemi, and Lynda W. Powell, "Term Limits in State Legislatures: Results from a New Survey of the 50 States" (paper prepared for delivery at the annual meeting of the American Political Science Association, Philadelphia, Pa., August 28–31, 2003).

16. Bruce E. Cain and Thad Kousser, "California in Crisis: Term Limits," *California Journal* (August 2003): 22–24.

INDEX